The Cosmetic Gaze

The Cosmetic Gaze

Body Modification and the Construction of Beauty

Bernadette Wegenstein

The MIT Press
Cambridge, Massachusetts
London, England

This book was set in Stone Sans and Stone Serif by Toppan Best-set Premedia Limited. Printed and bound by CPI Group (UK) Ltd, Croydon, CR0 4YY

Library of Congress Cataloging-in-Publication Data

Wegenstein, Bernadette.
The cosmetic gaze : body modification and the construction of beauty / Bernadette Wegenstein.
    p. cm.
Includes bibliographical references and index.
ISBN 978-0-262-23267-8 (hbk. : alk. paper)—978-0-262-52966-2 (pb. : alk. paper)
1. Body image—Social aspects. 2. Aesthetics—Social aspects. 3. Human body—Social aspects. 4. Surgery, Plastic—Social aspects. I. Title.
BF697.5.B63W4195   2012
306.4′613—dc23
2011032822

The MIT Press is pleased to keep this title available in print by manufacturing single copies, on demand, via digital printing technology.

Contents

Acknowledgments

This book is dedicated to my children—Alexander, Charlotte, and Sebastian.

I want to thank the following people for their valuable input and collaboration on this book: Geoffrey Alan Rhodes, with whom I made the documentary *Made Over in America* (2007) about U.S. reality television makeover culture; the authors who contributed to "Reality Made Over: The Culture of Reality Television Makeover Shows," a special issue of *Configurations* 15.1–2 (2008) that I guest edited, and who have been immensely influential with their ideas and expertise on the topic—Julie Albright, Virginia Blum, William Egginton, Kimberly Jackson, Pamela Orosan-Weine, Mark Poster, Brenda R. Weber, and Joanna Zylinska; Nora Ruck, who was a vital part of the genesis of chapter 1 during her research period at The Johns Hopkins University in 2008 (I thank Nora in particular for her research input on Sir Francis Galton and on monsters); the very helpful reviewers of the manuscript and of the journal *Body & Society*; and Doug Sery from the MIT Press, who kept me going with his unprecedented patience and belief that I would deliver this manuscript even while producing a second documentary and having a third child (thank you, Doug). Thanks also to my encouraging and precise production editor, Deborah Cantor-Adams, and manuscript editor, Rosemary Winfield, at the MIT Press, as well as Troy Toyer for his careful proofreading.

Special thanks go to all fifty-nine image rights holders, who either waived their fees or gave me their images for a reduced price. The book would not be the same without these important illustrations. Thanks to Melanie Bühler for obtaining these rights and images, as well as to Brian Cole and Reid Szcerba for preparing the images for this publication.

My husband, Bill, has been indispensable in the completion of this book and in everything else I do in my life. He is my inspiration.

Parts of chapters 1 and 3 are forthcoming in *Body & Society* (17.4, December 2011) as the collaborative essay "On Physiognomy, Reality Television, and the Cosmetic Gaze," written with Nora Ruck. Other parts of chapter 3 are in the essay "Machinic Suture: Technologies of Beautification," in *Throughout: Art and Culture Emerging with Ubiquitous Computing,* edited by Ulrik Ekman (The MIT Press, 2012).

Introduction

The origins of the word *cosmetic* go back to the Greek *kosmetikós*—relating to adornment. The verb *kosmein* means both to arrange and to adorn. *Cosmetic*, then, is derived from *cosmos*—something that was there to begin with but was there precisely to be put into order. A correlate to this order that precedes itself is the intimate self-identity that is the ultimate object of the gaze and that is, like the cosmos itself, already structured by a preceding adornment. The self, at its origin and center, is cosmetic all the way down. The cosmetic gaze believes in the body as the *cosmos*, the original (holy and whole) place, and at the same time is the operative force in its construction as endless adornment.

In my previous book, *Getting under the Skin: Body and Media Theory* (The MIT Press, 2006), I focus on how the strategies and operations of today's social and cultural gaze have "gotten under the skin." By directing us to look at "organs instead of a body" within the visual culture of the globalized West, this gaze has generated a breakdown between the interiority and exteriority of the human body. Over the last four years, my critical attention has been drawn toward "the cut" itself—that place of transfixation where the movement distinguishing outside from inside comes to a stop. The media of enhanced perception—such as medical imaging technology, high-definition television, and ubiquitous computing—seemed to be revealing the operations of a gaze whose object is the cut itself as the embodiment of potential transformations. The *cosmetic gaze* is thus transfixed by a plane of potential that lies below the skin and is accessible only via the action of cutting (with old-fashioned scalpels or the less invasive ways enabled by digital technology). This plane is far from a mere voluntaristic fantasy. It is always a platform for projections that are limited by a special moment in a body's history when the self was perceived as truly "good and beautiful." The cosmetic gaze thus perceives all bodies in light of some potentially transformative completion, while at the same time transfixing that potentiality on the phantom remnant of a "true" self that is fixed in time.

The cosmetic gaze is deployed in individuals but is nurtured and evolves in the media of culture. The cultural media through and in which bodies come to self-awareness direct these bodies toward the goal of a "better you" in both the ethical and the aesthetic senses. The thought process inherent in the cosmetic gaze can thus be imagined as follows. After a self is dissembled and reassembled as I describe in *Getting under the Skin*, it becomes re-created in a "better" way. The gaze carves out (to use one of the sculptural metaphors of the cosmetic surgery industry) what in the body obscures its perfection and leaves behind only what is beautiful and meant to be seen by others. This new self is what Meredith Jones has called the "rebirth" theme in makeover culture, whereby rebirth is intimately related to the death and mourning of an "old self."[1]

In this book, I show how the cosmetic gaze facilitates such rebirth and how it builds on a body concept that has collapsed into its mediality—that is, the complex of media through which it comes to know itself and represent itself to others. Although we have, since the late 1980s, either celebrated or grieved this collapse between medium and body (see "The Medium Is the Body," my final chapter in *Getting under the Skin*), today's construction of self is building on this medial ground with some self-confidence. Like the "organ instead of a body"—the Deleuze-inspired metaphor I use in *Getting under the Skin* for the body concept of the twenty-first century—this self yearns for independence from its body but does so as media. Instead of having a body, this self appears on TV. What we experience in today's beauty discourse, as I develop it in many examples in *The Cosmetic Gaze*, is a bettered self that has been reborn from its own flesh and is now, like a digitally remastered character from a classic Hollywood movie, immortal.

Although the revelation of the cosmetic gaze has been enabled by the new media environment of the twenty-first century, there is nothing new about the cosmetic gaze itself. In the first chapter, "Tracing the Cosmetic Gaze: From Eighteenth-Century Physiognomies to Racial Theories of the Third Reich," I turn to Johann Kaspar Lavater's eighteenth-century physiognomic treatises, proceed through nineteenth-century Darwinism and the development of eugenics, and end with the racial theories of the Third Reich. This first historical step demonstrates how the well-intentioned gaze of eighteenth-century physiognomists who were intent on performing an ethical reading of a person's appearance—according to the rules of the Platonic *kalókagatheia* and using Sir Francis Galton's photographic composites in the hopes of finding and optimizing the "average" British face—could pave the way for the discriminatory and deathly eugenic gaze of the Nazi regime. This first chapter sets the tone for chapters 2 and 3 by positioning the values and intentions of the cosmetic gaze both historically and conceptually.

Chapter 2, "The Dark Side of Beauty: From Convulsive Beauty to Makeover Disfiguration," builds on the categorical premises of chapter 1—how Western culture learned to look for, distinguish, and categorize the human body, particularly the face, as "beautiful," "ugly," "useful," or "useless." As a result of such categorization, a new notion arises that incorporates both beauty and ugliness in what the surrealists called "convulsive" beauty. Under the influence of this notion, the deformed body becomes a recognized and justified place and rises to a new aesthetic position of celebrated other. The chapter revisits the Lavaterian notion of deformity, particularly of the "monster," and ends with a discussion of what I call the new beauty.

Chapter 3, "Machinic Sutures: Twenty-first-Century Technologies of Beauty," moves chapter 1's historical exploration into the twenty-first century and continues where that chapter left off, leading to today's reality makeover business. This chapter looks at the cosmetic gaze's late twentieth- and early twenty-first-century areas of application and operation and asks whether current technologies of beauty have overcome the grief and trauma caused by the results of the Darwinian turn and the racial theories responsible for the elimination of particular facial or bodily types. The chapter also examines how today's media practices embody the cosmetic gaze in reality makeover shows like *The Swan*, video games like *The Sims*, pornographic Web sites such as *I Shot Myself*, and facial recognition software such as E-FIT and EFIT-V, which is used by British police to identify criminal subjects on watch lists.

Chapter 4, "Editing Women: The Cosmetic Gaze and Cinema," leaves the diachronic trajectory of the book to concentrate on one particular area of the cosmetic gaze's expression—cinema. This chapter focuses on questions of "female beauty" and "female suture" on the screen. The chapter examines mainstream and independent films—including horror films, comedies, and psychological thrillers such as *The Face of a Woman* (1941), *Les Yeux sans visage* (1959), *Dans ma peau* (2002), *In the Cut* (2003), and *Time* (2006)—that incorporate or comment on the cosmetic gaze's influence on the viewer.

Because feminist film theory has some of its origins in the psychoanalytically inspired notion of the male gaze, the final chapter recapitulates the book's arc of slowly unearthing a feminist position from the deep cultural sediments of misogyny. Thus, the book begins with physiognomy as instituted by men and eventually identifies physiognomy's role in the deployment and transmission of the cosmetic gaze. An exploration of the cutting of women in cinema must start with psychoanalytic concepts to suggest how the idea of the cosmetic gaze might finally displace that of the male gaze in explicating the continuing power of the cinematic apparatus in our lives. Although its dominant exertion over the bodies of women has required a revelation stemming from feminist thought, the cosmetic gaze spares no one. The cinema, like many other screens that paper the walls of the house of being, never ceases to show us our bodies as they could be and hence draws life from the cosmetic gaze that it transmits.

1 Tracing the Cosmetic Gaze: From Eighteenth-Century Physiognomies to Racial Theories of the Third Reich

For *sight* is the most piercing of our bodily senses; though not by that is wisdom seen; her loveliness would have been transporting if there had been a visible image of her, and the other ideas, if they had visible counterparts, would be equally lovely. But this is the privilege of beauty, that being the loveliest she is also the most palpable to sight. Now he who is not newly initiated or who has become corrupted, does not easily rise out of this world to the sight of true beauty in the other; he looks only at her earthly namesake, and instead of being awed at the sight of her, he is given over to pleasure, and like a brutish beast he rushes on to enjoy and beget; he consorts with wantonness, and is not afraid or ashamed of pursuing pleasure in violation of nature.

—Plato, *Phaedrus*[1]

When Americans flocked to the spectacle of women revealing their surgically enabled transformations on reality television's *Extreme Makeover* in 2002, many thought that a radically new world had begun. But the seeds of today's makeover phenomenon reach far back before the medical and mediatic technologies that make such spectacle possible. The *gaze* is a cultural construction that brings forth our codependent needs to see and to be seen.[2] Here it serves as a transhistorical category that traces a relationship between a historical field of vision, its apparatus, its users' agencies, and the underlying social contract that allows the gaze to be projected onto a "screen" that a culture looks at and believes in. The screen is a site that a society looks at to find itself represented. It is the place that the gaze is destined to look at and to be made for. As Kaja Silverman has said, it is the "site at which the gaze is defined for a particular society."[3] The screen expresses a visual regime of a society. The screen onto which the cosmetic gaze is projected includes the body itself as well as the formats discussed in this book, including reality TV and Internet sites for "bad cosmetic surgery." For people whose desire for change has literally materialized in their own flesh, their bodies become a screen on which culture can see or fail to see itself reflected. This body screen that displays a society's desire for change is discussed at length in chapter 3, where people talk about how being surrounded by made-over bodies produces a desire for one's own makeover but also produces a gaze that is circular: I see myself in the bodies of others, and the bodies of others tell me how I look or could look.[4]

The *cosmetic gaze* is one through which the act of looking at our bodies and those of others is informed by the techniques, expectations, and strategies of bodily modification. It is also a moralizing gaze—a way of looking at bodies as awaiting a physical and spiritual improvement that is present in the body's structure as an absence or a need. As Nely Galán, the creator and producer of Fox Broadcasting Company's reality makeover show *The Swan* (2004–2005), said about candidates for a successful makeover: "you have to want to better yourself, inside and out."[5]

This first chapter traces some of the history of the short circuit between inside and outside transformations, which is essential to the operation of the cosmetic gaze. The Swiss theologian and priest Johann Kaspar Lavater (born in Zurich in 1741) was well known for his physiognomic treatises, which were widely read throughout Europe in the late eighteenth century. He laid the ground for the Darwinian physiognomy of Sir Francis Galton and his development of eugenics in the nineteenth century and also for the physiognomy of the racial theorists of Germany's Third Reich.[6] This chapter examines several guiding questions: What did eighteenth-century physiognomy identify as character traits in a person's outside appearance? What were Johann Kaspar Lavater's intentions as a theologian and a priest as he sought to reveal a person's inner psyche? How did Lavater perceive and interpret the female appearance, and how might such female physiognomy be indicative of nineteenth- and twentieth-century attempts to "read" people's appearances? How did eighteenth-century physiognomic knowledge, which was based on the subjectivity of the observer, influence nineteenth-century objectivity-driven attempts at categorizing human appearance via the lens of the photographic apparatus? How did nineteenth-century eugenics inform the racial theories of the Third Reich in its intent to exterminate the deviant body, inside and out, from society? Finally, which media and apparatuses have propagated the cosmetic gaze—

from Lavater's drawn portraits and Galton's photographical composites to the anthropometrically defined and intuitively discovered ideals of the "Aryan body" in Nazi Germany? Ultimately, today's makeover practice is indebted to a cosmetic gaze whose mechanisms were widely deployed in eighteenth-century European culture.

While one could begin in the Middle Ages or even in antiquity, my study builds on the identification of a medical gaze—directed under the body's skin—that has been in circulation in the Western world since the anatomical discoveries of the fifteenth and sixteenth centuries. In early modernity, a separation began to be theorized between an individual body and a social body,[7] which led to the concept in high modernity of the body as, in the words I used in *Getting under the Skin*, "a 'project' to be worked on and accomplished as a fundamental aspect of the individual's self-identity."[8] The eighteenth century thus represents a significant moment for the history of medicine, a moment that Michel Foucault famously identified as the birth of modern medicine.[9]

What characterizes this moment in medical history is the examination of the body by the medical expert or doctor. As Barbara Duden puts, "It was only toward the end of the eighteenth century that the modern body was created as the effect and object of medical examination. It was newly created as an object that could be abused, transformed, subjugated. According to Foucault, this passivity of the object was the result of the ritual of clinical examination."[10] As a result of examining a person while alive (and not just dissecting a cadaver), the doctor's dissecting gaze creates a private body. As Duden explains, "The reality of this 'body' was the product of these descriptions."[11] In other words, this medical gaze was translated into a "scientific discourse" that was capable of describing the individual according to its bodily symptoms—what the individual sees on her own body and reveals to the doctor, who sees and describes the patient by asking, "What do you have?" The discipline of physiognomy, as pointed out by Carsten Zelle, was revived in the late eighteenth century as a result of an increased tendency to view "oneself as unique and independent."[12]

Physiognomy, when it becomes a human and medical science, ascends to the status of studying the "truly authentic self," an endeavor that twenty-first-century makeover culture continues. Thus, to analyze the cosmetic gaze from a cultural-theoretical viewpoint, I am dependent on the historical assumption of this self that sees (itself) and is simultaneously seen (by the doctor). The following study of Lavaterian physiognomy was also based on the reality of a man's observations and his interpretations. The "reality" of the Lavaterian portraits, thus, is a result of the pastor's gaze, of his ability to put his observations into words, and of a scientific discourse that lent him a vocabulary to describe what he saw.

My investigation of a cosmetic gaze in late eighteenth-century Europe is therefore in historical congruence with a body that was then under examination by a medical gaze that turned the body inside out. This modern body concept, which also informs the Cartesian intellectual tradition—is both the result of and condition for the physiognomic reading of the body traced in this chapter. As Patrizia Magli has put it, "Physiognomic perception is a form of daily knowledge."[13] This correlation between an outside appearance and an inside constitution—or between an extended body and a thinking thing or soul, to put it in Cartesian terms—has been a preoccupation at least since the fifth century BCE, when the discipline of physiognomy was linked with medicine and discussed as pseudo-science by ancient doctors such as Hippocrates, for whom it constituted a conventional signifying relationship. Whether there was a strict belief in this signifying relationship or whether it served to prove the existence of a universal and divine harmony, what drives the history of physiognomy— from Aristotle to the phrenology of Franz Joseph Gall—is the belief in the power of the face as the most symptomatic place for the soul to "reveal" itself and to be read. There is, as Magli says, "a tendency to freeze the ineffable qualities of a face in a system of strictly codified equivalences."[14] This freezing of an "ideal face" makes it possible to look underneath the skin in search of the code that explains an interiority, and it also reveals a moral code that explains a human behavior. In this way, the human body, particularly the face and its traits, becomes a symptom—something that leads elsewhere (to God) or that misleads by "hiding" something underneath. I return to this point at length in chapter 4, where I read the history of the cosmetic gaze against the history of cosmetic surgery and makeover as represented in film. For now, to better understand how Lavater reaches knowledge of what to look for in the "beautiful" and the "ugly," I begin with a short background on the zeitgeist of late eighteenth-century Enlightenment Europe, the time when Lavater's eye was active.

The Concept of *Kalókagatheia*: "The Good and the Beautiful"

The concept of *kalókagatheia*—from *kalós* (beautiful), *kai* (and), and *agathós* (good)—assumes a correspondence between beauty of bodily form and a beautiful disposition in the soul. Plato wrote about it in many of his dialogs and other writings, such as this one from *The Republic*:

—Therefore, if someone's soul has a fine and beautiful character and his body matches it in beauty and is thus in harmony with it, so that both share in the same pattern, wouldn't that be the most beautiful sight for anyone who has eyes to see?

—It certainly would.

—And isn't what is most beautiful also most loveable?

—Of course.[15]

Although in Plato's times the term *kalókagatheia*[16] or *kaloi kagathoi* (its more common spelling) referred to "gentlemanly nobility"—the quality of being raised right or possessing the proper culture[17]—the term itself is not easy to trace.[18] It went through various interpretations from antiquity to the Enlightenment, when in the first half of the eighteenth century it was finally fused into the concept of the "beautiful soul."[19] In the sixth century BCE, Theognis and Pindar used the term *kalókagatheia* to indicate an intrinsic relation between physical beauty and ethical perfection and therefore to refer to a true nobleman.[20] During the classical Greek era around the fifth century BCE in Athens, the term commonly was used to refer to someone who came from a "good" or privileged family and who was therefore honorable. The lamp sellers, cobblers, leather dealers, and other workers, as Aristophanes lists the "non-good-and-beautiful" in *The Frogs* (405 BCE), were opposed to the upper crust of the *kaloikagathoi*. It was in the interest of the Athenians to be part of this upper crust or nobility.[21] It was not assumed, however, that the quality of being beautiful and good would be innate, and it was possible and even respectable to acquire *kalókagatheia* through *paedaia* or education. Thus Xenophon, a contemporary of Plato, presented *kalókagatheia* as one of the primary subjects in a Socratian education. For Xenophon, the good and beautiful manifested itself in the right relationship to God (*dikaiosyne*),[22] which emphasized the "good" in *kalókagatheia*. For him, the good deed or the morally good behavior outweighed the beautiful in that the latter brought fewer material rewards. But moral behavior would be readable on a person's face. In his

Memorabilia (431–355 BCE), Xenophon talks about how reaching the height of moral nobility is reflected in the face and gestures of a person and how one has more pleasure when watching a *kalos kai agathos*:

Socrates: And which is the pleasanter type of face to look at, do you think—one on which is imprinted the characteristics of a beautiful, good, and lovable disposition, or one which bears the impress of what is ugly, and bad, and hateful?[23]

Xenophon's notion of the relationship between the beautiful and the good is therefore closely related to the gaze. What is morally good appears to be beautiful, and a beautiful soul will "shine through" the face, which is the "window to the soul." Aristotle, in the fourth century BCE, put a preliminary end to the marriage of the "good" and the "beautiful" by noting that these are very different concepts.[24] His concept of *kalókagatheia* emphasized the "good" and also rid itself of the "beautiful."[25] Aristotle further challenged the notion of an inborn virtue. Leaders, *aristoi*, were supposed to be chosen according to their lifestyle and conduct and not according to their birth into a noble family. The Aristotelian ethics led the philosopher to propose as an ultimate goal for the *kaloi kai agathoi* his or her own felicitousness.[26] This relationship between the good and the beautiful would remain an ethical debate for post-Aristotelian philosophers such as Epictetus, Plutarch, and Demosthenes.

The concept was revived by the Neoplatonic[27] interpretations of the Egyptian-born philosopher Plotinus (204–270 CE). The following passage from the Plotinian *Enneads*—from the sixth tractate, entitled "beauty"—was written seventeen hundred years ago, but the connection that Plotinus ascertained between an inner beauty that needs to be carved out (as if by a sculptor)—revealing the beauty of the soul that is somehow hiding underneath—seems to come from contemporary makeover discourse and beauty self-help instructions. Here is Plotinus in a section about "inner vision":

Withdraw into yourself and look. And if you do not find yourself beautiful yet, act as thus the creator of a statue that is to be made beautiful: he cuts away here, he smoothes there, he makes this line lighter, this other purer, until a lovely face has grown upon his work. So do you also: cut away all that is excessive, straighten all that is crooked, bring light to all that is overcast, labour to make all one glow of beauty and never cease chiseling your statue, until there shall shine out on you from it the godlike splendor of virtue, until you shall see the perfect goodness surely established in the stainless shrine . . . and never can the Soul have vision of the First Beauty unless itself be beautiful.[28]

Plotinus's perfected statue features a beautiful soul as a result of utter-most moral being. But the philosopher also points out that the soul cannot grasp or see beauty unless it is itself beautiful. So, too, does the Lavaterian physiognomic universe of the late eighteenth century read the human body, particularly the face, as an entryway into the soul's universe as well as point to the soul's need to see or experience beauty. Both the term's original Platonic meaning as well as its Neoplatonic meaning adopted by Plotinus were fervently discussed among eighteenth-century German Enlightenment philosophers. In his essay entitled "Is Physical Beauty a Messenger of the Beauty of the Soul?," for instance, Johann Gottfried Herder begins with the observation that those who have been ennobled by nature can only triumph, while all others may go either to a hospital or back into the mother's womb to be reborn.[29] He ends the essay on a similarly ironic note about the subjectivity of the one who sees: "every-body judges according to his own eyes, and why would I wake up the other from his sweet dream, if he is delighted by it?"[30]

The eighteenth century can be roughly divided ideologically into a first half beholden to ancient Rome and a second half to ancient Greece.[31] During the early eighteenth century in Germany, England, and France,[32] in the rationalist spirit of rereadings of Virgil, Horace, and Cicero, Plato's writings were considered obscure and ambiguous. In 1762, the London *Monthly Review* announced that "Plato is unfashionable."[33] As Christopher Celenza points out, Platonism had seen much better times—with such revivalists as Plotinus, St. Augustine, and Marsilio Ficino—before the late eighteenth century, when the "first 'modern' historian of philosophy, Jakob Brucker . . . denounced the esoteric brand of Platonism as a confused hodge-podge of ill-digested ideas harmful to the progress of true, 'rational' philosophy."[34]

But the latter half of the century saw a turn toward ancient Greece, culminating in the other extreme of ancient Greece revivalists, such as Denis Diderot, Johann Joachim Winckelmann, Wilhelm von Humboldt, and poets like Friedrich Schiller and Friedrich Hölderlin.[35] As a result of this German graecophile tradition, which continued to thrive in the nineteenth century, the Hellenic concept of *kalókagatheia* was also revived. In his pedagogical essay on a "plan for an academy for the cultivation of the heart and mind of young people" (1758), Christoph Martin Wieland returns to the concept *kalókagatheia* and reinterpreted its meaning as such:

The goal, therefore, of their education was to form or cultivate [*bilden*] their young citizens into what they termed *kalókagatheia*. By this word, they understood all of the excellences and perfections that distinguish a free and noble human being from a slave and from a humanlike animal. . . . To this end, which alone is worthy of human nature, they inculcated in their youth as early as possible a taste for the beautiful and the good, along with the best moral and political notions.[36]

Drawing an Instinctive Connection between Physical and Moral Beauty: Lavater's Physiognomy

The spirit of Wieland's resuscitation of *kalókagatheia* was also at the forefront of Johann Kaspar Lavater's (1741–1801) science of physiognomy. The Swiss pastor's popularity after the publication of his *Physiognomical Fragments for the Promotion of the Knowledge and Love of Man* between the years 1775 and 1778 cannot be overstated. The work was translated into all major European languages within a short time of its German publication and was released in numerous styles and formats, including pocket versions that people could carry with them to consult when making new acquaintances. In many ways, Lavater became a kind of relationship adviser who was constantly in demand by society matrons for his scientific insights into the mysteries of human character.

For Lavater, there is no doubt that morality and outer appearance are connected: "Beauty and ugliness have a strict connection with the moral constitution of Man. In proportion as he is morally good, he is handsome; and ugly, in proportion as he is morally bad."[37]

For Lavater, morally beautiful states of being express themselves beautifully on the body, particularly on the face. Morally ugly or bad states of the soul express themselves with a negative countenance. In his view, the face is a general expression of a current state of mind, just as it is in the classic art of rhetoric, in which the face is supposed to underline and express a speaker's feelings.[38] It is not a question of whether people have inborn beauty or ugliness or of whether they are good or bad people. Instead, the movement is inverted: what is in someone's soul will be visible on his countenance. But Lavater also limits his position by noting that virtue beautifies and vice uglifies, intensifying what is already there to begin with. He admits that socioeconomic circumstances such as climate, profession, illness, and profession are influential to appearance. Most important, though, improvement is always possible and desirable. Although certain predispositions of the mind and body are inherited, you can better yourself: "that the whole bony system with the fleshy parts, the whole frame taken together—figure, colour, voice, gait, smell—every thing, in a word, has a relation to the face, and is liable to degradation or improvement[39] together with it. . . . But if . . . Man be liable to fall, he is able to rise again, and capable of attaining an elevation of virtue superior even to that from which he fell."[40]

In a series of drawings produced on two consecutive days in 1797 (figures 1.1 and 1.2), Lavater depicts a gradual transition from ugliness (November 16) to beauty (November 17). Starting from the "ugliest ugliness," he creates sometimes hardly noticeable changes in the physiognomy of a profile whose gender is equally hard to guess at the beginning but is clearly female by its beautiful stages. The series could serve as a visualization of the great chain of being, an array of species stretching from God down to the lowest living being. In much nineteenth-century thought, the chain of being was also a chain of beauty,[41] and it certainly was so for Lavater. From this perspective, the beautiful individual is closest to God, and the ugly individual approximates the kingdom of animals. But Lavater maintains that the most deformed among men is still nobler than the most beautiful animal.

Lavater's insistence on a full range of humanity in physiognomy was motivated by his religious desire to find the true essence of human nature, which he felt reveals itself through the outer appearance of man:

Each creature is indispensable in the immensity of the creations of God. . . . No man ceases to be a man, how low soever he may sink beneath the dignity of human nature. Not being beast he still is capable of amendment, of approaching perfection. . . . In every human countenance, however debased, humanity still is visible, that is, the image of the Deity.[42]

By believing that every human can approach perfection, Lavater sets the stage for a science that seeks the cause and expression of individual vice, which lessens each man's inherent perfection. He explains the moral position behind the matter of the outer appearance, a position motivated by a belief in the absolute "good" nature of human beings:

I have seen the worst of men, in their worst of moments, yet could not all their vice, blasphemy, and oppression of guilt, extinguish the light of good that shone in their countenances, the spirit of humanity, the ineffaceable traits of internal, external perfectibility—the sinner we must exterminate, the man we must embrace.[43]

Figure 1.1
Johann Kaspar Lavater, *The Ugliest Ugliness* (*Die hässlichste Hässlichkeit*), November 16, 1797. The caption below the drawing reads: "The unnaturally prominent forehead; the wild eyebrows; the angular and blunt nose; the lacking upper lip; the preponderant lower lip, which almost reaches the end of the rather short nose; the small chin becoming a goiter; [all these characteristics] determine ugliness and stupidity. The eye is goodish."

Figure 1.2

Johann Kaspar Lavater, *Progress toward Beauty* (*Fortschritt zur Schönheit IV*), November 17, 1797. The caption below the drawing says: "The arch of the forehead is a little more open and beautiful; eyebrows and eyes a little more delicate; the nose a little more majestic; mouth and chin a little more grandiose; but the lower lip should be a bit less prominent and more set back. To the whole [appearance], we admit beauty."

Although in the nineteenth and twentieth centuries the extermination of undesirable traits was transposed onto entire populations, Lavater intends no such exclusions. The sinner who is to be excised is part of an individual, a set of character traits that physiognomic research will enable science to define and isolate. Lavater thus retains a notion of free will and believes in the fundamental ability of people to practice virtue. Nevertheless, the physiognomist in Lavater is able to reveal whether someone was born as a good person, a *kalókagathos*, or if he has pushed himself to be better through practicing *paideia*.

Lavater's approach to his work was thoroughly eclectic and subjective and often fused empirical observation with unscientific methods, depending on his intuitions. He even admits to forming judgments about faces he sees on the street instantly and without any reflection: "when a face with which I was wholly unacquainted, so forcibly struck me, notwithstanding my near-sightedness and distance from the street, I instantly formed a decided judgment upon the case. Reflection had no share in it."[44] Lavater further reveals that only when he turned away from the study of books and to the study of nature and the "images which represented her" was he able to fulfill his principal ideals, which in a Neoplatonic fashion were to be found not in nature but in the human form: "to discover the beautiful, the noble, the perfect; to define them, to familiarize them to my eye, and to give fresh energy to the sensations which they excited."[45] These judgments result from an assumed universal instinctive grasp of correspondences between outer and inner beauty. In Lavater's own estimation, the differences of character that manifest themselves on the surface of an individual face respond to and provoke universal reactions that touch the core of our moral and intellectual being:

Place a man perfectly handsome by the side of one homely in the extreme; and no one will say of the former, "He is an ugly fellow," nor of the latter, "He is charmingly beautiful." Let the handsome man disfigure his face by grimaces, and every person who looks at him, were the spectators collected from every nation under heaven, would cry out with one voice: "That face is ugly, disagreeable, hideous!" and the moment he returns to his natural form, "It is beautiful, agreeable, graceful."[46]

Lavater's chief physiognomic method was intuitive. It was a direct expression of his imagination and the moral instinct that fueled his drawings. In a letter, he advises Count Thun of Vienna that every student of physiognomy first needs the "physiognomical sensation of drawing,"[47] and he proposes to proceed from a holistic perception of a face to a more detailed one by describing first the whole form and then each particular feature. The description should further entail the proportions of the face. On the basis of these descriptions, a drawing of the person in question should be produced in his or her absence. The key to physiognomic success is thus to "describe and draw, draw and describe."[48]

But who is looking at us through these portraits? In the case of the 280 portraits in the plates accompanying Lavater's *Essays on Physiognomy*,[49] the people looking at us are of various natures. In addition to establishing groups divided by degrees of beauty and ugliness, Lavater characterizes his subjects into categories like awareness (*Aufmerksamkeit*), mental weakness (*Geistesschwäche*), vice (*Laster*), passion (*Leidenschaft*), religion (*Religion*), and women (*Weiber*). About the latter, Lavater provides a range of possible looks, some in combination with religious behaviors, awareness, authenticity, and female moral qualities such as motherhood. Given Lavater's confession that he lacked opportunities to observe women, cultural imaginings were probably more important than empirical research in his attempts to observe women:

I must premise, I am but little acquainted with the female part of the human race. Any man of the world must know more of them than I can pretend to know; my opportunities of seeing them at the theatre, at balls, or at the card table, where they best may be studied, have been exceedingly few. In my youth I almost avoided women, and was never in love.[50]

Lavater's Concept of Female Beauty: Devotion versus Masquerade

Despite these claims of ignorance, Lavater had a lot to say about femininity and about female appearance. The first issue he struggles with is whether we can believe female appearance or whether we must assume that what we see conceals for the most part an underlying deception. Lavater invites us to learn the skills of physiognomy so that we can read a woman's outer appearance, which may trick us. In his appealing graphic illustrations in the German original edition, physiognomy itself was represented as a secret weapon to decode the "hypocrisy of female appearance" (figure 1.3).

Behind the beautiful and confidence-inspiring face of a woman, we see a skeleton indicating nonbeauty and even death—the annihilation of

Figure 1.3
Illustration from Johann Kaspar Lavater, *Physiognomische Fragmente, zur Beförderung der Menschenkenntnis und Menschenliebe.*

beauty. In addition to his message not to trust a beautiful female face, he draws a parallel between life and death: what brings you life (woman) may also bring you death (through illness or other means). This is one of the oldest myths and truisms about the female body, which has lasted to modern times.[51] This issue of hypocrisy—of the possible deception behind a beautiful female face—is also at stake in Lavater's many examples of how he saw women perform in society as agents of mourning, motherhood, old wisdom, or "sanguine devotion."

The above description brings us back to the Plotinian notion of *kalóka-gatheia*, which claims that a lack of spirituality produces an ugly soul: "For a soul, ugliness consists in being impure, no longer unmingled, like gold tarnished by particles of earth."[52] Although Plotinus did not provide a physiognomic account of what an ugly soul would look like, Lavater did. He was able to detect beauty that disguised an ugly soul as though it were a mask. The true physiognomist acts as a moral guardian who helps men to discover what is hidden behind the mask of female beauty—appetite, affection, and cunning. To him, the masquerade is obvious, and his knowledge will keep him and others, whom he informs, safe from these women and the "dangerous charms of their shameless bosoms."[53] For Lavater the pastor, there is only one way to reach female authentic beauty—the beauty of female devotion (*Andacht*). The problem of the beauty of the "sanguine female" shown in figure 1.4 ("eyes and nose are spiritless") resides in her lack of an inner purity that is not spoiled by hypocrisy—that is, by outer display.

But what is the ideal appearance of a devoted woman, according to Lavater? How can she be pleasant looking and not deceiving? The answer to this is not simple. The physiognomist tends to divide a female face into two parts. The upper part is where the eyes, eyebrows, and nose are located, and for Lavater, it is the area that often houses intelligence and wisdom. We are able to detect this wisdom from the expression of the eye. At its best, female "noble silent wisdom" is of a certain confidence-inspiring mature age (figure 1.5).

Lavater prefers the upper area of the female face, like the eyebrows, to be astute. He also prefers the eye not to look up but straight forward or even downward, as in figure 1.5. His default reading of an upward directed gaze is that the person is a hypocrite, dreamer, or seducer. The lower part of the female face, on the other hand, tends toward softness. He may detect

Figure 1.4
Johann Kaspar Lavater, *Sanguine Female Devotion* (*Sanguinisch weibliche Andacht*), 1795. The caption reads: "Oh! She would so much like to rise, and she rises indeed above the earth; but the mass of the flesh is pending heavily from her spirit. The eye and nose are spiritless; but eye and mouth and chin are very sanguine, and phlegmatic. But it is not the face of a hypocrite."

Figure 1.5
Johann Kaspar Lavater, *Noble Silent Wisdom* (*Edle ruhige Weisheit*), 1796. The caption reads: "The accordance and simplicity of simple, softly curved contours without any foreignness, rigidity, stretching—is a main characteristic of wisdom. The eye bears the character of the nose, the forehead, the mouth, the chin. Everything innocence, clarity, soft purity, goodness, tranquil wisdom, nobility."

a "featherbrained mouth" (*dümmlicher Mund*) or a weak chin, but these do not seem to contradict positively connoted characteristics of astonishment and passion, which he often attributes to the lower face.

The overall interpretive framework depends on the extent to which the appearance expresses a moral stance. The relationship between utmost innocence (virginity or motherhood) and female beauty is evident in Lavater's chain of descriptions: "innocence, clarity, soft purity, goodness, tranquil wisdom, nobility." The more innocent a woman's appearance, the more noble or morally apt she is, and therefore the better she is in character. Another way of measuring a woman's character through appearance is devotion. Lavater, as a pastor, starts from the premise that men and women are made to be religious. But Lavater's gender preference becomes clear when he looks at at godless people: a man without God is destined to illness, and a woman without God turns into a monster:[54]

Man without religion is a diseased creature, who would persuade himself he is well, and needs not a physician; but woman without religion is raging and monstrous.

A woman with a beard is not so disgusting as a woman who acts the free thinker; her sex is formed to piety and religion; to them Christ first appeared; but he was obliged to prevent them from too ardently, and too hastily, embracing him.—*Touch me not.*[55]

What is evident from this description is that woman can never act alone, independently from man, who is the only free thinker. She also needs rules such as "touch me not" so that her immoral instincts (which are likely to be sexually charged) do not overcome her. To appear credibly religious, not a shimmer of a doubt—often depicted through wrinkled eyebrows or a long forehead—may be detectable on the face.

Sometimes Lavater's interpretations are arbitrary. No wrinkled eyebrows or in any way "suspicious" appearance are detectable from the below portrait of a "Jesuit coldness"[56] (figure 1.6). Nevertheless, Lavater claims to read a lot into this harmless-looking face.

Although Lavater's intuitions, as in the case of "Jesuit coldness," were entirely subjective and lacked grounds even within his own system of distinguishing the "beautiful" from the "ugly," he did have a cohesive way of attributing looks to gender. Beauty and morality are in a completely different relationship for men and women, however. Lavater's decision to depict a female profile as the emblem of beauty is therefore not a coincidence, as her beauty is already wired into her hardware:

Figure 1.6

Johann Kaspar Lavater, *Jesuit Coldness (Jesuitische Kälte)*. The caption reads: "Not a profound, but a cold understanding forehead. A clear lurking eye without philosophical acuteness—smart and seductive and difficult to seduce, the nose. Cold intelligent the mouth and chin. The whole [face] seems to be lacking delicacy and love."

Consideration and comparison of the external and internal make of the body, in male and female, teaches us that the one is destined for labour and strength; and the other for beauty and propagation. . . . The female skeleton gradually grows thinner and weaker from the hip upwards, and by degrees appears as if it were rounded.[57]

As the "second player," woman has been taken out of man, as Lavater states in accordance with the Hebrew Bible's book of Genesis, but by referring to the New Testament's book of First Corinthians (3.12), where he makes woman's adorning role even clearer. He references that "woman is not a foundation on which to build. She is the gold, silver, precious stones, wood, hay, stubble."[58] The problem remains one of *kalókagatheia*. How can something be bad but appear beautiful? How can a man enjoy these adornments but not be deceived by them in case they are morally unsound? Again, the outer appearance speaks for itself. In his plate entitled *Ignoble Pain of a Not-Good Wife*, we learn from the following description: "Too bad that the nose of an evil woman is very wise. Eyes, eyebrows and mouth show a bitter sharpness and an ignoble pain; the wrath of a heavy 'nag-wife' that is made for righteous quarrel and for torture." Lavater regrets that according to his own physiognomical rules, this evil woman's nose, "the foundation, or abutement of the brain,"[59] would not hold to its beautiful premise.

The wrath of an old woman, hag, witch, bad wife, or evil grandmother—which translates into her intimidating, monstrous appearance—has a long history in Western culture.[60] As Nora Ruck points out in her study of the deviant, monstrous body in Lavater's physiognomic theory, Lavater is not mostly bothered by the fact of the monster; the monster does not lend itself to physiognomic interpretation for it runs contrary to the rules of nature. Physiognomic rules do not seem to apply. But the physiognomist in Lavater is disturbed by the disharmonious relation of a certain body part or parts to the whole.[61] The absolute harmony between each part of the human body to the whole is of utmost importance to Lavater. It is a result of his monadic believe that "each trait contains the whole character of man, as, in the smallest of the works of God, the character of Deity is contained. . . . Every minute part has the nature and character of the whole. Each speaks the truth, the truth of the whole."[62]

The ideal outer display of a woman is supposed to be harmonious, the eyes should be straight looking and focused,[63] and there should be a symmetry within all facial parts. Harmony and symmetry are markers for all of Lavater's positive female characteristics—motherliness, female wisdom, and devotion (which is the most desirable trait of a female appearance). The key element in Lavater's cosmetic gaze, however, is simplification—based on personal judgment:

My continual endeavour is to simplify. The three things to which, especially, attention should be paid are the general form of the countenance, the relation of its constituent parts, and their curved lines, or positions, all which may easily be expressed by the most simple marks.[64]

In Lavater's gender theory, there is a clear divide between man (the founder) and woman (the ornament), on whose foundation no trust can be laid. The outer is an expression of the inner the purpose to which the sexes are dedicated—male to provision and action; female to chastity, devotion, and reproduction. Lavater gives us the essence of his theory of the sexes in a poem entitled "A Word on the Physiognomical Relation of the Sexes":

Man is the most firm—woman the most flexible.

Man is the straightest—woman the most bending.

Man stands steadfast—woman gently trips.

Man surveys and observes—woman glances and feels.

Man is serious—woman is gay.

Man is the tallest and broadest—woman less and taper.

Man is rough and hard—woman smooth and soft.

Man is brown—woman is fair.

Man is wrinkly—woman less so.

The hair of man is more stringy and short—of woman more long and pliant.

The eyebrows of man are compressed—of woman less frowning.

Man has most convex lines—woman most concave.

Man has most straight lines—woman most curved.

The countenance of man, taken in profile, is more seldom perpendicular than that of the woman.

Man is most angular—woman most round.[65]

Lavater sums up his gender episode with the significant metaphor that "man singly, is but half man; at least but half human. A king without a kingdom."[66] There is man, who has enslaved women in his kingdom but who is gasping at female beauty, whether it is deceiving or real. The nineteenth-century cosmetic gaze gives birth to Darwin's evolutionary account of the relationship between the sexes with truisms similar to Lavater's, such as "Man is more courageous, pugnacious and energetic than woman, and thus has a more inventive genius."[67] To put it in the words of Sir Francis Galton, Darwin's cousin and the founder of eugenics: "One notable peculiarity in the character of the woman is that she is capricious and coy, and has less straightforwardness than man."[68]

The next section demonstrates how the Lavaterian physiognomy and gender theory dominated nineteenth-century European culture, a century that Lavater experienced for only two days. He died in the aftermath of the French occupation of Zurich on January 2, 1801.

Lavater's Influence on Nineteenth-Century Culture

By the nineteenth century, Lavater's ideas had permeated many areas of European culture, literature, art, medicine, and emerging social sciences.[69] An interest in physiognomy was also fueled by the rise of Franz Joseph Gall's (1758–1828) phrenology, even though Gall's methodological bases for phrenology focused on the bone structure of the skull. Some of the principles of realism that galvanized the plastic arts of the nineteenth century were inspired by Lavaterian physiognomy, as seen in detailed physiognomical character descriptions from Balzac, Marcel Proust, Edgar Allan Poe, Oscar Wilde, and T. S. Eliot.

A direct comparison can be made between Lavater and the German scientist Franz Mesmer (for whom mesmerism was named), who laid the ground for nineteenth-century discoveries such as hypnosis, and the Italian occultist Alessandro Cagliostro, in that all of them drew on the late eighteenth-century wave of antirational sentiment.[70] By the time of Lavater's contribution, the physiognomical tradition had lost some of its impetus, as a general hostility toward superstition and the occult accompanied Enlightenment rationalism (as alluded to earlier in the discussion of the Neoplatonic revival of the concept of *kalókagatheia*). Montaigne expressed his skepticism in harsh terms, writing that "c'est une foible garantie que la mine; toutesfois elle a quelque consideration" (the face is not to be trusted; nevertheless, it is worthy of some consideration).[71]

Lavater's work, however, returned authority as well as popularity to the maligned science. His success had many sources, including his ability for marketing (as in the pocket editions of his work), a tendency to capture a zeitgeist, and the quality of his earlier editions, including his hand-drawn illustrations. On the other hand, Lavater's religious background, which may have earned him acceptability in some circles, was also cause for some skepticism toward his work. As Lucy Hartley points out, one problem associated with Lavater's physiognomy was his application of a religious paradigm to scientific content.[72]

In her physiognomic biography of Adolf Hitler's face, Claudia Schmoelders identifies an important historical connection between Lavater's physiognomical eye and his attention to the facial closeup, bequeathing to photography "the claim to evidence."[73] In Schmoelder's opinion, the physiognomist's diagnosis that an earlobe grown to the face is proof of a criminal disposition can be taken as a precursor to the medical and criminological photography of Lombroso and his school of criminal anthropology.[74] Schmoelders concludes that between 1780 and 1914 the physiognomist's hope that an exterior bespeaks the merits (or crimes) of the interior had made tremendous strides. Slowly but surely, the discipline of physiognomy conquered the sciences and the juridical fields (including anthropology, psychiatry, and racial theories). Literature was also highly influenced by physiognomy. Schmoelders points out that Lavater's visual physiognomy—and I would include the criminal anthropological attempts by Lombroso and the racial eugenics practiced by the Nazis—was a "physiognomy directed downward"[75] toward the identification of criminals and the ill, who did not fit the parameters of the healthy body. Literature, on the other hand, often turned the competence of the cosmetic gaze into a "physiognomy directed upward," praising the physical aspects of a person, transferring this visual closeup to a rhetorical closeup, or convincing a reader of a character's virtues and flaws.

One of the masters of the "physiognomic narration" was Marcel Proust. In his *Remembrance of Things Past* (published between 1913 and 1927), for instance, Marcel recounts Charles Swann's encounter with Odette de Crécy, the woman that Marcel expected the womanizer Swann to fall in love with. Swann did not "see" Odette's beauty, however, but was disturbed by the disharmonies in Odette's face: "Her profile was too sharp, her skin too delicate, her cheekbones were too prominent, her features too tightly drawn, to be attractive to him [Swann]. Her eyes were beautiful, but so large they seemed to droop beneath their own weight, strained the rest of her face and always made her appear unwell or in a bad mood."[76] Swann deduces from Odette's disharmonious appearance a "bad mood"—an emotion or an emotional expression that he disliked about Odette.

In the following section, the portraitistic, physiognomic eye's ability to implement an adorning gaze with the possibility of seeing a better, more beautiful body is "outsourced" to an apparatus other than the naked eye. The human eye is replaced by the photographic, physiognomic eye, which authenticates the body by exact measurement, drawing affirmative (and less intuitive) conclusions that assume legal status and a more authoritative claim to "objective" truth.

Darwinian Physiognomy, Eugenics, and Snapshots of Objectivity

For Lavater, the essence of man was his soul, and the body was a mirror of that soul, but an increasing number of scientists in the nineteenth century considered the body to be the essence of man. Among these was Sir Francis Galton (1822–1911), cousin of Charles Darwin,[77] who is remembered for his advances in statistics, twin studies, fingerprinting, and composite portraiture and for naming and defining *eugenics*.[78] Galton's work provides a rich contrast to Lavater's, especially since Galton expressed physiognomic ambitions, too. Galton was impressed by Darwin's insights, and in his 1869 treatise *Hereditary Genius*, he set out to prove that human faculties are not divine givens but transmitted from generation to generation. For Galton, character and intelligence were as hereditary as biological traits were, and as with Lavater, his key to discovering the nature of a man's character lay in the face.

Born into an age with technological possibilities that were unknown to Lavater, Galton was highly skeptical of the methodological value of drawings. He considered the differences in human facial features exceedingly numerous and too minute to be measured by the naked eye. A depiction of a face would have to account for all facial traits, but Lavater focuses on only a limited number of facial features. We can get an idea of Galton's reckoning by an episode he recounts in his *Inquiries into Human Faculty and Its Development*:

I lately watched an able artist painting a portrait, and endeavoured to estimate the number of strokes with his brush, every one of which was thoughtfully and firmly given. During fifteen sittings of three working hours each—that is to say, during forty-five hours, or two thousand four hundred minutes—he worked at the average rate of ten strokes of the brush per minute. There were, therefore, twenty-four thousand separate traits in the completed portrait, and in his opinion some, I do not say equal, but comparably large number of units of resemblance with the original.[79]

Galton considers traits to be the smallest units of a whole. Because the face is made of many units, it is unlikely that a painting or a drawing could achieve real likeness. A drawing, which is a rough sketch of a portrait, can be a suggestion of a person but not a likeness. Considering that all facial features together reveal a man's real nature, it becomes relevant to ask why the likeness between a face and its reproduction used for scientific study is of such vital importance to Galton. To overcome the difficulties inherent in drawing, Galton retreats to a technology he believes to be objective—photography.[80] To put this technological choice in a media-theoretical context, for Galton, the camera became the technological object through which he established his own "scientific gaze" of people's faces and through which we are supposed to align our gaze and our belief in the categorization that Galton proposes.[81] The gaze, in other words, becomes the camera, an apparatus whose function is to "put us into the picture."[82]

This is Galton's project—putting the valid representation of a single man into the picture. But this is only the first step in a series of procedures. Galton is looking for the identification of groups whose members share the same hereditary raw material. His method of composite portraiture starts by identifying members of groups whose inherent nature is to be analyzed (such as criminals) and by taking a photograph of each member under the same aspect (full face) and under the same conditions of light and face. These photographs are taken one after another within the exposure time usually required to take a single good picture. Unlike Lavater, who informs his readers about his spontaneous sentiments of drawing, Galton provides his readers with a six-step process:

(1) I collected photographic portraits of different persons, all of whom had been photographed in the same aspect (say full face), and under the same conditions of light and shade (say with the light coming from the right side). (2) I reduced their portraits photographically to the same size, being guided as to scale by the distance between any two convenient points of reference in the features;

... (3) I superimposed the portraits like the successive leaves of a book, so that the features of each portrait lay as exactly as the case admitted, in front of those of the one behind it, eye in front of eye and mouth in front of mouth. .... (4) I fastened the book against the wall in such a way that I could turn over the pages in succession, leaving in turn each portrait flat and fully exposed. (5) I focused my camera on the book, fixed it firmly, and put a sensitive plate inside it. (6) I began photographing, taking one page after the other in succession without moving the camera, but putting on the cap whilst I was turning over the pages, so that an image of each of the portraits in succession was thrown on the same part of the sensitised plate.[83]

The result of the composite process is an averaged figure that is supposed to bring into evidence "all the traits in which there is agreement, and to leave but a ghost of a trace of individual peculiarities."[84] It did not occur to Galton that drawings and photography could take part in the visual realities produced by them. In his view, photography produces picture that are not qualitatively different but rather are more precise than a hand-drawn picture because it can depict more facial traits and thus achieve a greater likeness.

The applications of Galton's composite portraiture[85] are at least fourfold: it can produce typologies of races; it allows a comparison between the average face of parental generations with that of their offspring; it produces the likeliest image of historic personages; and it reveals the real character of a single man. Galton argues that photography is better than drawing because it can capture a single expression at a given moment in time. Composite portraiture becomes a true physiognomical technology by presenting the essence of a man's inborn character. By the time *Human Faculty* appeared, Galton had turned to figures such as Alexander the Great, to family portraits, and to portraits of "healthy" and "ill/criminal" types (figure 1.7).

The groups that Galton juxtaposes in figure 1.7 are the "healthy type," the "ill type," and the "criminal type." The healthy type includes officers and privates from the Royal Engineers. Galton infers from this composite "an expression of considerable vigour, resolution, intelligence, and frankness."[86] The criminals summarized in this figure are thieves, murderers, and people convicted of other serious crimes. Galton remarks about these composites that "the individual faces are villainous enough, but they are villainous in different ways, and when they are combined, the individual peculiarities disappear, and the common humanity of a low type is all that is left."[87] According to Nora Ruck,[88] the healthy type and the criminal or

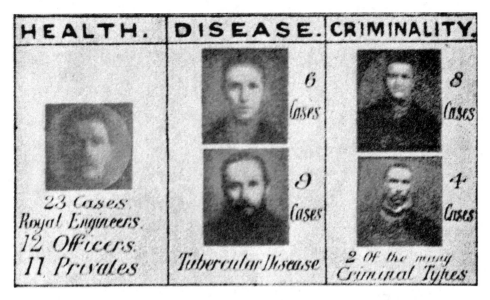

HEALTH.	DISEASE.	CRIMINALITY.

6
Cases

8
Cases

9
Cases

4
Cases

23 Cases
Royal Engineers.
12 Officers.
11 Privates

Tubercular Disease

2 Of the many
Criminal Types

Figure 1.7
Specimens of composite portraiture: health, disease, and criminality. From Francis
Galton, *Inquiries into Human Faculty and Its Development* (London: MacMillan,
1883), 9.

low type therefore represent the two poles of an imaginary bell curve portraying the nature of the "British race." Galton believes that each race has
such an ideal form on which all individuals are based and deviates from
it in minor ways. The healthy type exhibits a desirable deviation from the
average, whereas the criminal type embodies an undesirable deviation.

Although Lavater's intuitive method of internalizing the character traits
he found in the world onto an "internal screen" was ostensibly descriptive,
Galton's proceedings were prescriptive from the outset. Galton thus
sketches a sociopolitical program for creating a world that has rid itself of
deviant groups. The belief in the unquestionable will of a divine creator
had to some extent prevented Lavater from drawing sociopolitical conclusions from his physiognomic observations. A century after Lavater and in
the midst of the Darwinistic turn in the European sciences, though, Galton
could openly confront the religious authorities and proclaim that man
"should look upon himself more as a freeman, with power of shaping the
course of future humanity."[89] He used the Greek term *eugenes* meaning
"good in stock" or "hereditarily endowed with noble qualities"[90] to coin

the term *eugenics* to describe how the course of evolution could actively be advanced. In fact, the *eugenes* are synonymous with the "good and beautiful," the *kaloi kagathoi* of the classical Greek era (described above). The aim of eugenics thus lay in the improvement of a given stock. The term also emphasizes the biologistic nature of Galton's counterproposal to a religious world view. In 1904, twenty years later, Galton proclaims that eugenics is the new religion of the British race and that its installation demands a three-step process:

First, it must be made familiar as an academic question, until its exact importance has been understood and accepted as a fact. Secondly, it must be recognized as a subject the practical development of which is in near prospect, and requires serious consideration. Thirdly, it must be introduced into the national conscience, like a new religion. It has, indeed, strong claims to become an orthodox religious tenet for the future, for eugenics cooperates with the workings of nature by securing that humanity shall be represented by the fittest races.[91]

With Galton, Lavater's notion of the good and the bad and their connection with beauty and ugliness experienced a translation into the language of evolution. What was formerly identified as the good is now the well adapted, and the bad has become the badly adapted. Galton's project is still a physiognomic one insofar as he sees the body as an expression of underlying qualities; however, Galton's body no longer expresses the "soul" or "character" of a person but instead reveals the "hardware" of its constituency, indicating its genetic deep structure.[92]

For Galton, the aim of eugenics was the representation of each class (or race) by its best specimens. He was not especially interested in other races, although he believed in the superiority of the British race. For Galton, though, the average Englishman of his time was not as well adapted to his environment as he should be. The solution to this problem lay in supplanting the average with the desirable deviation—the healthy type. To this end, Galton suggested banning marriages that were unsuitable from a eugenic point of view and encouraging suitable marriages. Galton did not advance what became known as negative eugenics (decreasing the fertility of the genetically disadvantaged or mass homicide for those considered deviant), but he did lay both the ground and the terminology for a fascist regime to exterminate those "not fit[ting]" through radical programs of ethnic cleansing.

According to Sharrona Pearl,[93] the nineteenth-century turn to interiority did not do away with physiognomic principles altogether. The popularity that physiognomy enjoyed in nineteenth-century Britain, of which Galton's composite portraits are just one example, started to decrease by the end of the century. From then on, physiognomy took on the manifestation of either "radical exteriority" or "radical interiority." The first form is most evident in the classificatory methods (such as craniometry) used by anthropologists and eugenicists. Unlike physiognomy in its Lavaterian formulation, the discourse of radical exteriority as present in much anthropological research and eugenics at the turn of the century focused on the visual classification of collectives and aimed at making claims about actual or constructed groups. The discourse of radical interiority, on the other hand, turned physiognomic principles upside down.

To return to the question of the gaze in relation to a cultural screen onto which these images of good and bad character traits are projected, we can say that Lavater mapped these images onto an internalized normative screen based on a Christian Neoplatonic world order and that Galton externalized the construction process of the image onto the "rational" apparatus of photography. Whereas Lavater was proud of his intuitive capacity to judge, a capacity that was gained through describing and drawing and his overall knowledge of mankind, Galton was afraid of the inevitable errors of subjective judgment and therefore entrusted an "other" (a machine) to make the ultimate judgment. Ultimately, however, neither of these men's world views damaged human dignity to the extent that Galton's contemporary, the Italian psychiatrist and criminal anthropologist Cesare Lombroso, did.

Deviant Bodies: Criminals and Women = Monsters[94]

According to Michel Foucault (1926–1984), the body since the classical age has been overall a prescriptive and normative one that is subject to disciplinary power or what he terms *biopower*.[95] The story of the rise of biopower, which he tells across many books, is also one of the inclusion of traditionally marked and excluded bodies into social normativity. In the case of what he terms the *carceral society*, the rise of the prison as society's preferred form of legal enforcement "fails to eliminate crime" but "has succeeded extremely well in producing delinquency."[96] According to this history, behavioral and bodily deviancies are gradually incorporated, mapped, and ultimately controlled as part of a regimented spectrum of normalcy. Although Galton laid the groundwork for the naturalization of the criminal and thus of moral and physical deviance, biological determinism of the criminal did not become a widely held notion until the Italian psychiatrist Cesare Lombroso (1835–1909) founded the discipline of criminal anthropology in the late nineteenth century. Lombroso, a medical doctor, was interested in the "abnormal" mind and body of the criminal and the madman, and for him, lawbreaking was a result primarily of biological and only secondarily of psychological and social factors. In an encompassing attempt to explain the natural deviation of the criminal from the "normal" rest of society, Lombroso turned to the concept of *atavism*, denoting a drawback to an earlier period or a lower stage of evolution. Maintaining that the born criminal represents a lower evolutionary stage, Lombroso claimed that he shared common characteristics with primitive man (man of earlier epochs), with savages, and with members of "'inferior' groups like women, southern Italians, or Africans."[97] Just as Lavater's great chain of being ranged from God to the lowest human being, for Lombroso the criminal is closest to the animal in this chain, to put it in his own atavistic terminology. Lombroso examines the groups that were beginning to elicit anxiety in late nineteenth-century Europe and America and concludes that women, nonwhites, the poor, and children are physically, psychologically, and morally inferior to white men.

A hundred years before Lombroso, the philosopher Cesare Beccaria (1738–1794) coined the category of "the free will of criminals" in *On Crimes and Punishment* (1764). For Beccaria, punishment was not revenge but a means to create a better society. His operating term was the *free will* of the individual, whether criminal or not. Punishment thus served to deter members of society from committing crimes and to prevent the criminal from repeating his crime. For Lombroso, any penalty is a punishment of an individual and not for a crime. Due to his belief in biological determinism, he insists on the absence of free will in the criminal. Consequently, in opposition to Beccaria's condemnation of capital punishment in favor of "perpetual slavery," Lombroso opts for the criminal's elimination from society, including taking his or her life. Penalty, including capital punishment, becomes society's way of protecting itself from atavistic tendencies.

In *Criminal Man* (the first edition was published in 1876, and the final fifth edition in 1896–1897), Lombroso collects what he claims is convincing evidence that the physical characteristics of primitive man return in the born criminal (*delinquente nato*), a man with "evil inclinations."[98] These include low, sloping foreheads; overdeveloped sinuses, jaws, and cheekbones; prognathism (an apelike forward thrust of the lower face); oblique and large eye sockets; dark skin; thick and curly head hair; large or protuberant ears; and long arms.[99] Lombroso finds these features best represented in the black and Mongol races and—according to his theory of atavism—in prehistoric man. Based on anatomical predispositions (such as microcefalic or small craniums) that he found, for instance, in the male criminal Vilella of Calabria, Lombroso identified several criminal character traits—an absence of moral and affective sensibility, laziness, an absence of remorse and foresight, great vanity, and fleeting, violent passions. He wondered how society could blame Vilella or punish him if his violent passions were "innate."

Lombroso was not alone in coming up with scientific methods to categorize the anatomies of "inferior" groups like women and blacks into what can be called "the physiologically different" from white man. The discipline of phrenology—which taught that the brain consists of separate faculties (the number of which varied according to the various schools) that govern certain aspects of human behavior and are each developed differently in the various races—was already widely spread and adapted at the time of Lombroso's *Criminal Man*.

Samuel R. Wells, for instance, a traveling professor of phrenology who offered popular lectures and analyzed heads across the United States,[100] published an illustrated handbook of phrenology and physiognomy in 1871 in New York (figure 1.8). For Wells, certain races, particularly the Caucasian, have superior skulls that host superior human faculties:

the skulls of races and nations also differ widely in form, and these differences are found to correspond with known differences of character. In the Caucasian it will be seen that the forehead is prominent and high, the coronal region elevated, and the back-head moderately projected. . . . It indicates great intellectual power, strong moral or spiritual sentiments, and a comparatively moderate development of the propensities. The special organs in which the Caucasian brain most excels, and which distinguish it from those of all less advanced races, are Mirthfulness, Ideality, and Conscientiousness, the organs of these faculties being somewhat smaller in savage and barbarous tribes.[101]

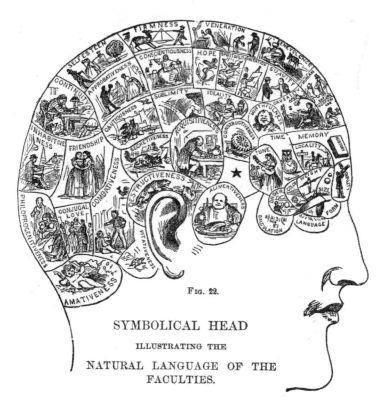

Figure 1.8
A phrenological map of human faculties. From Samuel R. Wells, *How to Read Character. A New Illustrated Handbook of Phrenology and Physiognomy for Students and Examiners with a Descriptive Chart* (1895) (Rutland, VT: Charles E. Tuttle Company, 1971), fig. 22.

Wells tried to resist the conclusion that is inherent in the above quotation—that female, Negro, or Indian skulls produce inferior or potentially criminal characters—by noting that it cannot be "assumed that one race or ethnic group holds a distinct intellectual advantage over another."[102] But his choice of words implies otherwise. The forehead of the Caucasian is described positively as *prominent* and *high*, and the foreheads of the North American Indian and Negro are described negatively as being "broad and very prominent at the lower part, but tend to retreat. "[103] For example, Wells read character into the two foreheads shown in figure 1.9: "If the lower part of the forehead predominate, as in fig. 169, perception will be found in the

THOUGHTFUL.

OBSERVING.

FIG. 168.—HEPWORTH DIXON.†   FIG. 169.—A LOWLANDER.

Figure 1.9

Illustrations of two male profiles. From Samuel R. Wells, *How to Read Character, A New Illustrated Handbook of Phrenology and Physiognomy for Students and Examiners with a Descriptive Chart* (1895) (Rutland, VT: Charles E. Tuttle Company, 1971), figs. 168–169.

ascendant; and if the upper portion be largest, as in fig. 168, there will be more thoughtfulness or reflection and less observation—more philosophy and less science—more of the theoretical than of the practical."[104] But Wells manipulates his audience's viewpoint in these two drawings. The face with the "high" forehead, which is supposed to be more thoughtful, is featured looking down, which makes making the forehead look longer. This face also has a name: Hepworth Dixon. The "bad forehead" of the "lowlander" (not named) is shown from a straight profile, which in its representation in the book looks shorter and emphasizes the more "observant and practical" character trait, which results from the predominating lower part of the forehead. The fact that the "philosophically inclined characters" would generally be pictured with a beard or eyeglasses indicates that Wells is not objective in his classifications. Rather, these representations can be compared to the before and after pictures that are popular in today's makeover industry and that are generally subjected to image manipulation.[105]

Although phrenology and criminal anthropology shared similar approaches to reading the criminal or deviant body, in that both are looking for hard evidence that is evolutionarily motivated, Lombroso distanced himself from the phrenologists by arguing that they were too "qualitatively deterministic,"[106] were not experimental enough, and relied too much on methods like anthropometry.[107] Even though Lombroso was strongly dedicated to anthropometry, which he called an "ark of salvation from the metaphysical, a priori systems dear to all those engaged in the study of man,"[108] and was especially fond of craniometry, the methods ultimately fell short of his expectations:

Lombroso had anticipated that measurements of dead and living bodies would reveal correlations between criminal dangerousness and such mundane features as body weight, height, proportions of the limbs, and cranial capacity. Many of his studies would, however, reveal only minute differences, useless for the identification of dangerous individuals.[109]

Despite becoming critical of the methods due to their misuse by neglectful scientists, Lombroso nonetheless continued to employ them. He claimed that the discrepancies between him and most of the authorities in the field "flow from the fact that the variations in measurement between the normal and the abnormal subject are so small as to defy all but the richest research."[110] By 1896, Lombroso had measured a total of 6,608 French, German, and Italian criminals. Lombroso's compulsive measuring can be read as an indication that he was looking for *something*. As Horn points out, in Lombroso's semiology the body was a bearer of signs that stand for that something, such as atavism or social danger. These signs were not in a causal relationship to behavior but were important to Lombroso in that they could predict criminal conduct. Physical difference was a sign for something that the doctor—in this case the psychiatrist Lombroso—could read as "marked" and thus potentially dangerous. Almost like a decoder of a mystery or a secret, Lombroso the semiologist was trying to read *into* the body to find the correlating character trait. But as Horn points out,[111] Lombroso's goal was not to identify the criminal, as Galton's composite method was designed to do. Instead, Lombroso was interested in the signaletics of dangerousness, of the fact that something could be wrong or off with an individual, and the possibilities of recognizing these pathological symptoms.

Lombroso was, in part, the product of a culture that had been inspired by the rules of the ancient *kalókagatheia*, resuscitated by Christoph Wieland not even a century before Lombroso's *Criminal Man*. Wieland's socioeconomical observations on how "a free and noble human being" could easily be distinguished "from a slave and from a human-like animal" had been enriched by anthropometrical data and findings in evolutionary biology and psychology. Lombroso's cosmetic gaze was thus informed by a combination of two different discourse regimes—reading human appearances according to the rules of *kalókagatheia* and relating them to nineteenth-century findings in biology and psychology (including the euphoria inherent in the new belief in scientific authority and truth). As much as I would like to repudiate Lombroso's criminal anthropology, I agree with Horn that "dismissive readings of either nineteenth-century or twentieth-century sciences of the criminal body as pseudoscience"[112] are counterproductive. We must instead consider the cultural background of Lombroso's deterministic interpretations of the real bodies of the criminals and the people with disabilities that he studied.

Lombroso's paradoxical theories of "normal" versus "abnormal" are apparent in his anthropological account of criminal women, which influenced studies on female crime until the 1970s.[113] For Lombroso, femininity is always potentially pathological, and at the lowest evolutionary stage of atavism, it becomes monstrosity (this is discussed in more detail in chapter 2). But even the best and most trustworthy of feminine traits remain suspicious because a beautiful masquerade can hide that very *something* that Lombroso was searching for and by which he was driven. Lombroso seems to suspect that women's pathologies are always latent and that their criminality can therefore erupt at any time. Women, due to biology, can offer their bodies to men at any time, turning them into the "female equivalent of the male born criminal," the prostitute.[114]

In his preface to the *Criminal Woman* (1893), Lombroso makes clear where woman stands in relation to man in her evolutionary stage: "In the human race she appears equal or superior to the male before puberty— equal in strength and stature, even in intelligence; but gradually she falls behind, leaving proof of that precocity that is standard among the inferior races."[115] The word *appear* expresses Lombroso's deepest suspicion for the female. It may seem that a woman is superior, but she is in fact not because (as Lavater would add) her femininity is a camouflage that prevents her from true divine devotion (in Lavater's case) and that hides her promiscuity (in Lombroso's case). In his chapter "The Female in the Animal World," Lombroso stresses the fact that despite certain female animals' superiority over their male counterpart (such as the female spider *Tegenaria domestica*), "males are almost always superior in anatomical structure."[116] Lombroso explains that this "female superiority" in the animal world is necessary to guarantee a species' survival and therefore is related to the "necessary evil" of reproduction. Thus, at the lowest end of Lombroso's *female chain of being* is promiscuity or promiscuous sexual conduct that is present in all women and may turn them at any point into criminals or prostitutes. Although Lavater offered an endearing "gender-poem" that pointed to gender difference as positive complementary polarity ("man is the most firm—woman the most flexible"), in Lombroso's account of sexual difference, men and women do resemble each other—at the lowest stage of evolution (the criminal or atavistic stage). In other words, primitive and criminal people lack the strong differentiation of the sexes that Lombroso believed to be essential for civilized peoples. Lombroso's belief in sexual difference leads him to treat female and male crimes separately. He insists that "the word *beautiful* has different meanings for the two sexes, and its meaning is less specific for woman"[117] because man chooses woman for her beauty, while "woman does not appreciate beauty because her sexual sensitivity is weak."[118] Throughout *Criminal Woman*, Lombroso consistently employs the white man as a measure against which he first defines normal woman and, by extension, criminal woman. Relying on a curious mixture of sources, including results by other anthropologists, historical anecdotes, examples drawn from literature and painting, and even proverbs,[119] Lombroso claims to prove, with considerable argumentative and empirical effort, that the female correlate to the male criminal is not the female criminal but the prostitute. Again, he accords this to atavism, since the savage woman is to him essentially a prostitute and as such enslaved to the (sexual) will of man. Although the criminal man is marked by an array of physical degenerative signs and Lombroso considers him to be therefore uglier than the normal man, it is not so with the prostitute:

In prostitutes we have women of great youth in whom the "beauty of the devil," with its abundance of soft, fresh flesh and absence of wrinkles, masks anomalies. . . . Certainly makeup—a virtual requirement of the prostitute's sad trade—

minimizes many of the degenerative characteristics that female criminals exhibit openly. Where delicacy of feature and a benevolent expression are useful, we find them—a truly Darwinian phenomenon.[120]

As with Lavater, here is a theory of beauty as masquerade. Women, naturally bestowed with an "instinct for lying,"[121] hide their moral and intellectual shortcomings because they are cheaters in the competitive game of sexual selection. To Lombroso, prostitutes are especially prone to the use of makeup or toiletries: "lies in action, used by woman as ammunition in the sexual battle."[122] But he considers prostitution a far less malign counterpart of male criminality. He even writes in his preface that "I certainly need to state, very clearly, that she [woman] is less perverse and less harmful to society [than the male born criminal]"[123] and that prostitution "would not exist without male vice, for which it is a useful, shameful, outlet."[124]

Apart from measuring heads and bodies, Lombroso used photographs in his collection of criminals from around the world. Galton relied on the photograph to reproduce a "truth" of an average type in an approach of "pictorial statistics,"[125] but Lombroso used photography in a different way. The fifth and last edition of *Criminal Man* (1896–1897) featured an *Atlas* of illustrations and photographs of criminal types (figure 1.10). Colleagues from around the world sent him their collections to increase the criminal anthropologist's master database. He also reproduced images from newspapers and journals, such as *The New York Police Journal*, which permitted him "the study of the Anglo-American type of criminal."[126] When commenting on these photographs, he concludes that "the criminal type is so strong as to force one to wonder whether some of the portraits are no more than different shots of the same person."[127]

Despite all these different facial types (and the fact that I believe the similarity is expressed—if at all—more through facial hair than anatomical differences), Lombroso claims that these born criminals (especially the murderers) resemble each other in the following abnormal characteristics— a large jaw, a scanty beard, enlarged sinus cavities, a shifty gaze, thick hair, and jug ears. He also lists asymmetry, femininity, sloping foreheads, and prognathism as unifying criminal characteristics.[128] But as Horn points out, Lombroso's *Atlas* was only in part about the documentation of individual offenders. Others (like the French law enforcement officer, biometricist, and promoter of anthropometry Alphonse Bertillon) had started before

Figure 1.10
An album of criminal photographs. From Cesare Lombroso and Guglielmo Ferrero, *Criminal Man*, trans. and with an introduction by Mary Gibson and Nicole Hahn Rafter (Durham: Duke University Press, 2006), 203.

him in his classification of the outlawed in what he coined "signaletics."[129] The *Atlas* was really about psychiatric diagnostics. Lombroso tried to read the (bad) character traits lying beneath the skin of these faces. He did not just classify them and engage in the calculation of a mathematical average, as Galton did and as he did by listing similarities that were not as evident as he claimed they were. If anything, the production of an average would not satisfy Lombroso in his scopophilia for the deviant, since he was looking at the outlawed, the uncommon. As Horn puts it, "precisely because the 'type' was not common, it was necessary to multiply rather than collapse or superimpose the pictures of the heads and faces of the dangerous, and to look and read with attention both to family resemblance and to idiosyncratic difference."[130]

Probably the best example of Lombroso's perverted-eye diagnostics are his photographs of criminal children and their "dangerousness." When I look at the girl shown in figure 1.11, I see a child too sad to cry. The little girl is folding her arms in front of her chest. She looks disappointed, unloved, and sad. But Lombroso saw in this picture an expression of immorality and a loss of innocence.[131] When I look at the girl shown in figure 1.12—a photograph of a Flemish girl taken in 1942 by Erna Lendvai-Dircksen as an example the "Germanic popular face" (*germanisches Volksgesicht*)—it seems that one girl could have easily been the same model for both photos. What is different is that the criminal girl's hair has been cut off and that her gaze is directed downward, into the grounds of her poverty, and not staring upward at an unknown but concrete place, as in the Flemish girl's case.[132]

Both Galton and Lombroso believed in the fixity of types, and their physiognomic gaze—despite its difference—was thoroughly fixating and particularly in Lombroso's case dangerously discriminating. Due to their commitment to a deviance-free society, the two scientists had in mind the removal of undesirable social elements. However, Lombroso concluded that the deviant was a necessary evil in the "symbiosis" of all members of a society, since the born criminals "promoted not only destruction, but also renovation of the social order."[133] That combination of physiognomic competence with a totalitarian political agenda eventually led to efforts to eliminate "deviance." During Germany's Third Reich, the Nazis turned Galton's and Lombroso's prescriptive physiognomic gaze into the eradication of *the* deviant body of its time—the Jewish body. Although Galton

Figure 1.11
Cesare Lombroso, A young girl with a shaved head, from *Criminal Child*, taken from
David G. Horn, *The Criminal Body. Lombroso and the Anatomy of Deviance* (London:
Routledge, 2003), 41.

Figure 1.12
A young Flemish girl with short blond hair. From Erna Lendvai-Dircksen, *Das germanische Volksgesicht* (*The German Popular Face*) (Bayreuth: Gauverlag, 1942), 12. The caption reads: "Contemplativeness and willpower are Germanic genetic material."

and Lombroso never instrumentalized their theories for an overall racial theory in the service of a totalitarian ideology leading to genocide, their goal was similar to the Nazis' in that they were all looking to produce or preserve a "better race." In the twentieth century, two centuries' worth of rules of physiognomy as well as the rediscovered ancient rules of *kalóka-gatheia* were reapplied in a deadly combination.

Excising the Deviant during the Third Reich

Galton's and Lombroso's project of prescribing rather than describing physiognomies was taken further in Nazi Germany, where people were influenced by the racial theories of Hans F. K. Günther (1891–1968), who was known to his contemporaries as *Rassen*-Günther (race Günther). Günther's "racial science" was published in 1930 (I return to it below), but in Germany in the 1920s, physiognomic thought was being stimulated by developments in visual media, particularly the moving image.[134] The first half of the twentieth century also was filled with imagery and appraisals of the "German countenance," drawing on common stereotypes for German genetic material—blond hair or the generally "fair type," including hair, eye, and skin color (see figure 1.12). In the German photographer Erna Lendvai-Dircksen's picture book series *Das germanische Volksgesicht* (1942), for instance, her introduction to the volume about Flanders claims that "the twentieth century is the century of the rebirth of the Germanic. In the heart of the Germanicness, the Third Reich, this departure [*Aufbruch*] had to occur."[135] Under the picture example of a little Flemish girl, Lendvai-Dirckens writes: "Contemplativeness and willpower are Germanic genetic material."

The gaze itself is the expression of a desire to finalize its output on a neutral objective "cultural screen"; it is not the expression of a subject's interpretation. For Lendvai-Dircksen, the Flemish girl is thus deprived of any subjective interpretation (whereas I wonder about what she is looking at and why she seems very serious) and is interesting only for the sheer data of her appearance. The camera eye is no longer involved in a process of "seeing and drawing" an outside appearance of a person or of looking for a psychiatric diagnosis of the character (as was the case with Lombroso). Rather, it is trying to look inside and bring out a person's genetic material, as the caption points out.

Within this scaffold of a physiognomic culture of seeing, Willy Hellpach (1877–1955)—a psychiatrist, social psychologist, and former politician of the German Democratic Party of the Weimar Republic—delivered a talk to his fellow psychiatrists at a conference in Nuremberg in October 1933, nine months after the National Socialist Party's rise to power and the installation of Adolf Hitler as chancellor. In a direct reference to Lavater, Hellpach meditates on the question of distinguishable German folk physiognomies and thus on the contemporary controversy about racial differences and differences in human phenotype. Pointing to well-known differences between European southerners and Germans,[136] he rhetorically asks how many "original European races" there may be, a question that from today's perspective would refer to whether race is a biological or a social category.[137] In contrast to most racial scientific theories of his time, Hellpach reflects on the ways in which speech practices and the entire habitus of a population shape physiognomy. Hellpach nevertheless affirmatively acknowledges the concept of race.[138] He believes in a "dynamic of whole-bodyness [Ganzkörperlichkeit]" that forms a face on the basis of a spoken language, that activates certain facial muscles, and that thereby forms a certain countenance and a certain people's mien [Gebaren]. As he puts it in his talk: "The physiognomic conditions of race and constitution will no doubt merge into the modeling of the face."[139] The degree to which the face incorporates race and constitution will be either "plastophil" (more visible) or "plastophobic" (less visible). But according to Hellpach and his peers, no one can entirely escape some traces of race in his or her countenance.

Hellpach concludes his talk by pleading with psychiatry to include the entirety of expression [das Ausdrucksganze] of a patient in the diagnostics. His call against "mechanizing and atomizing" diagnostic methods and in favor of a holistic rather than hermeneutic analysis, he joins the antimodern trend of opposing the objectivizing fantasies of feasibility and control of his time.[140] Nevertheless, in his final address, he is concerned with what he considers the most urgent and important task of the future, and it is built on the ability to read faces:

The strongest and finest human organ of expression—the countenance—is also a mirror that reveals the soul's hygiene [Wohlartung] or degeneration [Missartung], its harmony of form [Wohlbildung] or malformation [Fehlbildung]. A countenance can reveal to the knowledgeable eye to a shattering extent that its bearer is either a "eugenes" or a "euplastos"! Creative hygiene (eugenics) and leading harmony of form (euplastics) will provide us with command over nature, a command that is more important than technical command of the machine—the command over human nature![141]

Hellpach refers to the importance of Lavater's pioneer work and expertise in reading the "national face" (*Nationalgesichter*) on the basis of "blood and earth," language and customs. These characteristics are not fatalisms, as Hellpach the ethnologist concedes, but they are "put into our hands" both as received heredity and as task.[142] It did not take long for Germany's politics to change and for the official racial theorist of the National Socialists, Hans F. K. Günther, to modify the language of Hellpach's naïve ethnological attempts.[143] Fatalism becomes the central point in Günther's reading of the German face, and there was little "task" left to accomplish for a "face-owner" who simply did not fit into Günther's mask. Everything about it was fatalistic.

The Bavarian comedy writer and satirist Oscar Panizza wrote an anti-Semitic satire called *Der operierte Jud* (*The Operated Jew*) in 1893 (reprinted in 1914). The story makes fun of the "awkward" or "ugly"[144] appearance of an eastern European Jew, Itzig Faitel Stern,[145] who undergoes a "total makeover" (including surgery) to rid himself of his "ugly Jewish ancestry" and to "pass" as Siegfried Freudenstern to be able to marry the German Protestant Othilia Schnack. Panizza provides physiognomic descriptions of someone who did not fit into the desired model of the anti-Semitic Third Reich. A new enemy figure was found or resuscitated to take the place of Lombroso's deviant female monster—the Jew.[146]

But this "monster," unlike with the divide of the "other gender," spoke from within and was not easy to disqualify for mental retardation and other atavisms, according to Lombroso's theories. Not only did the comedy writer Panizza describe his subjects in ridiculing detail, but his descriptions also give us a viewpoint that was from within. Although Panizza no doubt "viewed Jews in a traditional anti-Semitic fashion," as Jack Zipes points out, he also "admired Jews for their intellectual powers and mercantile talents."[147] In response to an open contest call on "How to Improve Our Race," Panizza comes to the Jews' defense: "even the Jews, despite their physical decrepitude, have developed better minds (especially mercantile Jews) so that the German race cannot keep up with them."[148] Panizza was a regime critic of Wilhelminian Germany and the Catholic church and hence a political *enfant terrible*, and he also had a history of mental illness in his own family (and spent sixteen years in mental clinics), probably as a result of or in combination with his own case of syphilis. According to Zipes, these personal factors contributed to Panizza's opposition to eugenics and Darwinist theories for improving the human race that were circulating in the late nineteenth century—despite his anti-Semitism. In other words, "the Jew, Panizza perceived, was part of himself."[149]

In terms of the satire's narrative, Panizza identifies with the German commentator and Itzig Faitel Stern. Zipes even stipulates a schizophrenic relationship between the first-person narrator and the third-person object: "two sides of the same individual, one dissecting in a detached and ruthless way the passive compliance of the diseased and malformed subject, who eventually destroys himself by seeking to conform to the normative Aryan standards of German society."[150] But when Panizza describes Itzig Faitel's eastern European Jewish looks, even he cannot do it without a reference to Lavater:

Itzig Faitel's countenance was most interesting. It is a shame that Lavater had not laid eyes on it. An antelope's eye with a subdued, cherry-like glow swam in wide apertures of the smooth velvet, slightly yellow skin of his temple and cheeks. Itzig's nose assumed a form which was similar to that of the high priest who was the most prominent and striking figure of Kaulbach's painting *The Destruction of Jerusalem*. To be sure, the eyebrows had meshed, but Faitel Stern assured me that this meshing had become very popular.[151]

The Operated Jew is also Stern's makeover story. As Itzig Faitel is made over into Siegfried Freudenstern, he has his hair colored and straightened (from dark curls to blond straight hair); he gets his language rehabilitated, since one of the most dominant features of his "awkward Jewishness" is (and this is clearly Panizza's obsession) his Yiddish dialect; and he gets engaged to the German, blue-eyed, and light-haired Protestant, Othilia Schnack. Stern's willingness to "pass" leads him to undergo several orthopedic surgeries by the renowned professor Klotz to straighten out his "Jewish legs." Despite all these efforts, however, his attempt to assimilate into the Christian culture and faith fails during the narrative climax of the wedding when Stern's "real face" is discovered and slips through his masquerade as a goy. Panizza lists some of the facial traits that revealed Stern's Jewishness, no matter how well he tried to hide them, and he does so by referencing Stern's monstrosity: "Of course, the formation of the teeth, the padded lips, the nasal pitch in Stern's face had to remain absolutely fixed to prevent a monster [*Scheusal*] from becoming visible. And whoever had an eye for such things could recognize the sensual, fleshy, and jutting Sphinx-like face in Freudenstern's profile."[152]

As Zipes points out, Stern's desire to pass as German will ultimately lead to his self-destruction.[153] When Stern finally gives up and "passes back," his amazing transformation gets undone: his blond straight hair turns into black curls again, and Professor Klotz's artwork is reversed to reveal—as Panizza ends his story—"a convoluted Asiatic image in wedding dress, a counterfeit of human flesh, Itzig Faitel Stern." From the narrator's perspective, the failure of Faitel Stern's makeover attempt is a good thing. It illustrates humankind's resistance to the aim of perfecting the human race with eugenic experimentation, which Panizza opposed. But there is another reason that Itzig Faitel's wish for bettering himself—inside and out—fails. It may be that it simply is not possible to "pass" because Jewishness—like a hidden female amorality—was something that no makeover can override. Stern would be better off revealing and standing stolidly by his Sphinx-like face. We can look at the makeover attempt from the other side of *kalóka-gatheia*: Jewish "bad character" comes out through physical appearance, as Sander Gilman puts it. In Panizza's story, the trait of mendacity always surfaces, no matter how well Stern tries to hide it.

Panizza's account of the physical appearance of Jews is relevant to the development of a cosmetic gaze at the turn of the nineteenth century to the twentieth century that no longer looks for just "beauty" but also seeks "health," as was already the case in Galton's eugenics and Lombroso's theory of deviance. Hence, the conceptualization of Jews as an ugly and sickly[154] race became one of the pillars on which Günther established his theory of the superiority of the Nordic race. In Günther's most popular work, *Rassenkunde des Deutschen Volkes*, which was published in fourteen editions between 1922 and 1930, he laid out his Nordicist ideology by dividing the European population into six races—the Nordic, Phalic, Eastern, Western, Dinaric, and East Baltic. Ethnologists, cultural anthropologists, and racial theorists of the Third Reich discussed the question of why and how non-Germanic races would be able to adopt the "privilege" of being of a light-colored, Nordic phenotype.[155] Günther, for instance, dedicates a subchapter of a chapter on contemporary Jews in his most influential volume on Jewish racial theory to "The light-colored and blue-eyed among the Jews."[156] The racial theorist traced Jewish light-coloredness to the fact that eastern Jews—more than southern Jews—had spread widely over eastern Europe and experienced contact with people like the "sha-kares" (*Shakaren*), a barbaric people who was said to have lived at the shore of the Northern European Sea and who, according to Günther, inherited the light-colored traits mostly from the East Baltic people.[157] Günther characterizes the appearance of the East Baltic peoples by way of traits that conform to the stereotypes of Jewishness and other rationalizations of the "marginal look," with such traits as small heads, wide faces, and short bent noses. He insists—often referring to other sources, such as Rudolf Virchov's investigations[158]—that throughout the nineteenth century there were very few racial mixes with the Nordic race that could have caused the unsettling outcome of light-colored Jews.[159]

During the Third Reich, Günther played the role of the objective, quan-tifying scientist. He heavily relied on anthropometry and suggested start-ing with measurements of height, weight, sitting height, and span length of the arms. The most important anthropometric measure for Günther and many physical anthropologists before him was craniometry. Günther divides the face horizontally (along a line running from one ear through the other via the eyes) and vertically in the middle. The entire craniometric roster of distance lines, surfaces, curves, and angles are then related to these two middle lines. The vertical line is used to measure the length of the head, and the length of the horizontal middle line indicates the breadth of the head. The relationship of breadth and length culminates in the facial index, which is the primary indicator of whether a person is a member of a long-headed (dolichocephalic) or a round-headed (brachycephalic) type. Günther typically describes the Nordic race as long-headed, tall, slender, blond, and blue-eyed.

Despite his overtly scientific habitus, Günther blames the natural sci-ences of the nineteenth century and early twentieth century for having disseminated a fundamental "nonpictorial [*unbildlich*] way of seeing and imagining"[160] across the German population. What most bothers Günther is that his German contemporaries do not seem to be able to perceive racial difference in their daily lives. For him, this is a matter of lack of knowledge, weaknesses in perception caused by a lack of training, and underexposure to the cosmetic gaze, which was a cluster of ideal features that Lavater taught to the physiognomists of his time along with his advice for a constant "seeing and drawing, seeing and drawing." The foremost aim of *Rassenkunde des Deutschen Volkes* is the reeducation of the (German) gaze that has been misled by the exclusively numerical quality of the sciences. The educational goal is the reawakening of a kind of sculptural instinct:

One could say: the sculptor in man is evoked only in the last instance in modern man [*am allerletzten wird im neuzeitlichen Menschen der Bildhauer aufgerufen*]. He who does not reconstruct internally the length or width of a head in the very act of seeing; he who is not tempted to internalize [*inbildliche Nachgestaltung*] the curvature of the eye, the chin, etc., through a configuration of lines and surfaces; he who does not always form or curve at the same time as he is seeing, misses a part, an essential part, of every appearance.[161]

The metaphor of the sculptor refers to a gaze that always has an array of plasticity and improvement in mind. It requires the mind's own moving and (trans)forming image. Günther's goal of spreading the physiognomic gaze of his time was soon realized by the Nazi regime. By September 1933, "racial science" was introduced as a compulsory subject in German schools, and extracts from Günther's works (among others) served as teaching materials for students.[162] By 1935, the year that the Nuremburg racial laws were implemented, racial institutions and societies had been formed to study and promote the purity of the "Aryan race." In that year, the Reichsführer Heinrich Himmler founded both the Society for *Ahnenerbe*, whose goal was to study the history and cultural heritage of the "Aryan race," as well as the registered society *Lebensborn Eingetragener Verein*, which promoted (particularly among the Schutzstaffel or SS and the Wehrmacht soldiers) marriage with "healthy Aryan women" to increase the birth of "Lebensborn children," who would lead the future German people and the entire world. The required sharpening of the racist gaze is also visible in widely used documents, such as the so-called family background investigation form (*Erbgesundheitsbogen*), which had to be filled out by applicants for the SS. This document established the health of one's family line and had to be submitted to and verified by Himmler. His instructions to those wishing to demonstrate this level of purity read as follows: "I want the members of the SS to build a racially worthy and healthy German family. Therefore, the future wives have to meet the strictest requirements in terms of appearance, health, and heritage."[163] These requirements begin by suggesting to SS doctors that they judge the woman to be married according to "general appearance." After this general impression, certain measurements, such as hip width, are "to be undertaken with sensitivity."

Himmler based his desire to attain ever higher levels of racial purity almost entirely on his subjective moral sentiments. Doctors were supposed to look at the men and women they were judging for reproductive desirability and intuitively approve or disapprove of the marriages of high-ranking officials. The gaze that was entrusted with the power to judge over these physical appearances belonged to those who had passed the initiation ritual of the Nordic race: they were members of the National Socialist Party. Galton's apparatus had been outsourced into the "anonymous machinery" of the Nazi party. A common defense heard among the perpetrators at the Nuremburg trials was to have "merely" acted according to the laws established by an anonymous political other. The perpetrators justified themselves by pointing out that they aligned themselves unconsciously with the gaze of this Nazi machinery. The gaze became deanthropomorphized, was detached from a particular screen, and activated it. It became the ultimate other.[164]

This move becomes visible in Willy Hellpach's postwar argumentation and defense of the German character (1953). Despite the genocide that this belief in German superiority had caused, Hellpach claims that the national character of the German people results in the following positive character traits—the will to work [Schaffensdrang], thoroughness [Gründlichkeit], love for order [Ordnungsliebe], resistance to form [Formabneige], self-will [Eigensinn], and enthusiasm [Schwärmseligkeit]. Although he criticized the Germans for having supported Hitler and his demagogy, he did not criticize the politics of the Third Reich in general. In an apologetic strategy in Der deutsche Charakter, Hellpach attaches the evil deeds of the Nazi regime onto the demonic figure of Hitler. In his chapter "Adolf Hitler: A Woodcarving," he writes, "how could it be that such a highly differentiated nation [as the Germans] with such a high level of education—long without illiteracy—would let itself be captured by the millions by this demagogue, not even offering an effective resistance to his evident crimes?"[165] For Hellpach, the war crimes are related to Hitler's "demonic power" and occurred because no restraint was applied to the dynamics of mass and power, which he claimed were a lethal combination if not used in measured form. In their defenses and "apologies," Hellpach and other ideologists of the "Nordic race" made use of a gaze that they held to be an innate and objective, a machinic gaze beyond the judgment of a single person's eye, such as Lavater's, that would be held responsible for the death of six million Jews.[166] The discipline of physiognomy and the rules of *kalókagatheia* were highly affected by World War II, to the extent that these rules and beliefs were largely put to sleep until the 1970s, when sociobiology and new approaches to evolutionary theory combined with new technologies of the late twentieth century and reawakened this "sleeping beauty" with digital composites and faceprint software programs. I return to this crucial moment in chapter 3.

The Reveal: Understanding the New Physiognomy

Claudia Schmoelder made a historical connection between Lavater's physiognomic eye and its attention to the facial closeup and the onset of photographic portraiture.[167] Lavater's excitement about a detail in a person's face and his ability to describe it can be said to have preceded Galton's photographic prescriptive eye, but what was inherited from one medium to the other was a claim to evidence. This section examines the relationships among physiognomy, portraiture, and photography and their respective claims to evidence or truth.

Photography's relationship to truth is not simple. It claims to preserve, but at the same time, as Christian Metz and others[168] have stated, it is the most "death-driven" and most fetishistic of all media: "The photographic *take* is immediate and definitive, like death and like the constitution of the fetish in the unconscious, fixed by a glance of childhood, unchanged and always active later. Photography is a cut inside the referent, a fragment, a part object, for a long immobile travel to no return."[169] Metz concludes that the photograph means both loss (by pointing to a moment that will never return) and protection against loss (by, through its capacity for externalization, preventing us from forgetting). Galton's ideal faces have been taken out of their natural context of lived experience and eternalized, literally "imprisoned" into a "frame of representation."[170] This frame no longer mourns its referent, however, and it is no longer indexically related to it. Instead, it points to an "ideal"—of superimposed variations of the "healthy," "ill," or "criminal" face—that was never there in the past but may be coming in the future. The outcome of this superimposition, the composites, can be described as "photographs from the future." What Galton failed to consider in his "scientific" use of the photograph, however, is that the gaze is structured circularly in that it also projects onto the screen the subject's self-awareness through the way he or she poses for the camera/gaze.

As Roland Barthes points out in his *Camera Lucida,* when I face the camera, something comes into being that was not there beforehand. He calls this something new, which happens before the gaze/camera has laid eyes on me, the *myself as other:* "Once I feel myself observed by the [camera] lens, everything changes: I constitute myself in the process of 'posing.' I instantaneously make another body for myself, I transform myself in advance into an image. . . . The Photograph is the advent of myself as other."[171] Unlike the video camera's moving images, the still camera can freeze the gaze and produce a "science-fictional referent-less fetish image" of a self as ill, healthy, or criminal. What we see in Galton's composites are the inscriptions of the fears of his times—the fear of being a deviant body or a body that indicates that something is wrong. What links Galton's desirable deviations to Erna Lendvai-Dircksen's "Germanic people's face" *(germanisches Volksgesicht)* is the fear of not seeing oneself in the image. The dramatic difference is that—unlike Galton's composites— these images point to real faces and not the faces of idealized species created by superimposition. They were created with real bodies and faces and by a rigid machinery of control. Someone who has one of the faces that could have produced the averaged ideal of the Germanic face belongs to a desirable species, and someone who does not will now die a real death, not the death of a photograph taken.

The constitution of the self through the photograph becomes evident in recent television reality makeover shows and their before and after pictures. Although the camera "kills life," it also creates new life in the sense of a new image and a new mental picture of oneself as other. This mental picture gets translated into a pose that anticipates the freeze.[172] For Susan Sontag, this pose reflects the image that one has of oneself as attractive, as a self that has learned to see herself photographically.[173] This inner photograph expresses the cosmetic gaze in that mentally the self sees itself already "a step ahead," as an improved "after-picture."

In the makeover show *The Swan* (discussed in detail in chapter 3), such a mental picture has become real. It is as if the superimposed "ideal

Figure 1.13
A woman covering her face with her hands. From *The Swan* television show, season
1, 2004. Courtesy gaLAn Entertainment/Fox.

faces" of Galton's composites have grown inside the public's imagination.
The viewers of the makeover show on Fox Television are put into the
visual position of the person who takes the picture and who mortifies
or freezes these women's bodies as we look at them through the mirror
(figure 1.13).

The viewer witnesses a "snuff film" of a mortified self that has become
"other" to herself at the moment of what the show calls "the reveal"—the
moment when the contestant sees herself in a mirror for the first time in
three months. The mental images that she has made of herself after multiple cosmetic surgeries dissipate, and we the photographers become witnesses to her mortification. Technologically, this is made possible by a
camera that lets us see through the mirror. We have become the ultimate
Peeping Toms of the already voyeuristic genre of a reality television that
engages the audience in the consumption of our own belief/disbelief game
show: "I know this is not true, but I still like to pretend it is."[174] The gaze
that we are asked to apply is truly cosmetic because it is equipped with
and informed by the technologies that make it possible to perceive each
and every body against the backdrop of its potential improvement. It is a
gaze that is entrenched in the digital media revolution offered by the late

capitalist media economy as embodied in reality TV formats. In other words, this gaze knows how to pose for a surgical camera that not only envisions a bettered self but makes it happen.

The reveal as it is used on *The Swan* is a ultimate model of the new physiognomy that plugs into the assumptions, images, and desires that compose the cosmetic gaze and deploys that energy in an instant. As Meredith Jones describes it, the television show's reveal segment combines the two-dimensional ability of the photograph to freeze an ideal moment with the three-dimensional lived body experience of a human subject undergoing a radical readjustment of her identity: "It is about representation and simulacrum whilst remaining utterly corporeal. It maneuvers inside an aesthetic and visual system where two-dimensional images and three-dimensional 'realities' are profoundly intertwined, and where flat images and actual embodied form beg to be reconciled. In the reveal body and body image are finally one: feeling, affect, and movement match— for once, and however briefly—appearance, exterior and reflection. This is the moment when two-dimensional and three-dimensional selves are reconciled."[175]

Just how does today's "culture of the quick fix make such transformation happen?"[176] Transformation was certainly at the core of Galton's as well as later eugenic sociopolitical agendas, but their notion of transformation was aimed at furthering the course of evolution. It was a decidedly teleological project that also aimed at the betterment of entire races or classes of people and the extinguishing of others. These normalization techniques via coercion have given way to self-normalization techniques through what Foucault also called the "technologies of the self." Although the eugenicists wished to impose their own moral guidelines on a population, today the situation is different. Jürgen Link employs the terms "protonormalism" and "flexible normalism" to account for the difference between coercive normalization strategies aiming at group distinctions and contemporary normalization techniques requiring individuals to constantly adjust themselves.[177] This results in what has been labeled "internalized racism," a concept that was developed in the 1980s by the Re-Evaluation Counseling Community and that has resurfaced in the current age of cosmetic surgery. It has, for instance, been reevaluated in the context of Asian Americans and Asians who desire upper eyelid operation to look more Western or European.[178] Jennifer Fero, a Korean who was adopted by a white American family, reveals in a powerful statement in the documentary *Adopted* (2008) that she experienced conflicted feelings and internalized racism while being raised by white parents:

There is this gap of benign ignorance because the adoption agency did not have lessons on race, on discrimination. You know, I even wonder if they do today. How many parents of Chinese daughters sit in classes about the Asian fetish that is out there and the multimillion-dollar industry that it is. Well, it's nice to have an Asian girl. They are submissive. . . . They'll do anything you want. There are thousands, if not millions of sex porn Web sites out that are specific on Asian women. My parents had a responsibility to say: "you are not an exotic whore." I internalized the racism because I play the part. I play the part. I am—that's my expertise as an Asian woman, and you know, that makes you pretty empty inside.[179]

In its internalized form, Jennifer's cosmetic gaze, which stemmed from a discrepancy of her own body image and the image she saw of her "ethnically invisible" parents and brother, can be compared to what Link calls self-adjustment or self-normalization. To fit into the Fero family, Jennifer incorporated the image that U.S. culture promotes of Asian girls into her own body image. Thus, the internalized racist discourse is not about the eradication of those who do not fit but rather about a subjectivity that urges one to realize those aspects within his or her own self that best reflect a cultural picture. By putting into drive the internalized cosmetic gaze, individuals like Jennifer are "finding" themselves. The result of this discourse is massive conformism, not exclusion or eradication.

Furthermore, the culture industry propagates limiting models of beauty to conform to, or as Egginton puts it "what is unlimited by technology. . . is finally limited by the models and templates society provides."[180] Consequently, the after images of *The Swan* contestants look like the averaged faces generated by current research in psychology. Marnie's before and after faces are shown in figure 1.14. To illustrate the extent to which the faces on this TV show have been averaged, I digitally exchanged the noses and mouths of three contestants. In figure 1.15, Marnie's face has been equipped with Cindy's nose and Kristy's mouth, but these changes do not produce profound changes in Marnie's face because her surgically enhanced face already is a composite. Lombroso probably would have read this erasure of difference as a sign for a lower level of civility in the great chain of being.

The late capitalist marketplace has few incentives to disrupt the media dominance of northern European beauty ideals. *The Swan* series 1 and 2 (2004–2005) included only four nonwhite contestants out of a total of thirty-two. Interrogating Euro-centric beauty ideals would present too complex a task because those ideals, as presented in the media, have their own relation to truth. Within the realm of the cosmetic gaze, the truth of beauty no longer depends on a real human referent (as in Lavater's times) or on an idealized set of traits (as in Galton's composites). Instead, authenticity is established in the lonely desert of the television experience, between an adorning camera eye and the entertained viewer's deliberate self-deceit. For Galton, the photograph represented the body of evidence, but in the logic of the makeover show, the body of evidence has literally been cut to pieces. With these surgically enhanced composite bodies, it is no longer a question of photographs losing their referent, as in Galton's times. These referents have resurrected through the hands of technology. These bodies have become "science fictional referent-less fetish images" and are looking back at us from an unreal place. But their imperative is nonetheless real: you must change.

What does this imperative of change mean in terms of the screen that the gaze is directed onto and that serves as frame for the cosmetic gaze? Lavater taught an automatized internalization of a gaze that projects an "ideal composite"—a cluster of remembered features—onto a surface that I call a *screen*. The gaze has a circular structure. It is shown by being generalized onto an interface or a screen that a culture can believe in, but it also looks back at its own enunciators—at itself—in a way that the self is incorporated in a screen that "gives shape and significance to how we are seen by 'others as such,' how we define and interact with the agency to whom we attribute our visibility, and how we perceive the world."[181] As Jacques Lacan has it, "I see only from one point, but in my existence, I am looked at from all sides."[182] (In chapter 3, I return to how the promise of the gaze's circularity is fulfilled with the help of digital technologies and environments as well as the reality, makeover, and entertainment complex.)

From Galton onward, the portraitistic-physiognomic eye's adorning gaze was able to see a better, more beautiful, and therefore improved body, and this gaze was replaced by the physiognomic-photographical eye, which authenticates the body by exact measurement and is able to draw affirmative (and less intuitive than Lavater's portraitisic-physiological eye)

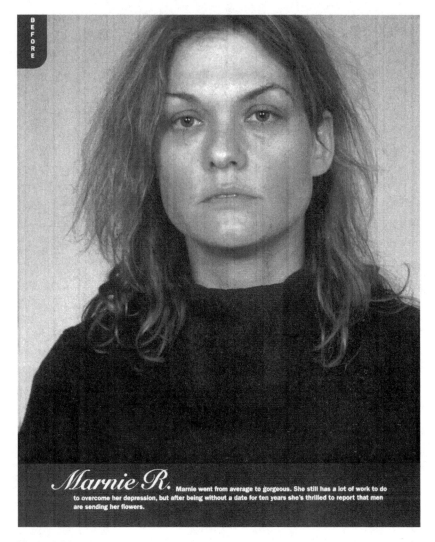

Figure 1.14
Marnie before and after facial plastic surgery. From Nely Galán, *The Swan Curriculum* (New York: Collins, 2004), 28–29. Courtesy gaLAn Entertainment/Fox.

Figure 1.14
(continued)

Figure 1.15
Composite photographs of Marnie made of Cindy's nose and Kristy's mouth. From
The Swan Curriculum. Digital touch-up by Glenn Feron, G.C.F. Graphic Fantasies.
Courtesy gaLAn Entertainment/FOX.

Figure 1.15
(continued)

conclusions that assume legal status and a claim to truth. The "objectivity" of photography is at stake from the onset of (portrait) photography. For Galton and Lombroso, especially, the "truth" of portrait photography refers to the fact that somebody was physically in front of someone else to have a photograph taken. But this is the same for a drawing. In both cases, an interpretative frame is the outcome of a particular gaze applied by the portraitist, regardless of the medium he or she was using. In relation to the referent, in other words, there is no difference in kind between a drawing and a photograph of a subject. The difference is in the degree of complexity of a judgment concerning that subject. Since the turn of the twentieth century, therefore, physiognomic theories have spoken of a more and more complex cosmetic gaze that is informed by more and more sophisticated technologies of beautification that are more and more specialized in the principles of symmetry and visual coherence. These new technologies and the resulting cosmetic gaze are analyzed in chapter 3.

But all attempts at seeing and recognizing faces are linked by the fact that such categorization also means the decategorization of deviance. Galton's regime depended on the visual identification of deviant physiognomies, and the first step undertaken by Germany's Nazi regime was a massive physiognomic training of the eye—a logic not fundamentally different from Galton's photographic attempt at "extinguishing" subjectivity with the pictures that had become "words of nature itself."[183] The next chapter therefore looks at Lombroso's attempt to define deviance, the conceptions of deviance underlying the distinction between beauty and ugliness, and today's "machinic suture" of a makeover culture, which produces "twenty-first century neo-cyborgs"[184] who have literally fulfilled the phsyiognomists' dreams to turn one's "better" inside outward.

2 The Dark Side of Beauty: From Convulsive Beauty to Makeover Disfiguration

Wherefore, I say, let a man be of good cheer about his soul, who has cast away the pleasures and ornaments of the body as alien to him, and rather hurtful in their effects, and has followed after the pleasures of knowledge in this life; who has adorned the soul in her own proper jewels, which are temperance, and justice, and courage, and nobility, and truth—in these arrayed she is ready to go on her journey to the world below, when her time comes.

—Plato, *Phaedo*[1]

The Platonic ideal of *kalókagatheia* inspired the cosmetic gaze that developed from the eighteenth century to the present (see chapter 1). This ideal guided the technological deployment of the cosmetic gaze in the service of a normalization of deviance, such that internalized beauty ideals often reflected and motivated political and bodily practices tending toward conformity, banality, and the eradication of cultural, ethnic, and racial otherness. The history of this gaze has been shaped by the men who made scientific observations of female bodies, which have served as a kind of ground-zero screen for the cosmetic gaze. The female body has borne both the ambitions of the gaze and the weight of its inevitable failures. What happens to the body as it stretches, twists, and slices itself in the service of the cosmetic gaze? How do its own desires and those of the culture around it shift as it sloughs off versions of itself in pursuit of an impossible ideal? Beauty is related to the good, but it is also related to desire, and desire is notoriously hard to placate with conformity or standardization. There may be, in other words, a surplus produced by the cosmetic gaze, such that the ability and will to modify the body in conformity with its ideals varies inversely with the intensity and incidence of models that scandalize, terrify, or merely break the mold.

As was shown in chapter 1, Plato's concept of beauty is related to both outside appearance (body) and interior essence (soul). For Plato, there is no point in achieving one without the other. Yet even this ideal needs to be left behind for an even higher good—wisdom. The Platonic ideal is to overcome the pleasures of the physical and spiritual worlds and to achieve wisdom, a "sort of purification"[2] in itself. On the way to achieving this wisdom, soul and body must not contaminate each other with their very different and, at times, opposite tasks:

—But the soul which has been polluted, and is impure at the time of her departure, and is the companion and servant of the body always, and is in love with and fascinated by the body and by the desires and pleasures of the body, until she is led to believe that the truth only exists in a bodily form, which a man may touch and see and taste and use for the purposes of his lusts—the soul, I mean, accustomed to hate and fear and avoid the intellectual principle, which to the bodily eye is dark and invisible, and can be attained only by philosophy—do you suppose that such a soul as this will depart pure and unalloyed?

—That is impossible, he replied.[3]

Physical beauty, which Plato found not in nature but in the human body—particularly in the handsome young boy—is ultimately also destined to a divine state of "eternal Beauty that exists beyond the boundaries of corporeal nature."[4] An indexical relationship exists between mortal beauty and eternal beauty, which is why Plato attributes a greater responsibility to beauty than to other virtues, as he explains in the *Phaedrus*: "As opposed to other abstract ideas, such as Justice, Temperance, Courage, and so on, Beauty alone has a physical correspondent in nature that thus makes it the privileged mediator pointing the way from the world of sense to that of the soul."[5] It is therefore beauty's challenge and responsibility to lead the right way. This is why being beautiful also always implies the imperative to be or do good. Finally, this relationship underlies human desire, what motivates us to act. As Plato puts it in reference to love in the *Symposium*, "Is not the good also the beautiful?"[6] For Plato, physical beauty has an enormously important role to play in life because it is the only mortal virtue whose physical manifestation serves as both an index to moral perfection and also a potential motive force for self-improvement.

In the *Hippias*, Plato has Socrates quote a man's question to him: "How, if you please, do you know, Socrates, what sort of things are beautiful and ugly? For, come now, could you tell me what the beautiful is?"[7] Surprisingly, Hippias does have a concrete answer for Socrates, not just a philo-sophical-rhetorical one: "For be assured, Socrates, if I must speak the truth, a beautiful maiden is beautiful."[8] This chapter reevaluates Hippias's answer in light of today's culture of surgical makeover beauty and contemporary theories of evolutionary psychology. Does the correspondence between beauty, goodness, and truth—the operative relation for the construction of beauty from Plato to Johann Kaspar Lavater—still hold? Is today's beauty still "borrowed" from God, as suggested in the above dialog, or is it merely man-made and therefore subject to constant reevaluation and change? We also cannot avoid rethinking beauty's traditional adversaries—from the notion of monstrosity (alluded to in chapter 1) to the discovery of beauty's "convulsiveness" by twentieth-century avant-garde artists and philoso-phers—as potentially sharing its place as motors of desire. By reveling in this "dark side"—in the moment of decomposition and dismemberment of the beautiful body—the twentieth century was able to create a notion of makeover beauty that is simultaneously aesthetic and violent.

To undertake this exploration of beauty's dark side, I first look at the destruction of beauty in the Surrealist novel *Nadja* by André Breton, exam-ining his notions of "other" beauty and "beauty's hell." I then look into some examples of first-person accounts of distortion and deformation, including examples from twentieth-century mass culture, in which pur-poseful ugliness is marked as an alternative or "other" aesthetic ideal. The chapter ends with a discussion of the artistic celebration of the deformed body, one contemporary to the rise of a new notion of beauty that has been called *makeover beauty*, a notion built on the pillars of this history. This chapter conceptually and historically links the previous history of the cosmetic gaze—with its central dedication to an abstract and universalist value of beauty, whether God-given or represented in an individual's DNA—to a makeover beauty that incorporates a belief in the good and beautiful body into a culture that can fully realize such abstraction, fusing the good and the beautiful through the violent manipulation of bodies. In this age, then, Plato's love of beauty has been reborn as an aesthetic appeal that fixates on the destruction and disfigurement through which *kalókagatheia* can be achieved. As medical researchers have created the technology—in its medial forms, in medical advances, and in invasive procedures—for reshaping the body, art has explored the libidinal dimen-sion underlying such interventions by delving into the dark side of beauty.

Beauty's Irresistible Promise

The appeal of beauty, says Austrian philosopher Konrad Paul Liessmann,[9] is its promise of happiness. Liessmann references the legendary footnote by Stendhal in his essay *De l'amour* (*On Love*) from 1822, in which the romantic author says that for a man who chooses an "ugly" wife, she must nevertheless appear to be "beautiful." Beauty is thus the promise of happiness, not its fulfillment. The encounter with beauty raises expectations and desire but does not in itself represent happiness.[10] This is why, for Liessmann, the desire for beauty is intimately connected to its destructive potential. Beauty's promise coexists with the constant potential for its own nonfulfillment. Like desire itself, according to Plato's famous deconstruction in the *Symposium*, its coherence depends on a perpetual deferral of its satisfaction. This logic led Jacques Lacan to read Freud's long struggle to define Eros and Thanatos as the two fundamental drives underlying human existence as inevitably culminating in the realization that there is only one ultimate drive. Lacan named this drive after death because of its disruptive, destructive impulse to breach every barrier defining and distinguishing what a subject might hold up as a potential satisfaction for its desire.[11]

Beauty is always a risk. Looking at it means to commit to the danger of becoming "infected," "bitten," or "addicted" to it. In a romantic Stendhalian sense, beauty is the hopeful sign that the world's imperfection can be overcome, not least by overcoming our sense of mortality. This is the case in today's makeover beauty, which promises an eternal refresh button that can be pushed whenever someone wishes to erase the signs of age or defer the event of death. This idea of beauty as something that brings us beyond life and its constraints comes with a price, though. It is not something that can be easily achieved. At times, it can be dangerous: something can seem "too beautiful" to look at; one can be "blinded" by beauty.[12] But in the fear of looking at beauty lies something else—the idea that beauty, especially female beauty, is a masquerade, as Lavater feared. Underneath beauty's perfection and seduction are hidden the abyss and the ugly, which can erupt at any time (the "necessary evil," as Cesare Lombroso said). There can be no history of beauty that does not reflect on the fear of ugliness that lies underneath it and that may reveal itself as death under the beautiful skin of a young woman, to quote Hippias's example of ultimate beauty.

This fear is evident in countless tales and stories. The Gypsy fairytale "The Moon"[13] starts out like many other tales with a father who gives land and possessions to his sons before his death. Every son gets a specific duty, but the youngest and "most beautiful" one is given responsibility for the money and animals. After the father dies, his wife gives birth to a girl who is the most beautiful thing in the world, except for one big flaw: she is born with teeth in her mouth. As a baby, she covers her mouth with her hand to hide the abyss of her beauty. The sister-vampire is shut off in a room so that no one outside the family knows about its shame. The youngest son then leaves on a journey, during which he encounters a woman who is "truly beautiful," but she is hidden in a tower. The tower has no door, so he sees her only through the window (which may be in his interest anyway, since this way he does not have to share her with anyone). When he returns home to ask his mother if he can marry this beautiful woman, he is met by his vampire-sister and finds that his mother and brothers are dead. The wind tells him that the sister killed them and will kill him, too. The brother looks at the blinding beauty of his sister and starts running way, but she follows him. The chase takes them through the woods and ends at the tower, where the brother tries to reach his fiancée through the window. At this point, the vampire-sister grabs him by the legs while his fiancée holds onto his arms. The young man is stretched to the verge of being torn apart between the dangerous beauty of the sister and a promising loyal relationship with the new woman. The story ends with the moon coming to the young man and telling him that he has to endure.

Although any single interpretation of this tale will probably be overdetermined, this and other fairytales thematize a fear of femininity and feminine beauty. In fact, a long tradition of medieval misogyny saw no contradiction in treating woman equally as "devil's gateway and bride of Christ."[14] As William Egginton has argued, woman takes on this curiously bifurcated identity because culture has made her the embodiment of the border separating man from impossible satisfaction. She becomes both the symbol of the original sin that stole man from paradise and the pathway that could potentially lead him back.[15] What we see in the Gypsy folktale "The Moon" is yet another manifestation of fundamental feminine duplicity: the beauty that kills and the beauty that potentially saves are perpetually in strife over the destiny of a man's soul.

Nadja, or Beauty's Convulsiveness

Prior to the modern period, art had a variety of purposes, but as Arthur C. Danto puts it, "from the eighteenth century to early in the twentieth century, it was the presumption that art should possess beauty."[16] For this reason, the early twentieth-century avant-garde produced a cultural sea change when the Post-Impressionist art exhibitions shocked their first audiences with a "palpable absence of beauty."[17] The modernist painter and critic Roger Fry, who organized some of these exhibits, nevertheless argued "that the new art would be seen as ugly *until* it was seen as beautiful."[18] According to Danto, the avant-garde movements of the early twentieth century had the philosophical audacity to promote the premise that, depending on the viewer's aesthetic education, anything can be found beautiful and that beauty therefore is not inherent to any form or shape until discovered by the interpreter.

Although European Enlightenment thinkers such as David Hume and Immanuel Kant differed widely in their understanding of aesthetic taste, they nonetheless agreed that there was an intimate relation between beauty and morality. For Hume, good taste derived from discrimination, which in turn betrayed a sensitive mind. As he puts it, "in each creature, there is a sound and defective state; and the former alone can be supposed to afford us a true standard of a taste and sentiment. . . . Where the organs are so fine as to allow nothing to escape them, and at the same time so exact as to perceive every ingredient in the composition: This we call delicacy of taste."[19] For Kant, aesthetic taste can only be subjective, since it requires the sensibility of a perceiving subject, but he theorizes that the subject that pronounces an aesthetic judgment is implicitly demanding a universal agreement with that judgment, a demand that parallels the unconditional universalism of his ethical theory.[20]

Although Romantic aesthetics allowed art's content rather than just its appearance to take center stage, which largely did away with a facile parallelism between beauty and morality,[21] the Romantic ideal still held beauty as the ultimate aim of art, even if it allowed for enormous variation in how that beauty was attained. But not until the convulsions of the early twentieth century did artistic practice begin to imagine aesthetic experiences that were opposed to the traditional Euro-centric ideals of beauty. The avant-garde, in Danto's words, "helped show that beauty was no part of the concept of art, that beauty could be present or not, and something still be art."[22] Such relativism was the first step in dethroning beauty as the ultimate standard of artistic achievement, and it was finally "assassinated" by Dadaist Tristan Tzara. By the 1960s, beauty entirely disappeared from the notion of "good art" and its philosophy.

The artists at the theoretical core of the avant-garde, Dadaism, Futurism, and Surrealism all dedicated themselves in some sense to "ugliness." They did so by

exhibiting disturbing upheavals in psychological coherence at the level of the individual mind or social body. Understood, in part, through psychological models for understanding human sexuality, the surrealist method presents the impact that restrictive social mores made on the human psyche through visual and literary depictions of shocking psychological regressions that result in transgressive behaviors.[23]

This dedication to an aesthetics of "disturbing upheavals" is perhaps nowhere so evident as in the writings of André Breton, author of the influential *Surrealist Manifesto* (1924), who ended his 1928 novel *Nadja* with a paean to a beauty that will be "CONVULSIVE, or it will not be at all!"[24] He defined the simplest Surrealist act as consisting "of dashing down into the street, pistol in hand, and firing blindly, as fast as you can pull the trigger, into the crowd."[25]

Although Breton's manifestos and statements point to a new conception of aesthetic creation as being primarily violent, disruptive, and obscene, his novel *Nadja* reveals the underlying connection that I have been intimating between such an aesthetics and the traditional role of woman and the female body. The mystery and potential abyss that underlie the figure of woman in Western culture have long played the role of spurring male creativity, but in their work and thinking about art, Breton and other avant-garde thinkers revealed the extent to which violence, destruction, and dismemberment have always been an integral part of this fantasy. Misogynist imagery and rhetoric run rampant in Surrealism, often in predictably traditional ways, but the almost naïve combination of such traditional misogyny with their aesthetics of violence allows avant-garde production to access an underlying truth about the nature of our basic conceptions of beauty.

Breton's character Nadja is woman as tantalizing mystery, a motif that, on its own, would make *Nadja* about as innovative with respect to literary history as a panning shot of New York City would be for cinematic openers. Breton's contribution lies in how the narrator explores his own relationship toward this mystery and what it means for his understanding of beauty.

Breton's narrator can approach Nadja only through ruminations on language and its indeterminacy, as if she herself were a kind of automatic writing: "She had told me her name, the one she had chosen for herself: 'Nadja, because in Russian it's the beginning of the word *hope*, and because it's only the beginning.' Just then she thinks of asking who I am (in the most limited sense of these words). I tell her. Then she returns to her past, speaks of her father, her mother."[26] Nadja is not named but names herself. She is autochthonous, resisting even the most basic tenet of identity—that we receive it from our parents—a contradiction that Breton highlights by saying, in passing, that she speaks of her father and mother. The name she chooses for herself elicits a sense of becoming and possibility but nothing concrete. Again, identity is eschewed.

Such is the fate of the narrator's various attempts to understand Nadja. As he writes somewhat later: "She uses a new image to make me understand how she lives: it's like the morning when she bathes and her body withdraws while she stares at the surface of the bath water: 'I am the thought on the bath in the room without mirrors.'"[27] The imagery here suggests nothing more than beautiful surfaces whose depths stubbornly refuse to reveal their meaning. The narrator strives and strives for answers, but his efforts produce only more enigmatic poetry at the edge of her being. Even his desire to cease this endless striving ends up formulating itself in a poetics of bodily surfaces, such as in the famously enigmatic phrase he attributes to Nadja: "I want to touch serenity with a finger wet with tears."[28] Even the standard English translation does not quite grasp the enigmatic charge of the original French line, "Je veux toucher la sérénité d'un doigt mouillé de larmes," which is better rendered as "I want to touch the serenity of a finger wet with tears." In other words, what the narrator expresses in his rendering of Nadja's words is the mysterious serenity of another person's body—in this case, a finger whose skin can be imagined glistening with the moisture of teardrops.

In keeping with misogynist fantasies, the correlate to Nadja's mystery is her almost total passivity. Nadja is always presented as depending on men and as constructed by their desires and fantasies:

Who is the real Nadja—the one who told me she had wandered all night long in the Forest of Fontainebleau with an archeologist who was looking for some stone remains which, certainly, there was plenty of time to find by daylight—but suppose it was this man's passion!—I mean, is the real Nadja this always inspired and inspiring creature who enjoyed being nowhere but in the streets, the only region of valid experience for her, in the street, accessible to interrogation from any human being launched upon some great chimera, or (why not admit it) the one who sometimes fell, since, after all, others had felt authorized to speak to her, had been able to see in her only the most wretched of women, and the least protected?[29]

Even while the narrator's ruminations about her real identity circulate around images of her dependence on men and their passions, the words he reports as coming from Nadja relate her own sense of passivity, dependence, and even nothingness. The narrator writes:

I best recapture the tone of her voice and whose resonance remains so great within me:

"With the end of my breath, which is the beginning of yours."

"If you desired it, for you I would be nothing, not merely a footprint."

"The lion's claw embraces the vine's breast."

"Pink is better than black, but the two harmonize."

"Before the mystery. Man of stone, understand me."

"You are my master. I am only an atom respiring at the corner of your lips or expiring."[30]

But although these words ceaselessly repeat the traditional motif of the creative man's fantasy of a passive, inspiring muse, the narrator's self-reflexive ruminations in response to this traditional model of femininity provide the novel's innovative aesthetic. That this rumination is the book's central preoccupation becomes clear with its famous closing lines:

A certain attitude necessarily follows with regard to beauty, which has obviously never been envisaged here save for emotional purposes. . . . neither dynamic nor static, I see beauty as I have seen you. As I have seen what, at the given hour and for a given time which I hope and with all my soul believe may recur, granted you to me. Beauty is like a train that ceaselessly roars out of the Gare de Lyon and which I know will never leave, which has not left. It consists of jolts and shocks, many of which do not have much importance, but which we know are destined to produce a *Shock*, which does. Which has all the importance I do not want to arrogate to myself. In every domain the mind appropriates certain rights which it does not possess. Beauty, neither static nor dynamic. The human heart, beautiful as a seismograph. . . . Beauty will be CONVULSIVE or it will not be at all.[31]

Nadja the novel ends, then, with a reflection, as philosophically intricate as any by Hume or Kant, on aesthetic theory. Nadja, it turns out, is an allegory of this conception of beauty. She is neither dynamic (her passivity ensures this) nor static (as she is far too ephemeral). The narrator's ultimate desire is the ceaseless repetition of the shock that brought her into his life. But the very idea of shock belies ceaseless repetition. Because only the experience of shock, as opposed to the source itself, can be repeated; beauty can only be convulsive, ever changing. It cannot rest on eternal principles, on universal standards, or on harmonies that are intrinsic to nature and man. Breton's exploration of that traditional canvas of creative man—woman's body and soul and the mystery of her identity and desire—has led him to the ultimate reversal of aesthetic principles: beauty must always become its opposite if it is to survive at all.

"The Birthmark" and Other Autobiographies of Ugliness

There was a sea change in aesthetic theory after Romanticism, but even in the Romantic literary tradition, traces can be found of the dark side of beauty that explodes in post-Romantic art. Two stories, one from the mid-nineteenth century and another from the end of the twentieth, explore the theme of deformity's relation to female beauty. In Nathaniel Hawthorne's 1843 story "The Birthmark," the proximity of "defect" and "beauty" is described through the experience of the scientist Aylmer, a scientist "proficient in every branch of natural philosophy," who after marrying the beautiful Georgiana comes to realize that he is tormented by the hand-shaped crimson birthmark on his wife's cheek, which—as the story emphasizes—is an even bigger problem on her "nearly perfect" face:

One day, very soon after their marriage, Aylmer sat gazing at his wife with a trouble in his countenance that grew stronger until he spoke.

"Georgiana," said he, "has it never occurred to you that the mark upon your cheek might be removed?'"

"No, indeed," said she, smiling; but perceiving the seriousness of his manner, she blushed deeply. "To tell you the truth it has been so often called a charm that I was simple enough to imagine it might be so."

"Ah, upon another face perhaps it might," replied her husband; "but never on yours. No, dearest Georgiana, you came so nearly perfect from the hand of Nature that this slightest possible defect, which we hesitate whether to term a defect or a beauty, shocks me, as being the visible mark of earthly imperfection."

"Shocks you, my husband!" cried Georgiana, deeply hurt; at first reddening with momentary anger, but then bursting into tears. "Then why did you take me from my mother's side? You cannot love what shocks you!"[32]

The Surrealist riposte would be that one can only love what shocks. Indeed, the physical response that Georgiana perceives in her husband and that ultimately leads her to submit to his experimentation, is nothing other than a "convulsive shudder."

Although the story's conscious aesthetics are the contrary of the post-Romantic embrace of beauty's dark side, Hawthorne's narrative goes to similar lengths to reveal the troubled relation between man's creative urge toward the surface of a woman's body and the potential destruction that accompanies that urge.

Georgina cannot recover from the damage of her scientist husband's convulsive shudder and trusts him to remove her birthmark, a symbol of her "liability to sin, sorrow, decay, and death." But this interference with nature has fatal consequences. By removing his wife's imperfection, Aylmer kills Georgiana, "for this little hand on her cheek represented, as she explains to him, "nature's hand on her."[33] Seen in the context of late nineteenth-century attempts to excise deviance with the help of technological devices (chapter 1), Hawthorne's story seems prophetic and even cautionary. Georgiana's apparently superficial defect is not merely a flaw to be brushed away but—following the rules of *kalókagatheia*—reveals itself to be deeply rooted: "this crimson hand, superficial as it seems, has clutched its grasp into your being with a strength of which I had no previous conception. I have already administered agents powerful enough to do naught except to change your entire physical system. Only one thing remains to be tried. If that fails us we are ruined." This is the story's inevitable outcome, since the treatments that render his wife perfect also render her lifeless.

In an interesting twist, Hawthorne reflects on the role that technological reproduction plays in this short circuit between beauty and death. When Aylmer realizes that there is no way to save his wife, he switches to his last reserve, the daguerreotype photograph—in what Virginia Blum has called an "anticipation of Baudrillard's account of the simulacra."[34] To "save" her image, he proposed to take her portrait by a scientific process of his own invention. It was to be effected by rays of light striking upon a polished plate of metal. Georgiana assented; but, on looking at the result, was affrighted to find the features of the portrait blurred and indefinable; while the minute figure of a hand appeared where the cheek should have been. Aylmer snatched the metallic plate and threw it into a jar of corrosive acid.[35]

In Blum's reading of the story, at this point we realize that Aylmer's "scientific expertise" is a special form of aesthetic science and that "his work is more allied with the emergent technology of the daguerrotype than it is with the natural sciences."[36] In a double betrayal of nature, both the birthmark and the technology become objects of controversy. Instead of showing the portrait of a new Georgiana, the daguerrotype reveals and highlights her flaw in the form of a hand on her cheek. As Blum comments: "this episode reverses the story's conclusion insofar as the hand supplanting the beautiful face is an ironic refusal of Aylmer's photographic goal to make the body permanent, immortal, two-dimensional; here the body exceeds the image, whereas by the end the image will overwhelm the body."[37] For Blum, Aylmer's fixation on his wife's birthmark, which is extended in his attempt to fix her image to the daguerrotype, can be read as a metaphor of man fixated on beauty. Although the story is a "warning" not to mess with nature, it is also an exploration of the meaning of beauty and our attempts to define and capture it. This urge may have its origin in a desire to elude death, but Hawthorne reveals it to be a strategy that courts death. Finally, the story is an important early testimony to the anxieties that are connected to the process of makeover—the dependency on the image and the resulting ethical issues, the responsibility of the "photographer-surgeon" to "restore" the female body to some image of perfection, the transference of the gaze (once Aylmer saw the birthmark, Georgiana could no longer be happy), and the correlation of the husband/wife relationship turned into surgeon/patient relationship (to which I return in chapters 3 and 4).

In contemporary literature, the short story "Face" by Alice Munro, also about a birthmark, presents a narrative inversion of Hawthorne's tale. The narrator describes his sense of "abnormal self" as empowered—despite the difficulty and otherness it produces. The story is also about a fixation on a birthmark, not by a spouse but by a friend. The narrator starts out by describing which side of his face is "normal":

One side of my face was—is—normal. And my entire body was normal from toes to shoulders. . . . My birthmark not red but purple. Dark in my infancy and early childhood, fading somewhat as I got older, but never fading to a state of inconsequence, never ceasing to be the first thing people noticed about me, head on, never ceasing to shock those who had come at me from the left side.[38]

Rather quickly, the narrator describes his sense of guilt for being monstrous looking and as a result for having created, as he says, a "monstrous rift" between his parents. Reading this story feels nothing like reading the shameful confession of Hawthorne's story. The only indication for a weakened self-image that "Face" reports is the story of the narrator's friendship with Nancy, a neighbor's daughter, whose mother he suspected of being his father's mistress. Nancy used to terrorize him as a child, smearing her face with red paint and asking, "Now do I look like you?" His mother defends him like a lioness, calling Nancy a "nasty little beast" and never letting her son play with Nancy again.

A few years later, the birthmarked son comes home from boarding school. His experience there was better than expected. He was given the nickname "Grape-Nuts," but since most students had a nickname, he did not feel singled out by it. He vaguely remembers Nancy, and his mother provides more information about the girl:

one bright fall morning, Nancy's mother had come upon her daughter in the bathroom, using a razor blade to slice into her cheek. There was blood on the floor and in the sink and here and there on Nancy. But she had not given up on her purpose or made a sound of pain. [. . .] 'It was the same cheek,' she said. 'Like yours.' . . . 'Trying the best she could to make herself look like you.'[39]

The narrator at first pretends not be touched by this incident, suggesting that Nancy could have gotten cosmetic surgery to fix her face. But after being stung by a wasp on his eyelid and hospitalized, he meets a nurse whom he can't see because of his eyelid and who reads to him. We are led to believe that it may be Nancy, who is curing her old friend: "Suddenly her quick hand was laid on my mouth. And then her face, the side of her face, on mine. 'I have to go. Here's just one more before I go.'"[40] The birthmark here is presented not as offense to normalcy but as an opportunity to find uniqueness and truth. A love emerges between former enemies because the narrator's face is unique and because the little girl Nancy may have fallen for it, despite or perhaps even because of its ugliness: "Something had happened here. In your life there are a few places, or maybe only one place, where something has happened. And then there are the other places, which are just other places."[41] This is the modern, success-story version of Hawthorne's "The Birthmark," one that turns his Romantic fantasy into an allegory for the testimonies of today's makeover culture.

Real autobiographies of disfigurement are also structured like "success stories." The success is twofold: an internal self-help process teaches the person how not to look into the mirror or how not to see oneself as ugly, and an external process helps the person through surgery, implantations, and other technologies. Recent testimonies raise the question of whether ugliness has found its place as part of makeover culture's mantra for change. In her *Autobiography of a Face*, Lucy Grealy[42] tells the story of growing up as a child with a facial disfigurement. She was nine years old when she was diagnosed with cancer in the jaw and lost a third of her face in surgery. Over the course of her childhood, Lucy undergoes numerous reconstructive operations of the face, until a final one in Ireland leaves her with an acceptable facial image. As a child, Lucy feels so different that she empathizes more with animals than with people: "I thought animals were the only beings capable of understanding me."[43] First ponies and then horses become Lucy's soul mates, her "one real source of relief."[44] Similar to the little girl Nancy in Alice Munro's story "Face," who became fixated on the birthmark of her neighbor, children refer to Lucy as "the ugliest girl they have ever seen." There even comes a time when it is decided that she is "too ugly to go to school," and she is home-schooled. When Lucy wears a plastic witch mask on Halloween, she feels liberated because nobody stares back at her. Wearing this mask, which conforms to the code of appearance on that particular day, she is able to be "breathing in normalcy."[45] The cosmetic gaze is paired with the moralizing gaze in Lucy Grealy's captivating testimony of ugliness. She talks about feeling a sense of deep shame for her appearance: "More than the ugliness I felt, I was suddenly appalled at the notion that I'd been walking around unaware of something that was apparent to everyone else. A profound sense of shame consumed me."[46] It seemed completely impossible for Lucy to abstract her identity from her facial disfigurement: "I *was* my face, I *was* ugliness."[47] Over the course of curing her cancer, Lucy turns the feeling of being ugly into being special. She starts by redefining her otherness as something positive: "I was special. Being different was my cross to bear, but being aware of it was my compensation."[48]

In a next step, she imagines a situation that is an inversion of the above-mentioned Gypsy folktale "The Moon," where beauty hides the abyss. Instead, Lucy imagines that her ugliness is hiding a beauty beneath: "Maybe this wasn't my actual face at all, but the face of some interloper, some ugly intruder, and my 'real' face, the one I was meant to have all along, was within reach. I began to imagine my 'original' face, the one free from all deviation, all error. I believed that if none of this had happened to me, I would have been beautiful"[49] Because of the transformational power of the physical makeover, Lucy feels that she can be beautiful if her "real self" can be revealed. She imagines her face as something fluid, in transition, of which she has merely reached one point: "my face had only changed into the next shape it was meant to have."[50] In both of these statements, Lucy reveals the core point of the makeover discourse: the change of the exterior body ideally reveals what is hidden or inscribed underneath, what was there before the body's adornment or before the cosmos itself. Lucy refers to this imagination as "this strange fantasy of beauty."[51] I return to this point at the end of this chapter.

Lucy's story ends with her successfully embracing her new body image. After numerous operations, she finally is able to have a face. She reminisces about her past, when she avoided the encounter with her mirror image: "my trick of the eye was the result of my lifelong refusal to learn how to name the person in the mirror. My face had been changing for so long that I had never had time to become acquainted with it."[52] Lucy tries to become acquainted with this new image, and as she successfully recognizes herself, the book ends. The story comes to a closure when Lucy's gaze stops second-guessing herself, her face, and her ugliness. As stated in the afterword, the book "understands how none of us ever feel we are pretty enough while it makes us question the very concept of beauty."[53]

Jessica Queller has also contributed important documentation for understanding beauty's dark side. But in her case, the disfiguration is self-imposed. After losing her mother to breast cancer, Jessica is diagnosed with the BRCA "breast cancer" genetic mutation, which elevates the likelihood of developing breast or ovarian cancer by 80 percent. She describes hearing the news about her gene mutation as if it was an actual diagnosis of cancer: "as soon as someone tests positive for a BRCA mutation, she *is* treated like a cancer patient."[54]

After carefully evaluating her options, she decides to have her breasts removed—a double mastectomy as a self-imposed cancer-prevention measure. Jessica does not come to this decision easily. A self-described "buxom Jewess,"[55] her sense of beauty has been having a pretty face and being thin, leggy, and busty. From childhood on, her mother, a fashion designer, tells her she resembles the film actress Natalie Wood. To imagine herself with breast implants, therefore, makes her wonder whether she will "feel deformed"[56] and lose her natural Natalie Wood-like beauty. In fact, the idea of becoming a monster reappears during her decision-making process, when she compares herself to the "celebrity's anti-Christ": "here I was, transformed by stress and anxiety into a monstrous, histrionic Joan Crawford."[57]

Jessica's decision is very much influenced by her sense of beauty. Can she imagine herself with a boob job? Her research includes meeting with other BRCA-positive women who have had mastectomies done, such as Suzy, whose breasts she inspects in the bathroom of a Starbucks café: "Suzy didn't look scary or deformed—her breasts were beautiful."[58] Finally, Jessica decides to have the surgery done. It is now time to say good-bye to her breasts, carriers of her own sense of beauty and femininity, and have them replaced with silicone ones: "I sat on the floor of my bedroom in front of a large mirror and gazed at my naked breasts for an hour. It sounds ridiculous, but I felt sad for them. They needed to be sacrificed in exchange for my health."[59] In Jessica Queller's autobiography, health and beauty are described as synonyms. The idea that her breasts, which she has always thought of as beautiful, could potentially "kill" her, as she puts it, is unbearable. Her newly implanted breasts not only give Jessica a lower chance of cancer (which is not meant as normative statistical information but rather expresses her frame of mind) but also empower her sense of self, of who she always wanted to be. At the end of her makeover story, she expands her experience into other realms of personhood: "I was born with a name that I found diminishing;[60] I realized I had the power to change it. I inherited a gene that statistically ensured I would get cancer; I took action to prevent it. . . . I believe in utilizing biotechnology to promote health."[61] Jessica's story thus reads like a biotechnological manifesto for change and for a sense of body-self that is always in transition and open for change. The title of her book carries this notion in it: *Pretty Is What Changes*. Her autobiography is a story about taking a destructive measure to allow a new beauty to arise—the beauty of health. This aspect of make-over beauty has an enormous forum and following, as evidenced by *New Beauty* magazine (newbeauty.com), which is based on the notion of a healthy beauty: "NewBeauty believes that looking good and feeling good are one and the same."[62] The online magazine is a forum for advertising cosmetic surgery with both invasive and noninvasive measures.

In light of Lucy Grealy's and Jessica Queller's autobiographies, Alice Munro's birthmark tale, "Face," reflects the normalization of an aesthetic revolution that began with the Surrealists. They activated beauty's dormant dark side, which was present in negative form in stories like Nathaniel Hawthorne's "The Birthmark." After their redefinition of the goal of aesthetic appreciation and the time required for general acceptance of such a cultural revolution, a story like Munro's can celebrate the everyday attractiveness of a mark traditionally known for its ugliness.

Munro's story, however, suggests that there is a potential for pathologizing the love it describes. Little Nancy has a troubled relation to her friend's mark. Can her desire for the mark be interpreted as a superegoic compensation for her original aggression against the narrator? In a similar way, a recent film, *Quid Pro Quo* (Carlos Brooks, 2008), presents the outlier phenomena of amputees by choice and would-be paraplegics as in a facile causal relationship with a kind of original trauma. In the film, Nick Stahl plays a paraplegic who is befriended by a woman who wants to be paralyzed, just like him. The film's rather predictable plot twist comes when it is revealed that she was the child driver who crashed into his parent's car when he was a child and left him paralyzed. Her trauma has played itself out in her psyche as a desire for the ultimate "quid pro quo," which the movie laughably provides when her sacrifice leads Stahl's character to regain his ability to walk.

But behind the pathologization, whether subtle or overt, the prevalence of such texts reveals that beauty's dark side has become mainstream. Hans Bellmer's contorted female nudes and dismembered dolls may still provoke an eerie feeling in viewers, but they are also and always were works of eroticism, as were many of the avant-garde's works (figure 2.1).

The erotics of mutilation that are evident in Bellmer's photographs pass with some ease to an erotics of deformity that has been deployed by numerous contemporary artists but perhaps most famously by Aimee Mullins (figure 2.2). Although she is known for her aesthetic innovation

Figure 2.1
Hans Bellmer, *La Poupée (The Doll)*, 1934. © 2011 Artists Rights Society (ARS), New York/ADAGP, Paris.

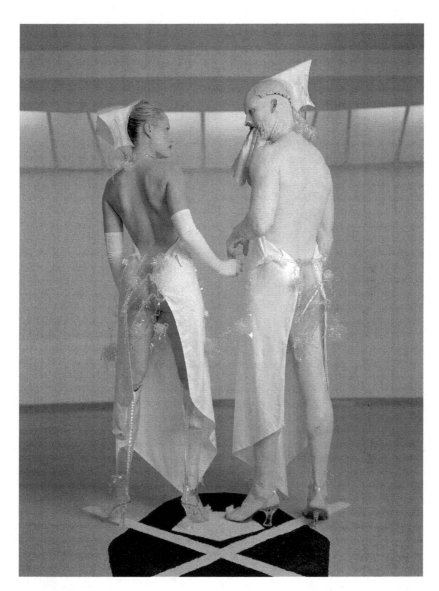

Figure 2.2
Production still from Matthew Barney, *Cremaster 3*, 2002. © 2002 Matthew Barney, photo Chris Winget, courtesy Gladstone Gallery, New York.

of her use of her own body (her legs end just below the knee), I mention her in this context for the unproblematic eroticism of her appearance, despite the shock she wishes to impart. As Marquard Smith writes about her appearance in Matthew Barney's *Cremaster 3*, "If her presence does offer mild surprise (or what people call shock value), it still does little more than pay lip service to the affirmative politics of disability identity and . . . seems to make little difference to her fetishization or her complicity with—or implication in—her own enfreakment."[63]

From Visible to Invisible Monsters

Although Mullins and Barney deploy mutilation and deformation without departing from the realm of the erotic, the Korean performance artist Lee Bul's body performances and drawings of monstrous proliferating forms at times short-circuits the connection between femininity and the monstrous by completely leaving out eroticism.

In her twelve-day performance *Sorry for Suffering—You Think I'm a Puppy on a Picnic?* (1990), for example, Lee Bul walked the streets from Gimpo Airport, Korea, and throughout various sites in Tokyo while dressed head to toe in a soft, mobile sculpture that merges the "fantasies and nightmares of biomechanical couplings, the fusion of flesh and polymers,"[64] thus provoking an image of a uncategorizable uncanny (figure 2.3). Her *Monster Show* (Le consortium, Centre d'art contemporain, Dijon, 2002) includes sculptures composed of elements alternating from tentacle-like appendages to vaguely female-seeming body parts. The potential for erotic connections remains, however, as in her monumental *Hydra II*, whose inflated tentacular mass features an enormous projection of the artist in high boots and net stockings, with her legs spread wide. What is the link between femininity and monstrosity that Lee Bul is trying to explore?

The word *monster* goes back to the Greek root of *teras*, meaning "horrible" and "wonderful" at the same time. As Rosi Braidotti points out and as Lee Bul demonstrates, monstrosity and femininity have a lot in common.[65] Women and particularly mothers have been associated with the abnormal (nonmale) ever since Aristotle's *Generation of Animals*. In his *Monstrorum historia* (1662), Ulisse Aldrovandi, the "Bolognese Aristotle," categorizes the various hybridizations of monsters. For Aldrovandi, these monstrosities were a mistake of nature (*erratis naturae*). The only way he

Figure 2.3
Lee Bul, *Sorry for Suffering—You Think I'm a Puppy on a Picnic?*, 1990. Courtesy of the artist.

can conceptualize the monster is by thinking of it in opposition or in lack of the norm, the "normal male body." Aldrovandi then categorizes these monsters in terms of hybrids between humans and animals (e.g., *Foemina facie Simiae*, a woman with a monkey's head), excess (e.g., *Monstrum bicorpor unico capite*, a monster with two bodies and one head), or lack (e.g., *Infans scifis nasibus*, child without nose).[66] As Rosi Braidotti points out, the idea of the monster as lack or dislocation is structurally comparable to the realm of the feminine, which also lies outside of the male norm.[67]

According to K. E. Olsen and L. A. Houwen, the figure of the monster changed from the classical era's nonhuman entity that had to be defeated (such as the Hydra or Medusa) to the Christian Middle Ages' monster that was "humanized" by being translated into the order of divine creation.[68] The "abnormal" body with its outgrowths from "normalcy" then became something failed but nonetheless part of the creation of a God who expressed his omnipotence through the range of human creation. This "transformation from an existential to an ethical view of monsters"[69] incorporated a wide range of "otherness" into the idea of the human, including the idea of the deviant and also the feminine body as other.

According to Barbara Duden, the eighteenth century saw the creation of an "isolated, objectified, material body" as an object of cognition.[70] This epistemological condensation was accompanied by the establishment of many of today's medical disciplines. One of these was orthopedics, a discipline that originally studied the prevention and correction of deformities in children. The French medical doctor Nicolas Andry de Bois-Regard, founder of the orthopedic discipline, explains how he named the discipline:

As to the Title, I have formed it of two Greek Words, viz. *Orthos*, which signifies straight, free from Deformity and *Paidion*, a Child. Out of these two Words I have compounded that of Orthopaedia, to express in one Term the Design I propose, which is to teach the different Methods of preventing and correcting the Deformities of Children.[71]

The deformities that Andry had in mind, however, did not primarily concern what we today call "genetic defects." He focused on more mundane problems, such as those produced by poor posture, as emblematically shown in his illustration of "a tree bound to a stake in an effort to correct the curvature of the trunk" (figure 2.4). The culture of the mid-eighteenth century had a precise way of thinking about the relationship between a

Figure 2.4
Nicolas Andry de Bois-Regard, "A Tree Bound to a Stake in an Effort to Correct the Curvature of the Trunk," 1741. Courtesy of National Library of Medicine, National Institutes of Health.

proper body and one in need of adjustment, and the vectors between these two states ran exclusively in one direction: in this illustration, the stake is the model for the deformed tree.[72] Those who could not conform or be corrected formed an outcast group that was once occupied by mythic creatures. They would become monsters. And it was not lost on eighteenth-century observers that these monsters were born of women.

One theory that circulated at the time attributed the creation of monsters to a woman's thoughts or psychological state at the time of gestation. In a striking example of maternal imagination, Johann Kaspar Lavater recalled a pregnant woman who watched the execution of a man who was beheaded and had his hand cut off. Her child was born with the right hand missing.[73] The myth that a deformed body could be created by a mother's imagination was a commonplace of the eighteenth century and prevailed throughout the Enlightenment and beyond.[74] Even if the genealogy of the monster retained its basis in superstition, by the early eighteenth century the existence of monsters had been relegated to medical explanation, and their irregularity had been normalized,[75] thus inspiring not horror but repugnance.[76]

Lavater presents his own theory on the subject in a section on "Marks, which Children bring into the World upon them—on monsters, giants, and dwarfs," in which he states that the monster results from a badly proportioned relationship between parts and the whole. The monster is "a living and organized being, who has a conformation contrary to the order of nature, who is born with one or more members too much or too little, in whom one of the parts is misplaced, or else it is too great or too small in proportion to the whole."[77] Lavater, unlike Cesare Lombroso after him, is repelled by the sight of the monster. He admits to being tempted to "turn away his eyes from those abject creatures, from those deformed images, from those hideous and grotesque masks, the refuse of mankind."[78]

Comparing Lombroso's account of monstrosity to Lavater's suggests a lot about the one hundred years that passed between these two authors. In Lombroso's case (discussed in chapter 1), the notion of monstrosity cannot be separated from that of femininity, as if the two were aspects of the same being. For Lombroso, the rare liaison of the female and the criminal produces a creature so disturbing that he uses a term that has long been employed to denote everything that runs against the course of nature—*monster:*

In addition, the female born criminal is, so to speak, doubly exceptional, first as a woman and then as a criminal. This is because criminals are exceptions among civilized people, and women are exceptions among criminals, women's natural form of regression being prostitution, not crime. Primitive woman was a prostitute rather than a criminal. As a double exception, then, the criminal woman is a *true monster*. Honest women are kept in line by factors such as maternity, piety, and weakness; when a woman commits a crime despite these constraints, this is a sign that her power of evil is immense.[79]

Criminal woman is monstrous to Lombroso because she is virile in her outer appearance and often in her intelligence. The last passage of the quote further exemplifies that to Lombroso, motherhood is the only remedy for women's inborn lack of sensibility and empathy, for her inborn ability to lie, and for her many other shortcomings. In general, a lack of motherly instinct is constitutional for the female criminal, which for Lombroso once again proves his point that in primitives, savages, and criminals, the sexes are less differentiated. To be on the safe side, the sexes need to be visibly distinguishable, motherhood being one of the safest indicators for a clean femininity.

So what does Lombroso see when he encounters monstrosity, the screaming sign of uttermost female atavism? Lombroso's gaze corresponds best to the etymology of Latin *monstrare* (to show). He shows and exposes deviance. Unlike Lavater, he cannot turn away from it. In fact, we must read Lombroso's gaze as by definition perverted, in that he was mesmerized by and drawn toward deviation, not the norm. To him the "normal" does actually not exist, as we can see in its most extreme manifestation in his account of the female criminal. Woman is, by definition, abnormal. Her appearance of normalcy is highly suspicious to begin with, since she is always potentially dangerous. Why does Lombroso continue to measure and count data about cranial circumferences, hair color, age, sex, and provenance, even though many of his anthropometrical generalizations did not hold? What is he desperately trying to see? As David G. Horn points out, Lombroso was cagey about what he was looking for, comparing atavistic patterns to notes in a musical chord or to impressionist painting.[80] We may be forced to conclude that for Lombroso, beauty itself—*the* attribute of femininity in all its dangerousness—is actually coming from an ugly place or that (as the Surrealists later put it with far more self-awareness) beauty is convulsive. Only by understanding this inverted concept can we understand what Lombroso was so fascinated by and what Lavater tried to look away from—beauty contained in its opposite, its dark side.

Invisible Monsters (1999) by the novelist Chuck Palahniuk, who gave the world *Fight Club*, is narrated by a fashion model who becomes disfigured. The story circles around the event that creates the narrator as "monster" and is about what happens when a woman who is identified for her beauty becomes ugly. When the beautiful fashion model drives down the highway, she is shot in the face. The loss of her jaw disfigures her face (leaving her "half a face," as she says), similar to Lucy Grealy's case, incapacitates her (she has to eat baby food), and leaves her voiceless (she cannot speak). She recovers, befriends the transsexual Brandy Alexander, who is recovering from a sex-change operation, and spends the majority of the book with Brandy. Their meeting was meant to be, as the narrator tells us; their encounter is described as an allegory of female suffering as expressed through their desire and need for the cut:

Just don't think this was a big coincidence. We had to meet, Brandy and me. We had so many things in common. We had close to everything in common. Besides, it happens fast for some people and slow for some, accidents or gravity, but we all end up mutilated. Most women know this feeling of being more and more invisible everyday.[81]

Early in the novel, the narrator's monstrosity and invisibility are shown to be deeply linked to her femininity. She misses being marked: "Nobody will look at me. I'm invisible. All I want is somebody to ask me what happened."[82] The narrator's passing from the marked visibility of a fashion model into the marked invisibility of disfigurement drives the story, motivates the protagonist, and makes her suffer. She knows that to create a new being, she has to become visible again. But how? While Brandy is learning to speak like a woman as she passes from man to woman, the narrator is learning to speak without a lower jaw. They both are adopting new identities, one by choice (Brandy) and one by accident or the misfortune of being a woman (narrator). Brandy invents names for her friend, including Daisy St. Patience. The novel is told in a nonlinear sequence of memories and includes many side stories, such as the rivalry between the narrator and her fashion model friend Evie and that between the narrator and her homosexual brother Shane, with whom she competed for their parents' attention. At the end of the novel, the name of the "invisible monster," Shannon McFarland, is revealed. This is also when Shannon leaves behind the memory of herself as beautiful and when she finds the "truth" about her new image:

And I leave behind the story that I was ever beautiful, that I could walk into a room deep fried in a tight dress and everybody would take my picture. And I leave behind the idea that this attention was worth what I did to get it. . . . Sister Katherine brings me what I asked for, please, and it's the pictures, the eight-by-ten glossies of me in my white sheet. They aren't good or bad, ugly or beautiful. They're just the way I look. The truth. My future. Just regular reality. And I take off my veils, the cut-work and muslin and lace. . . . I don't need them at this moment, or the next, or the next, forever.[83]

This was not the experience that Lucy Grealy describes in her autobiography. She never really "accepted" her fate, as Shannon does in the novel. In the context of beauty's dark side, this "way I look" that Shannon finally accepts is reached only after being a victim to a shooting that is never explained in the book and after being reassembled by cosmetic surgeons ("a mummy coming apart in the rain") (a theme that I pick up again in chapter 4).

On Chuck Palahniuk's Web site, the author reveals his inspiration to write the story:

I wrote the first draft years ago sitting in laundromats and the only magazines to read were like *Savvy* and *Mademoiselle*, and I think *Glamour* and *Vogue*. So I sort of studied the language of those magazines; the language of fashion description, you know; 600,000 adjectives before you find the word *sweater* at the end. And I thought, why couldn't you write a book in this language? So I did, and it's about a fashion model who is always the center of attention until her face gets shot off in a drive-by shooting. And so she becomes culturally invisible and she realizes there is more power in people being afraid of acknowledging your presence than on people focusing on you all the time.[84]

Paluhniak gives us the plastic surgery fairytale version of Snow White and describes a feminine beauty that is driven toward its own destruction. In the tradition of Lavater and Lombroso, women in Paluhniak's world are by nature "invisible monsters." Their aging process genetically predisposes them to monstrosity. Not unlike *Fight Club*, Palahniuk's answer to this dilemma is to get cosmetic surgery, not to look younger but to fight back. His advice is to find a weapon that overpowers beauty. His suggestion, in the spirit of the Surrealists and their notion of beauty's convulsiveness, is a gun: "Mirror, mirror on the wall, who's the fairest one of all? The evil queen was stupid to play Snow White's game. There's an age where a woman has to move on to another kind of power. Money for example. Or a gun."[85]

Beauty is a guide to the good. Beauty is damnation and holds us bound to the physical world. As with the idea of beauty, the feminine body has been made to symbolize both the desirable and the monstrous, what saves us and makes us whole and what represents deformity. Perhaps that is why the modern beauty ideal is conflicted between the desire to eradicate difference and the fascination with the mutilations of all kinds that such eradication entails. Given this history, it is not surprising that the interventions created for the imposition of normalcy should be appropriated by those who seek a different beauty altogether.

The Case of Michael Jackson and Other Makeover Beauty Victims

In today's culture, the concept of beauty, once a marker of nature's harmonies, is no longer clearly distinguishable from the efforts, desires, and even cuts and deformations that go into making it. It is a culture of makeover beauty. In this culture, which has inherited both an avant-garde revolution in aesthetics and a traditional notion of beauty as expressing a natural order and a good soul, the technological possibilities of manipulating the body have rewritten Plato's *kalókagatheia* into a license to cut, deform, dismantle, and reconstruct. Whereas the traditional notion of beauty posited a signifying relation between internal essence and external appearance, the ethics of makeover beauty involve a wholesale collapse of this distinction. The "amazing transformation" that Americans watched every week for two years as contestants on Fox Broadcasting's reality television show *The Swan* competed to see who could change the most involved more than mere external beauty. In the words of the show's creators, the women had to change themselves inside and out. The change that appeared on the outside depended on changes that contestants made on the inside, adopting a new ethic of self-improvement that they would literally carve into their own flesh. (I return to a detailed discussion of this show in chapter 3.)

Michael Jackson's desire to transcend the categories of race, age, and gender led him to multiple surgical interventions (figure 2.5). He used and abused the cosmetic gaze to escape the appearance of blackness, maleness, and aging in what *Allure* magazine after his sudden death coined a "metamorphosis from adorable child of obvious ethnicity to boy-man with an

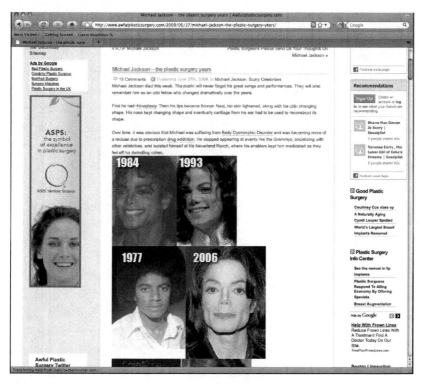

Figure 2.5
Photos of Michael Jackson from http://www.awfulplasticsurgery.com. Courtesy of Tara, Web host at Awfulplasticsurgery.com.

otherworldly visage."[86] Jackson's changing face can be seen as part of "passing," a term that Sander L. Gilman[87] uses for an attempt to be taken for a member of a group in which one was not born. With the help of surgical interventions, Jackson gradually lost many of the traditional facial markers of African American identity. Jackson also acquired an increasingly androgynous look over the years as his facial features became finer and less masculine. His masculinity, in turn, became a performance piece that was reserved for the stage.

Jackson's body modification moved in at least three directions—toward a diminishing of markers typically associated with his African ancestry, toward an ambiguity of gender, and toward an image of eternal youth or what he called his Peter Pan syndrome. In many ways, the last is the underlying essence of these changes, since remaining a child also means remaining in a constant state of change or potentiality. This desire to remain a child spread beyond his interventions into his own body. He also surrounded himself with children (a practice that led to several legal proceedings) and created a home in an amusement park. The opening line of *Peter Pan* became Jackson's motto: "All children, except one, grow up."

Through his body modifications, Jackson challenged the rigidity of the categories of age and black masculinity and indicated the central paradox of today's makeover culture. As he said in a 1993 interview with Oprah Winfrey, "I'm a black American. . . . I'm proud to be a black American. I'm proud of my race."[88] He also argued vehemently that the fact that he liked to sleep in the same bed with children did not mean that he was a pedophile. Jackson refused to accept categories like race and gender and seemed to be uneasy with the idea of belonging to any fixed category. The belonging itself seemed objectionable.

Meredith Jones considers the concept of the "white mask"[89] that Jackson created for himself as similar to the function of the mask of femininity in the gender dynamic discussed above. The problem was not the color of the skin itself; Jackson repeatedly insisted that he was a black man and was proud of that. The problem was that Jackson wanted to escape the confines of being marked per se. Perhaps this explains his tendency in later years to avoid showing his skin at all (figure 2.6).

I think that when Jackson said he was proud of being a black man, he was reaching for an inner platform from which to express his potential rather than accepting a publicly visible social or racial category. How this inner being finds expression can only be a matter of personal creation.

This inner being does not rest on any specific social category but derives from a holistic sense of personhood—what I am and what I strive to bring to the surface through the makeover possibilities available to me. This can be thought of as beauty, eternal youth, immortality, or a postgender or postracial identity. Jackson's "white mask" cannot be reduced to a mere disavowal of his race but demonstrates the complexity of questions of identity in today's America. In a culture under the sway of the one-drop rule, whereby a single drop of African blood is enough to consider a person black, Jackson's manipulation of the outward traces of his racial identity signaled a willingness and even desire to test the limits of such inclusiveness and at the same time showed his resistance to the marks of oppression left by his community's collective history. As sociologist Michael Eric

Figure 2.6
Michael Jackson and an unidentified child in Bahrain, 2006, *Rolling Stone*, special commemorative issue "Michael Jackson 1958–2009," 2009. Courtesy Reuters.

Figure 2.7
Film still from *Michael Jackson: Live in Bucharest. The Dangerous Tour* (1992).

Dyson put it in a *Rolling Stone* article after Jackson's death, "the reason black folk never turned their backs on him is because they realized he was merely acting out on his face what we collectively have been tempted to do in our souls: whitewash the memory and trace of our offending blackness."[90]

In some ways, Michael Jackson met the demands of the cosmetic gaze to its utmost perfection. In the 1990s, his made-over body became the icon for change and progress. In the famous opening of the Dangerous World Tour (1992) in Bucharest, Michael is being "shot out" from underneath the stage. While Romanian fans screamed, Michael stood still in this pose for about five minutes (figure 2.7). An icon of change, his statuesque body seemed frozen in its instability of time, gender, and race. Nearly twenty years later, during a rehearsal for his last tour, This Is It (scheduled for 2009 and 2010),[91] which never materialized due to Jackson's sudden and unexpected death on June 25, 2009 (eighteen days before the first concert of the tour), his eleven dancer-clones were shot out from under the stage in choreography that recalled the earlier iconic tour. Although Michael may have lost some energy over the years, it is doubtful that his dancers could repeat the stopping of time that the pop star caused for Romanian fans in 1992.

On the Web site Awfulplasticsurgery.com, Michael Jackson is remembered by some as a "scary celebrity," not because of his music and dancing but because of his appearance and the instability of his appearance. After his death, bloggers often commented on his appearance: "Michael Jackson died this week. The public will never forget his great songs and performances. They will also remember him as an odd fellow who changed dramatically over the years" and "He was such a good-looking man before 1993. I wonder who agreed to perform these unnecessary, unethical surgeries?"[92] In these Web obituaries, most bloggers say that he went too far. Tara explains her motivation for founding the blog Awfulplasticsurgery.com:

I started this website at the end of 2003 as a way to privately catalogue all the unneeded celebrity plastic surgery I had noticed cropping up over the past few years in Hollywood. Al Pacino had a facelift which ruined his unique handsomeness. It also seemed like every starlet or singer at the time (2003) such as Shannon Elizabeth, Susan Ward, Christina Aguilera, Britney Spears all had breast implants; it seemed like they were part of the Hollywood "uniform," like super white teeth. And all of aforementioned females had implants that looked . . . as if they had gone to a 'one size fits all' type surgeon.[93]

Tara's "catalogue of awfulness" is reminiscent of Cesare Lombroso's inventories in that they both separate the good from the bad makeover. About the "awful plastic surgery patient" cat lady Jocelyn Wildenstein (figure 2.8), Tara says:

I believe that a desire to be more attractive coupled with emotional problems drives awful plastic surgery patients, like Jocelyn Wildenstein. For patients like her, the initial plastic surgery results gave her an emotional boost. When it wore off, she decided to get more surgery, then more, and so on. I truly believe it was an addiction in her case. But I also think that the doctors who operated on her should have been prosecuted, because she is clearly mentally unwell.[94]

Tara's blog discusses the taxonomy of makeover and beauty's "dark side." Next to the comments posted about Jocelyn Wildenstein's surgeries—which, for instance, describe her as "alien" looking—there are advertisements for "natural" noninvasive procedures such as laser hair removal. The cat lady is clearly outside the norm, and this disturbs the blogger, who asks her the rhetorical question, "Could you look more normal?" Apparently the visibility of the destructive drive in the construction of today's beauty is organized along strict lines of what is acceptable and what is not. The advertisements that accompany the blog discussions of Jocelyn's abnormality suggest how selective that exclusion is.

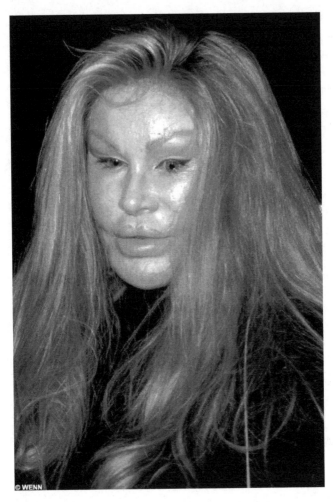

Figure 2.8
Jocelyn Wildenstein, from http://www.awfulplasticsurgery.com. Courtesy of Tara,
Web host at Awfulplasticsurgery.com.

As Meredith Jones has pointed out in *Skintight: An Anatomy of Cosmetic Surgery*, cases like Michael Jackson's and Jocelyn Wildenstein's ultimately have a normalizing function for the culture at large: "They are the special agents of an abject, hybrid otherness that cosmetic surgery—as emerging technology—requires to make itself legitimate."[95] In this market for representing extreme makeovers, the legitimizing function never seems to stray far from a desire to thrill at the excesses and failures that these technologies enable. As with Lavater and Lombroso, the definition of desirability seems to have a close, even symbiotic relation with the object that it ostensibly excludes. The recent market for such vicarious thrills includes documentaries like *Plastic Disasters* (HBO, 2006) and women's magazines with stories on cosmetic surgery disasters. One such disaster was that of French porn star Lolo Ferrari, "a full blown tragic figure: the Marilyn Monroe or Kurt Cobain of a world at the nexus of celebrity, cosmetic surgery and pornography."[96] Lolo's breasts made it into the 1999 *Guinness Book of Records* as the reportedly biggest human breasts with a dimension of 180 centimeters (71 inches), weighing 2.8 kilograms (6.2 pounds), and containing three liters of saline. Lolo's breasts, which she enhanced in about twenty-two operations, clearly exceeded a "norm." Some even think that her resistance to the patriarchical normalizing gaze was a feminist move because she was aware and willing to transgress it.[97] Indeed, the porn star exceeded every expectation of femininity. Her breasts, and with them Lolo Ferrari, stepped outside of the realm of the reproductive and sexual, which are the natural attributes of the breast. Her "completely artificial femininity," as she herself described it, went into a realm that may shock some and that some may read as having empowered her (figure 2.9).

After Lolo Ferrari's sudden death in 2000, her husband was charged with murder, but later it was decided that she had died of suicide. Bloggers were willing to forgive Michael Jackson, but they held Lolo responsible for her early death, and some even said that she "deserved" it:

That shit isn't natural either. They could've recycled all the plastic in this bitches chest and made a few bumpers for a couple SUV's. Lolo Ferrari, who was billed as "the woman with the biggest breasts in the world" and had a reputed 71-inch (177.5 cm) silicone-enhanced bust and was as ugly as her tits were big. As soon as they rule out that one of those tits of hers didn't get a mind of its own and roll up on her face in her sleep, I think they might have a case against the husband.[98]

Figure 2.9
Lolo Ferrari, from http://www.awfulplasticsurgery.com. Courtesy of Tara, Web host at Awfulplasticsurgery.com.

This blogger, Kuma, envisions Lolo's enhanced breasts as having gained a life of their own to "revenge" themselves, and it is hard not to think of Lee Bul's monstrous sculptures, in which female body parts take on a life of their own, threatening and massive—the perfect counterpoint to the required invisibility of a "successful" cosmetic surgery.

Such images of revenge could also have come from the 1964 science fiction horror thriller, *The Atomic Brain*, aka *Monstrosity* (which is featured on a Web site called Badmovies.org). In this film, an old widow has lost her beauty and wants to implant her own brain into the bodies of three young, beautiful immigrant women, who answer a help-wanted ad posted by a mad scientist. This "exchange" does not go unpunished. Jones seems to invoke a similar logic when she points out that Lolo Ferrari died a death by breast. She did not survive the "Survival of the Most Made Over." In makeover culture, it seems that the most made over tend not to survive. The following section examines normativity and how and where we learn to look for the better me and to melt into that "unmarked invisibility" that Sander L. Gilman talks about.

The New Beauty, or the Survival of the Made Over[99]

After World War II, *physiognomy* became a taboo word, especially in German-speaking countries. In recent decades, however, there has been a renewed upsurge of scientific interest in bodily beauty, although the term *physiognomy* is usually avoided.[100] Studies conducted by Cunningham,[101] for instance, claim to demonstrate that facial attractiveness is a universal notion that transcends the boundaries between different cultures. Following the seminal 1972 study of Karen K. Dion, E. Berscheid, and E. Walster[102] that proved that physical attractiveness influenced people's evaluations of others, psychologists have examined the relation between physical beauty and other positive attributes. Although these earlier studies focused on the effects of social stereotypes, today's attractiveness studies are experiencing a revival of what is called *Darwinian aesthetics.*[103] Victor S. Johnston, for instance, argues that "physical beauty is a sexual trait" and that physical attraction arises from an interaction between a perceiver's brain and a perceived face, both of which have been modified, in a complementary manner, by the actions of steroid hormones.[104] Attempts to question the supposedly natural relation of beauty and other positive qualities or to treat the equation in a historical perspective are referred to as "age-old maxims and precepts" like "(a) *Beauty is in the eye of the beholder,* (b) *never judge a book by its cover,* and (c) *beauty is only skin-deep*"[105] or as "popular writings."[106]

As Karl Grammer has argued, the idea that human beauty is exclusively in the eye of the beholder has had to be jettisoned in favor of a concept of beauty that understands it as a function of an observer and a complex of observed features, which have been naturally selected to optimize the search for the optimum sexual partner.[107] According to Darwinian aesthetics, which would have satisfied Lavater in his quest for harmony and symmetry, features considered universally attractive are attractive for a reason: proportionality and symmetry signify better health; an ideal ratio between hip and waist width in women indicates reproductive ability;[108] broad chins and jaws as well as height in men indicate high testosterone levels, suggesting strength and the ability to protect and provide for offspring. Moreover, some kinds of success in life can be experimentally correlated to the same traits that apparently define beauty. Male politicians whose facial traits best match these selective markers, for instance, tend to be more positively judged by the public than those who do not.[109] The signals for high testosterone levels have a secondary attractiveness guarantee, since testosterone incurs a high cost for an organism's immune system. In other words, a man with the signs of high testosterone also signals to a potential mate, "Check me out. I'm so healthy I can afford this chin!"[110]

The evolutionary approach to beauty even has theories to explain apparently counterintuitive features, such as why being thin (which would seem to indicate malnourishment) would be preferred over being fat (which would seem to indicate the ability to provide oneself with ample nourishment):

In poor societies, the rich impress the poor by becoming fat; which the poor cannot do; in rich societies even the poor can become fat . . . ; therefore, the rich must impress by staying thin, as if to say, "We have so little doubt about where our next meal is coming from, that we don't need a single gram of fat store." . . . Both standards require the investment of individual effort and resources.[111]

Apart from determining the effects of beauty on social interactions and attributions, current research in the field seeks to determine what beauty is and how it can be scientifically accounted for. In the early 1990s, for instance, Judith H. Langlois and her colleagues used a digital morphing program to create averaged computer-generated "composite faces." Several faces were photographed, and each was represented by 512×512 numeric gray values. These matrices were arithmetically averaged and used to create a series of achromatic composite facial images. The result of her research suggested that beautiful faces are actually averaged faces (figure 2.10).[112]

More recently, researchers have adopted the view that beautiful faces differ from average faces in a systematic manner, thereby indicating an optimal adaptation to the environment. Sexual selection is considered the driving force determining the ideal combination of facial features by sug-

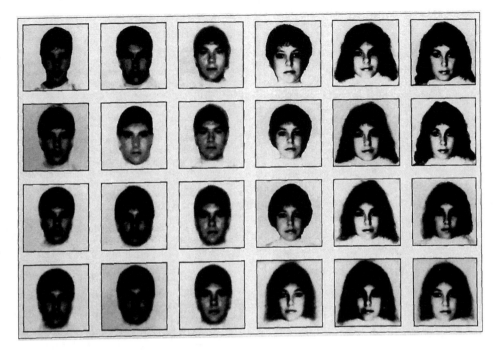

Figure 2.10
Photos of composite faces, from Judith Langlois, "Attractive Faces Are Only Average,"
Psychological Science 1 (1990). Courtesy RightsLink.

gesting genetic fitness. This model suggests that "a romantically attractive
face has neonate features in the center of the face, such as large eyes, and
sexual maturity features at the periphery, such as prominent cheekbones
for women . . . and large chins for men."[113]

Victor S. Johnston challenges Langlois's findings with the argument that
"the overlay averaging procedure used in these studies could blur facial
details, increase symmetry, and change proportions . . . and that as a result
all factors could enhance attractiveness."[114] In other words, Johnston challenges the operativity of Langlois's composites as applying a way of looking
that is informed by the technologies of bodily makeover—in this case, the
averaging composites' production of "more beautiful" faces. Johnston,
however, is an evolutionary psychologist and not a cultural theorist, and
for him this challenge can be overcome. In collaboration with M. Franklin,
he developed a computer program that allows individuals to "evolve" their
most attractive facial composite (see figure 2.10). Johnston finds that from

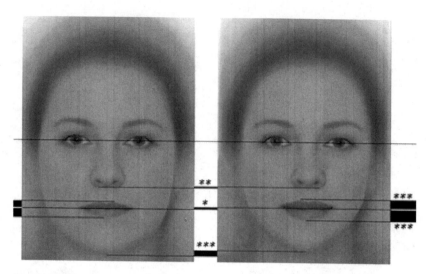

Figure 2.11

Photos of composite faces, from Victor S. Johnston, "Difference between Average and Attractive Female Faces," in "Mate Choice Decisions: The Role of Facial Beauty," *Trends in Cognitive Science* 10, no. 1 (January 2006). Courtesy Victor S. Johnston.

an evolutionary perspective—which correlates beauty and mate choice with sexual fitness—attractive female faces are not average but "display features indicative of higher levels of pubertal estrogens (full lips) and lower levels of androgen exposure (short narrow lower jaw and large eyes) than average females" (figure 2.11).[115]

According to Johnston and Franklin, this "average female face" (left) and its "attractive and younger looking female corrective" (right) differ in the elevation of the lower jaw and lips. In the younger-looking face, the eyes seem larger, the lips fuller, and the cheekbones appear higher, as if the face had been pumped with pubertal estrogens. This also corresponds to what Frederic Brandt, a celebrity dermatologist, notices, when a face ages: "What we notice when people age is that our fat pads start falling, the cheeks start dripping down, and we start losing volume in the upper face and it causes sagging in the lower face. You lose what we call the 'youthful convexities' of the face. And the convexities are the fullness and the roundness."[116] According to the resulting evolutionary explanation for attractiveness, an attractive face signals health to the potential sexual mate, who wants to ensure health for his offspring and thereby longevity for his own genes. In other words, youth is a placeholder for sexual and reproductive fitness, so that attractiveness becomes a survival strategy.

But none of these scientific authors has gained more popular interest than Stephen Marquardt, a maxillo-facial surgeon, developer of the "golden mask," and president of Marquardt Beauty Analysis LLC, Aesthetic Research and Diagnostic Analysis. Marquardt has combined detailed observations and recording techniques with a mathematical analysis based on the "golden ratio" or phi ratio of 1/1.618,[117] which is inspired by classical and neoclassical quantifications of beauty. He has invented a computer program (warping software) that measures the distances within the face and their approximation to an ideal facial mask[118] that he has constructed (figure 2.12). This is done not by relying on intuition like Randall Haworth or by morphing existing celebrity faces as in a photographical composite, but by warping (that is, approximating) the facial proportions to the golden phi ratio. For Marquardt, the closer a face is to the mask, the more attractive, beautiful, and ultimately healthy the person is for successful procreation.

As Marquardt points out, even "very unattractive" faces match the mask to a certain extent. He explains: "the 'average face' in today's Beauty Ranges was probably the most beautiful one three-hundred years ago. Today, we all fit into the mask. We may start out as neutral or even 'beautiful,' and with plastic surgery and make-up we can get *really* beautiful."[119] *Really* has to be understood here as literally: we have become real—a real person in the world, someone who can be experienced or seen on a reality show.

The mask can be downloaded from Marquardt's Web site and is intended for application. The doctor suggests that it can be used as a way to figure out which parts of the face need approximation to the mask so that makeup can be applied accordingly or even as a guideline for cosmetic surgery. Marquardt has been featured in several television documentaries. In the documentary *Made Over in America: A Voyage into the Land of Makeover* (2007), he recalls that after his appearances on TV, people asked him for advice on how to have their faces done according to the golden ratio or on what to look for in an ideal partner. Marquardt could be said to be a twenty-first-century version of the eighteenth-century relationship guru Johann Kaspar Lavater. In an interview with Cindy Ingle, Marquardt showed how a makeover show candidate could be improved according to the mask. The result of the new Cindy is close to the vision of her surgeon, Dr. Haworth. One thing, however, that the mask did not get rid of as much

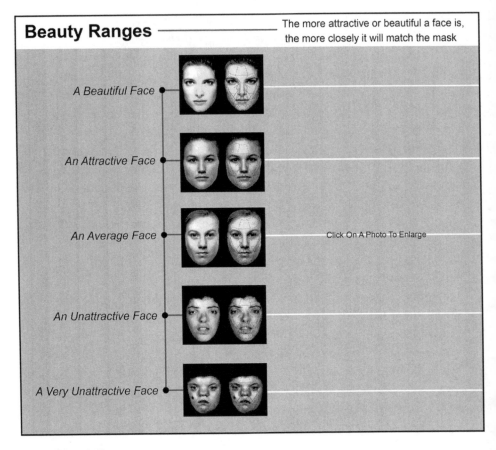

Figure 2.12
Photos of beauty ranges and the golden mask, from Stephen Marquardt, http://www.
beautyanalysis.com. Courtesy Stephen Marquardt.

as the surgery did is Cindy's "ethnic" native American and "chicana" look
(figure 2.13). When her eyebrows were raised in the golden mask, Cindy
looked, according to Dr. Haworth, more "Asian." The transformations
shown on the TV show *The Swan* were always a "whitification."

Recent research conducted in the area of data-driven facial attractiveness goes one step further in that it applies this particular cosmetic gaze—
the search for the younger more sexual productive self—into a "beautification
engine." Tommer Leyvand and his colleagues use a computer to match a
face to the golden ratio. The beautification machine they developed is
enhancing "the aesthetic appeal of human faces in frontal photographs

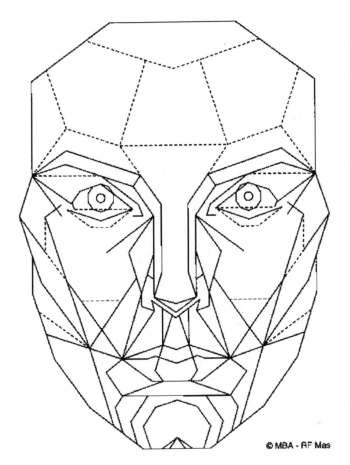

© MBA - BF Mas

Figure 2.12
(continued)

(portraits), while maintaining close similarity with the original" (figure 2.14).[120]

These after faces also fit Marquardt's golden mask better after having been put through the beautification engine. As Marquardt points out himself, the beautification engine is nothing else than the application of certain aspects of the golden mask. After analyzing these images from the beautification engine, Marquardt concludes that only the female golden mask has been applied to certain areas of the male and female face, such as eyes, nose, and lips. As a result, the "beautification"—according to Marquardt—is not complete and two-dimensional: "These researchers

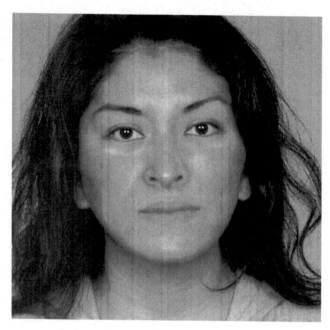

Figure 2.13
Film still of Cindy fitting into the golden mask, from unused footage from interview with Stephen Marquardt for *Made Over in America: A Voyage into the Land of Makeover* (Bernadette Wegenstein and Geoffrey Alan Rhodes, 2007). Courtesy Icarusfilms.

don't know what beauty really is. They just move a few things around, like changing the angle of the face, which creates more symmetry, but they don't really understand how a face functions."[121] When put through the beautification engine, though, these faces come remarkably close to the parameters of the golden mask (figure 2.15).

This data-driven approach to aesthetic enhancement is not as refined as Steven Marquardt's individually applied mask. But the beautification engine predicts certain human judgments on beauty. Although some suggest that this evidence supports an assertion of an ultimate grounding of human beauty in the realm of evolution or the theory of sexual attractiveness, this research stands for something far more radical. The machine, being built on the universal principles of beauty, knows us better than we know ourselves because the reality of those beautiful selves we long to "expose" can now be sutured together by the very media we use to express and know ourselves.

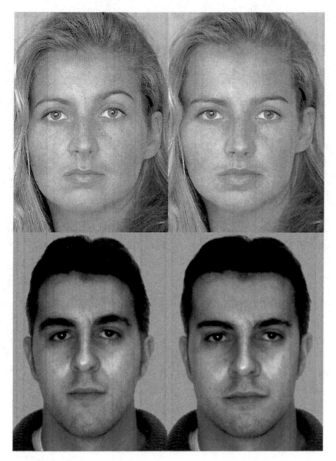

Figure 2.14
Photos of input facial images (left) and images generated by Tommer Leyvand and his colleagues to fit Stephen Marquardt's golden mask (right). The changes are subtle yet significant. Courtesy ACM.

The great philosopher of aesthetics Arthur C. Danto defines Hegel's "Third Realm of Beauty" as "the kind of beauty something possesses only because it was caused to possess it through actions whose purpose it is to *beautify*. . . . In this realm, things are beautiful only because they were beautified"[122] Makeover beauty is fully in the third realm, and the judgment from high modernity would seem to be that, whatever we say of it, such aesthetic practice remains trivial. Danto refers to Kant's contempt for the tattooed body, "when the body—after all the image of God—is already

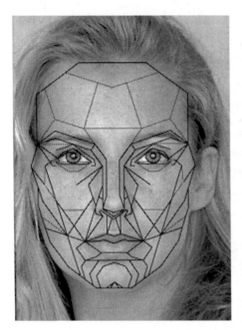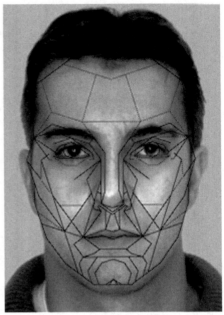

Figure 2.15
Photos of Tommer Leyvand and colleagues' "after" faces in Stephen Marquardt's golden mask. Courtesy Stephen Marquardt.

as beautiful as it can be."[123] But even something as apparently trivial as mere beautification can carry enormous ethical weight. As Danto goes on to say, "beautificatory practices themselves intersect at every step of the way with various moral imperatives, which specify what we may call the bounds of taste. . . . These aesthetic complaints can be, and typically are, over-ridden by moral considerations."[124] To take a case in point, the U.S. beauty industry grew from $40 million in sales in 1914, to $17 billion in 1985, and to around $20 billion today.[125] As Deborah L. Rhode documents, our current obsession with appearances has generated an industry valued at more than $200 billion a year[126] and leads to physical and emotional suffering and social, political, and economic discrimination. Far from being a trivial matter, makeover beauty is often literally a matter of life and death.

On the reality show *Survivor* and the recent *I'm a Celebrity. Get Me Out of Here!*, people have to prove their jungle fitness to those who feel threatened that they could be "left behind" in their various social environments by not fitting into the "golden mask." Cindy—thanks to *The Swan*—was able to say good-bye to her droopy "witch-nose" and her damaged body image to the beautification engine that rectifies and digitally refreshes faces. These examples share one common denominator—a presumed competitor who might survive instead of us. According to the new concept, beauty in an evolutionary sense is an indicator for physiological health, high immuno-competence, and successful procreation. The economic value of the "new new face" has never made more sense: if today's Hollywood stars don't improve and conform their appearances to a youthful survival-of the-fittest look, then they will not survive in their profession and will be replaced by the next generation.

In this "uncanny resemblance" to their selves of four films earlier, these actresses—like an uncountable number of women and men in our global electronic market who look just like the Olympians in figure 2.16—resemble an artist's rendering of their most glamorous celebrity moments.[127] To use Marquardt's universe, they all continue to fit the algorithms underlying the golden mask. But for Marquardt, this poses new questions of bioethics. Through these beautification engines, we are giving people a chance to survive who would have naturally died out. Their beauty no longer resonates with health and reproduction. This leads to a "conundrum," the surgeon says: "with these messages of eternal beauty we are screwing up our gene pool."[128] What I call in the next chapter the *machinic suture* has reached its limit here. An ideal of a subtly refreshed version of the real me requires the erasing of every trace of the technology that was used to create it, thus "falsely" mediating health and the possibility for healthy reproduction. But despite this "false announcement," this four-films-older new self increases the competitiveness on the image-driven global electronic market. As images, these faces are "healthy." For Jean Baudrillard, in the regime of the image, the real has been murdered and exchanged with a virtual version of it. This virtual can be reproduced no matter "how old" it is, by just one click.

This notion of the "four-films-younger" you (how an actor or actress looked about four or five years ago) comes from Tara of Awfulplasticsurgery.com. In an interview I conducted with her about her own cosmetic gaze and her own sense of beauty, she said:

I am a very visual person and have a good photographic memory. I'm also a bit of a pop culture addict. In the nineties, I noticed that some of the young actors I

DEMI MOORE
Age: 45

MICHELLE PFEIFFER
Age: 50

ELIZABETH HURLEY
Age: 43

NAOMI CAMPBELL
Age: 38

Figure 2.16

"The New New Face" (photos of four female film actors), from Jonathan van Meter, "About Face," *New York Magazine*, August 3, 2008, 29. © Getty Images.

followed were getting more polished. Shannon Doherty got breast implants, Jason Priestley had a rhinoplasty surgery, Tori Spelling bought breast implants, and from there, I started noticing other celebrities, some not so young or famous, also had gotten plastic surgery procedures. I think that noticing the alterations my favorites had gotten helped me train my eye. . . . And that is when I start looking for older photos of that celebrity, so I can see what they are possibly trying to hide.[129]

Tara's Web site monitors changes in celebrities' bodies. She has, in her own words, trained her eye to distinguish acceptable changes from bad work. In many ways, she embodies today's cosmetic gaze, dictating the versions of ourselves we should strive for and the ways that we go about implementing those changes. Her Web site reveals what Danto calls "the bounds of taste" as they exist in an age brought up on cosmetic surgery and reality TV. When I asked her what she thought real beauty was, she answered, "I think true beauty is within. Essentially, it is the sum of how you treat others in your environment, whether, human, animal, or inanimate object. . . . And a beautiful plastic surgery result is one that no one suspects is plastic surgery."[130] That these two statements somehow manage not to contradict each other tells us volumes about the cosmetic gaze in the age of makeover beauty. It is now fully normalized, invisible, a part of the way we inhabit our bodies today, and it shows itself through its supplemental extrusion, the dark side of beauty that revels in its own convulsions. The media and technologies that have helped get us to that point are the subject of the next chapter.

3 Machinic Sutures: Twenty-First-Century Technologies of Beauty

—*Socrates.* Further, in portraying ideal types of beauty, seeing it is not easy to light upon any one human being who is absolutely devoid of blemish, you cull from many models the most beautiful traits of each, and so make your figures appear completely beautiful?

—*Parrhasius.* Yes, that is how we do.

—Well, but stop (Socrates continued); do you also pretend to represent in similar perfection the characteristic moods of the soul, its captivating charm and sweetness, with its deep wells of love, its intensity of yearning, its burning point of passion? or is all this quite incapable of being depicted?

—Nay (he answered), how should a mood be other than inimitable, Socrates, when it possesses neither linear proportion nor colour, nor any of those qualities which you named just now; when, in a word, it is not even visible?

—*Socrates.* Well, but the kindly look of love, the angry glance of hate at any one, do find expression in the human subject, do they not?

—*Parrhasius.* No doubt they do.

—*Socrates.* Then this look, this glance, at any rate may be imitated in the eyes, may it not?

—Xenophon, *Memorabilia*[1]

The *cosmetic gaze* refers to how humans experience their own and others' bodies as incomplete projects that await the intervention of technologies of enhancement, which will help them better approximate their true self or natural potential. *Machinic suture* names the operation through which the supposedly prior or pure aspects of selfhood—my true self, how I desire to be, my body—have become so via the performative influence of augmented realities. These two concepts complement the contemporary paradigm of *ubiquitous computing* (or *pervasive computing*)—the complete integration of computing into everyday life. The cosmetic gaze and machinic suture do not presuppose physically ubiquitous computational machines, but digital technologies have been adapted to the operations of machinic sutures in various technological regimes.

Bodily experiences take place in and by means of mediated environments, and mediated environments are thoroughly embodied affairs. Virtual environments are important, but although Jay David Bolter et al. note that "the ontology of mixed reality is therefore different from that of VR [virtual reality],"[2] the existence and pervasiveness of both contribute to the current nature of the machinic suture. As Mark Hansen notes, *all reality is mixed reality*, so the conceptual distinctions between mixed reality and machinic suture are based on technology and subjectivity.

This chapter connects thematically to chapter 1 via various attempts—religious, scientific, and empirical—to find a "pure language"[3] with universal rules that can read and interpret the connection between a person's outer appearance and his or her inside ("character" or "soul"). Such a language is supposed to function as the Saussurian sign notion does (by arbitrarily linking a signifier to a signified), and by learning and appropriating the language, people can generate meaning. But something else drives this pure or universal language of physiognomy. At the core of this semiotic process—at the structuralist's "fraction line" between a signifier and a signified—a judgment is formed. In Lombroso's criminal anthropology, for instance, this judgment was based on an observation that a person's overdeveloped jaws and cheekbones were a sign of atavism, that they were typical of "prehistoric man" or "indigenous races," and that therefore people with these jaws and cheekbones more prone to "criminal behavior" than people who fit other kinds of observations (such as an observation that a white man's "prominent" and "high" forehead were signs of wisdom and intellectuality) (see chapter 1). This finding can be integrated into the broader historical picture by noting that this desire to see through the "mask of the face" was in part driven by a "science of the mind"[4] that was emerging in the late nineteenth and early twentieth centuries. This science was trying to read the mind inside out medically, cognitively, and psychoanalytically, and throughout the twentieth century it also found more and more accurate ways to render visually the internal sphere of the mind, such as via brain imaging technology.[5]

In this book, the link between aesthetic and moral judgment is encapsulated in the Platonic notion of *kalókagatheia*. This judgment has been absorbed by twenty-first-century Western culture as a way of looking for what has been marked as "better-beautiful" by an authoritative gaze spread through the eyes of physiognomists, racial theorists, and others. Today, this "better beautiful" version of the self has been identified as a commodity by aesthetic surgeons and software engineers who develop "beautification engines" of the "ideal you,"[6] and they are proliferated at the speed of light through our current media culture. This better you might feature a rounder jaw, a more even forehead, a smoother skin color, a wider smile, or a six-pack as opposed to a "pendulous abdomen." These are all examples of improvements, slight or drastic, that suit our bodies or our character better than the "original." This chapter is thus dedicated to understanding the logic of this gaze as it is applied via today's technologies and media. In one extreme case, when the pop icon Michael Jackson died of an overdose of prescription drugs, the world had already come to terms with his severely modified facial features. The issue was no longer that he had died of body dysmorphic disorder (the preoccupation or excessive concern with a nonexistent or slight physical defect in a normal-appearing person)[7] while attempting to escape from the visual categories of race and gender. Instead, after his death, the media reported that Jackson had died of medical reasons due to a variety of illnesses and incidents in his life—a broken nose, lupus, second-degree burns due to an accident during the shooting of a Pepsi commercial, and the pigmentation disorder disease vitiligo (which some felt caused Jackson's whitification).[8] But although the media emphasized the star's "medical" needs for surgeries, they overlooked another need—the need to fulfill fame's cosmetic gaze to its utmost perfection. The first section below examines today's most widespread and most important application of the cosmetic gaze—surgery—and the ways that it relates to fame and other illnesses.

The Subtly Refreshed Look of Cosmetic Surgery

Cosmetic surgery is, as Meredith Jones puts it, "makeover culture's quintessential expression"[9] and has a century of history—medically, culturally, theoretically, and practically. In today's Westernized world, nearly any "reason" is enough for someone to decide to go under the knife. But at the beginning of the twentieth century, when elective cosmetic surgery started to become available and attractive for the middle and upper classes, doctors willingly performed "real" plastic surgery (that is, reconstructive surgery) and but resisted cosmetic surgery as an unnecessary risk. In his brief introduction to *The Correction of Featural Imperfections* (1908), for instance, Charles Miller complains about the "apathy" of doctors:

A large number of the profession are at the present day apathetic regarding elective surgery for the correction of those featural imperfections which are not actual deformities, but such apathy cannot prevent the development of this specialty as the demand for featural surgeons is too great on the part of the public.[10]

As Elizabeth Haiken has demonstrated in her historical study of cosmetic surgery in the United States, the turning point for a demand on the part of the public, to put it in Miller's words, was the psychological concept of the "inferiority complex," a concept that was developed by the Austrian Alfred Adler and that developed popularity in the first half of the twentieth century:

The inferiority complex, in fact, became the final link in the self-reflexive argument plastic surgeons formulated to justify the practice of cosmetic surgery. Patients who developed inferiority complexes because of physical defects would find their economic status adversely affected, because those suffering from such complexes were unable to present themselves with the confidence necessary to ensure success in a competitive world. Conversely, those who could not obtain work because of their appearance would find that their psychic health was at risk: unable to support themselves and their dependents, they would develop inferiority complexes. In either case, surgery could make an important, even key, contribution.[11]

According to Cressida J. Heyes and Meredith Jones, "the language of inferiority complex has fallen away" in today's cosmetic surgery culture.[12] But the reasons that people give for undergoing elective cosmetic surgery still have to do with self-improvement—a psychological concept that is based on the principles of *kalókagatheia*: you must improve and better yourself to thrive. Women and men today choose cosmetic surgery as consumers (and not patients), and they do so for a widely varying set of reasons. Statistics say something about recent developments in the consumption of cosmetic surgery in North America.

According to the American Society for Aesthetic Plastic Surgery (ASAPS), in 2007—the last year that witnessed an overall surgery increase—11.7 million cosmetic surgical and nonsurgical procedures were performed in the United States for a total cost of $13.2 billion.[13] Of these cosmetic surgical procedures, 91 percent were performed on women. In 2007, men had 327,519 Botox injections, and women had 2,445,656. In that year, the top surgical interventions for men were liposuctions (57,980), and the top interventions for women were breast augmentations (399,440).[14] The percentage of male cosmetic surgery consumers is increasing but still minimal. In addition, eight out of nine surgeons are male.[15] More men are having cosmetic surgery done, and more women are becoming cosmetic surgeons, but it will take at least another century to overcome these unbalances.

ASAPS statistics also show that patients for cosmetic surgery procedures have gotten increasingly younger. In the United States in 2006, 16,477 rhinoplasties, 7,915 Botox injections, and 5,423 Hylaform/Restylane injections were performed on adolescents who were eighteen years and younger. The top surgery for U.S. adolescents in 2006 was rhinoplasty (1 percent had the procedure), and in 2007 it was otoplasty (cosmetic ear surgery) (2 percent had the procedure). An attitude survey performed by ASAPS revealed that 27 percent of eighteen- to twenty-four-year-olds would consider cosmetic surgery now or in the near future. In 2007, 21 percent of all cosmetic procedures were performed on racial and ethnic minorities (Hispanics, 9 percent; African Americans, 6 percent; Asians, 5 percent; and other non-Caucasians, 2 percent),[16] which constitutes a decrease of 1 percent from 2006. ASAPS claims that 56 percent of women and 57 percent of men approve of cosmetic surgery. Sociologist Anthony Elliott finds this trend resonates in other parts of the world, as well. According to a recent European survey, "most women now expect to have cosmetic surgery at some point in their lifetime."[17]

Anthony Elliott tries to make sense of the cosmetic surgery boom in the early twenty-first century by placing the demand for cosmetic surgery and the "new individualism of instant change"[18] within the broader phenomenon of globalization. He lists three global social influences—celebrity culture, consumerism, and the electronic economy of looking good. Celebrity culture is visible all around us in an avalanche of images of a "better self," "perfect-looking" celebrities from Hollywood, and "not so perfect-looking celebrities" from reality television. Even "reality celebrities" have become "real celebrities." The NBC reality show *I'm a Celebrity. Get Me Out of Here!*[19] remediates[20] these categories by making the old category of "celebrity" into the new reality version of "reality celebrity." The ten participants in this jungle survival experience appear thus as "nonfamous" reality TV stars—not particularly beautiful, intelligent, or gifted people. In fact, these participants had to Google each other to find out who they were and why they were "famous."[21] But both types of celebrity, the beautiful and the normal, are in some sense privileged and come together into a category that Chris Rojek calls *celetoid*. With this term, Rojek refers to "any form of compressed, concentrated, attributed celebrity."[22] The reality celebrity status is similar to the "real celebrity" in how the media treat them and how we perceive them. These two domains have drawn closer as reality celebrities become Hollywood stars (Jennifer Hudson, for instance, went from being a contestant on *American Idol* in 2004 to acting in *Dream Girls* in 2006 and winning the Academy Award for Best Supporting Actress in 2007). The category of celebrity is not rooted in recognition but in celebrity itself—celebrity for celebrity.[23]

Virginia L. Blum analyzes the desire structure that underlies the celebrity phenomenon by looking at some extreme examples, including MTV's television makeover show *I Want to Have a Famous Face*. For her, the contestants—such as the transsexual porn star Gia, who wishes to look like Pamela Anderson[24]—have a narcissistic desire structure. Blum problematizes the identification with the star ideal and interprets this act of inscribing the ego ideal into a subject's own body as a narcissistic move that brings the individual back to a "ground zero" of ego formation. At its worst, this narcissistic desire for the celebrity image can shift into a hysterical position of trying to morph oneself over and over again into a particular image, such as Cindy Jackson's famous surgical attempts to look like a Barbie doll.[25] But the desire for celebrity is not the only motivation behind a thriving cosmetic surgery industry. Another one is "shopaholism." Elliott points out that "much of the world as we know it we know through shopping."[26] This is particularly true in the United States, where the cultural environment of surburbia is defined by where one goes to shop. No flaneurs are walking the streets of suburbia and happening by chance upon a place or a store. The reason for going anywhere is scripted by the destination, which is usually a mall or plaza. But people do not have cosmetic surgery done simply to have another accessory, like a handbag, to adorn themselves with.[27] Rather, the commodification of an act like going under the knife is linked with the consumption of the images and stories of magical transformations that the media economy slingshots at us. The more we see "it," the more we see ourselves in it. Consumerism pairs with celebrity culture as it seeks its target—consumers of beautification discourse or "beauty junkies," as *New York Times* journalist Alex Kuczynski calls them in her account of her own engagement with the cosmetic surgery industry:

I am not obsessed with the way I look. Let me clarify. By "obsessed" I mean someone who stares at every pore of her face every hour of the day, who cannot leave the house in sweatpants, who is paralyzed by the fear that the world will find her unattractive, reject her, isolate her. . . . What I do is what we refer to in New York as maintenance. I am not preoccupied beyond therapeutic reach or common sense; I maintain. . . . It's become a way of life, part health routine, part beauty regimen, part political philosophy.[28]

This statement reflects the circular structure of the cosmetic gaze: one part of this consumerist behavior consists in looking at oneself for "maintenance," and another part involves looking at others. Kuczynski and others who study the cosmetic surgery industry research the best "maintenance products," examine makeover stories, and apply what they learn to themselves and to the fate and life stories others: "I read with fascination—with satisfaction, really—the books and articles by women who suffer from serious body dysmorphic disorder[29] and who have spent hundreds of thousands of dollars on cosmetic surgery, bankrupted their families, alienated their spouses."[30] With the consumption of stories of people who have felt dissatisfied about their looks,[31] Kuczynski moves into the third of Elliott's motivations behind the current culture of the quick fix— "the restructuring, remolding and re-sculpting of the self,"[32] for many reasons but principally as economic capital. Within the new global electronic economy of looking good, we capitalize on both the better look as well as the fact that we can change and are willing to do so: "In this new economy of short-term contracts, endless downsizing, just-in-time deliveries and multiple careers, one reason for self-improvement through cosmetic surgery is to demonstrate a personal readiness and adaptability."[33] The self-improvement stories that Kuczynski tells from her own and her friends' experiences (such as the professor of physical geography from Fullerton, California, who embarks on a surgery safari)[34] are (as Elliott notes) about our next-door neighbors and their "understandable" desires to look better on the global electronic market.

Some companies, such as the Czech private surgery clinic Iscare, even lure their employees, who may be earning more money in other places, with a bonus of free cosmetic surgery: "Under the incentive plan at Iscare, nurses can choose from an assortment of cosmetic surgical procedures, ranging from a €1,425 tummy tuck to a €1,300 face lift, in return for signing a three-year contract."[35] A thirty-one-year-old nurse, Petra Kalivo-dova, took Iscare up on this option and stated that she preferred to have free surgery than, for instance, a free car. The pressure to respond to a workplace's demands is also evident in the high-performance corporate world of "Richard Daley,"[36] a successful investment banker with a stellar résumé (Ivy League education and international work experience) that brought him to the London mergers and acquisitions division of a leading UK bank. Daley, age forty-three, says that he wants to undergo cosmetic surgery to eliminate a midlife belly that he has no time to "work off" and that he wants to appear "comfortable and relaxed."[37]

Similarly, Susan and Pat, two housewives from Newport Beach, California, told me in an interview[38] that their motivation for undergoing cosmetic surgery was not to look like entirely different people but to look and feel "subtly refreshed" (figure 3.1). Susan's goal was to make life "easier": "it's just sort of easier in a way, and it's feminine and just fun when your clothes fit you well and you look good. You know, you put on a dress, and it's nicer to have a strap dress and then have a curvy figure, and just do it easy." The pleasure of finding the "right clothes" is one of the main argu-

Figure 3.1
Susan: "We don't want to look like an entirely different person." Film still from *Made Over in America: A Voyage to the Land of Makeover* (Bernadette Wegenstein and Geoffrey Alan Rhodes, 2007). Courtesy Icarusfilms.

ments that are used by women who desire surgery, as Kathy Davis demonstrates in her field study of women undergoing cosmetic surgery.[39]

Susan mentions that a refreshed look helps people who are on the "job market" to become a spouse because "lots of men in this area are health-conscious and are looking for women with the same thoughtfulness and self-respect." The term "health-conscious" here is related to "healthy look" as an indicator in Elliott's global market hypothesis. In other words, in the global market of Newport Beach, these women have increased their capital.

As examples of capital gains, Susan mentions that a supermarket employee recently picked up a dropped item for her, and Pat remembers enjoying the time that a young waiter (in his twenties, probably some fifty years younger) turned to admire her at a recent brunch. But the main goal for Susan—who appears to be in her late thirties or early forties but would not reveal her age, saying that "a French woman never tells her age"[40]—was to gain respect from her community. She feels that having cosmetic surgery has translated into more respect: "A lot of doors open, everywhere. I went to my son's elementary school, and I made sure that I looked good because I would be received with more seriousness and treated more respectfully than if I looked grungy and went in with sweatpants. . . . you earn a higher degree of respect." This respect comes from others, but most important, you "owe yourself" this respect: "We want to feel good and take care of ourselves, respect our bodies. It's almost as if we did not do all this [eat well, dress well, have cosmetic surgery done], it would be disgraceful, disrespective. It's pretty basic. It's nothing vanity-oriented." This is similar to Kuczynski's basic maintenance program: it's nothing "special"; it's just what one does and what the culture demands. According to these perspectives, cosmetic surgery, which is an invasive surgical procedure that is conducted under anesthesia, is categorized as "healthy." The surgery has lost any risk factor. This belief is maintained even though Pat lost her own daughter—Susan's best friend growing up—to complications after a cosmetic surgery procedure.

Pat is between twenty and thirty years older than her friend Susan (figure 3.2). Her surgery is an example of a drastic intervention and reinvention of her face and is reminiscent of the "face lift" that was popular among women after World War II, when women became particularly concerned with aging. The common "face lift" helped them feel better about themselves and their world rather than feel a need to change it.[41] Pat's look

Figure 3.2
Pat: "I have had cosmetic surgery done and am making no secret of it." Film still
from *Made Over in America: A Voyage to the Land of Makeover* (Bernadette Wegenstein
and Geoffrey Alan Rhodes, 2007). Courtesy Icarusfilms.

adheres to the logic of the "Old New Face," as the popular dermatologist
and beauty product line developer Patricia Wexler puts it, pointing to the
example of Ivana Trump: "When she got a totally new face in the early
nineties—a new jawline, a new eyebrow arch—that was a *new* face. She is
now aging as a whole different person. The new version of the New Face
is that it shouldn't look new. It should look like you. It should look like
the *old* you."[42] The new face is the "subtly refreshed" version that Susan
wanted and is supposed to look like your four-films-older self (see chapter
2). The new face is an evolutionary likely resemblance of you—or a "fan-
tastic approximation," as Jonathan Van Meter calls it.[43]

   While Susan and Pat feel that they benefit from increased respect in
their community with their respective "new new" and "new old" faces,
"Richard Dyer" camouflages the pressure of a job and of aging, which
benefits him in his world of investment banking. Within the new corporate
economy, the body and its appearance are taken at face value. Not corre-
sponding to the demands of this "subtly refreshed look" may mean to fail
in many different ways. In the case of Susan, Pat, and Richard, it is the
fear that a younger, fresher-looking person could be favored over them—as

a better investment banker in London or as a better-looking mom in Newport Beach. The global body market is a competition.

All three of Elliott's sociological accounts for "making the cut" (celebrity culture, consumerism, and the renewed self in the new corporate economy) are united in one phenomenon—makeover television. As viewers sit comfortably in their living rooms, makeover television displays the ways that their own images can be made to approximate celebrity images, and the global culture of quick change reinvents the "easy looks." Watching these shows affects viewers' body images, their vulnerability, and their readiness to change. We consume these images as they consume us. The following two sections examine how the medium of reality television feeds into the human historical habit of watching the stories of others and why this particular format supports the global consumption of cosmetic surgery.

Realism: "It Could Be Me!"

In 2001, at the onset of the "reality TV revolution," *American Demographics* determined that 45 percent of all Americans watched reality TV and a fifth of these would describe themselves as "die-hard fans."[44] With this new format, television found a cheap, fast, and intimate format that merges the categories of truth and authenticity with realism. The "appeal of the real" on television owes its success story in part to the successful 2000 debut of CBS's *Survivor*: "By the first month of 2003—more than two years after the stunning success of *Survivor*—reality TV was increasing its hold on the airwaves with hits including *American Idol*, *Joe Millionaire*, and *The Bachelorette*. No longer an off-season summer phenomenon, reality TV has become a dominant prime-time programming staple, easily dominating the ratings in many of the most coveted time slots."[45]

Reality TV includes documentary-style shows, in which ordinary people are followed in their daily lives (as in *Family Plots*); docusoaps, which star celebrities (such as *Newlyweds* with Jessica Simpson or *Britney Cam* with Britney Spears); talent searches, in which ordinary people try to become celebrities (such as *America's Next Top Model* or the all-time favorite *American Idol*);[46] historical reenactment shows (such as *Colonial House* [PBS, 2004]), set in the American frontier of 1628); dating shows (such as *For Love or Money*); law enforcement, courtroom, or military shows (such as *Boot*

Camp and the British *Commando VIP*); reality game shows (such as *Survivor* and *Project Runway*, which may include a military component as with *Boot Camp* or a sport component as with *The Ultimate Fighter*); and lifestyle change shows (such as *Queer Eye for the Straight Guy*), including the booming subgenre of body makeover shows (such as *I Want a Famous Face*, *Pimp My Ride*, or *Ten Years Younger*), which can also feature game show characteristics (as with *The Swan*). These genres and subgenres incorporate the narrative strategy of "wish fulfillment": somebody appears on television, wishes for something, and receives it—despite dramatized difficulties.

Low production costs are behind the format's original boom. Reality TV was a response to the economic restructuring of U.S. and British television in the 1980s. The growth of cable television, video cassette recorders, powerful new television networks (like Fox), and local independent stations fragmented the TV audience. Because advertising revenues had to be spread among a larger pool of distributors, broadcasters felt pressured to cut per-program production costs. As Chad Raphael points out in his analysis of the political and economic forces behind the emergence of a genre that he calls "Reali-TV," there is an "inseparability of the television industry's economic needs and how this genre represents reality."[47] For Raphael, the economic crisis of television could have been solved by expanding infotainment or other programming. Instead, crime shows, tabloid gossip TV, on-scene shows, and documentaries were adapted to produce a new format that claimed access to "reality" and "truth."

But the "revolution" of reality TV's attempts to access the "truth" is not much of a revolution and was not unexpected. The dream of accessing the "absolute truth" via the moving image was with photography from its onset, through the indexical relationship between what is recorded (photography or moving image) and what "really is." The fascination with this relationship was expressed, for instance, by the Italian Futurists in their manifestos praising the speed and the simultaneity of the moving image. In 1916, Filippo Tommaso Marinetti and his Futurist friends formulated the manifesto *La cinematografia futurista* (*Futurist Cinema*). According to these men—who supported World War I and an Italian nationalist future—cinema was a supreme art form because of its "lack of past" and its "freedom of tradition," which allows it to express itself (in their famously proclaimed words) in freedom (*parole in libertà*). The Futurists were fascinated by the cinema's promise of simultaneity, which the authors translated into the following equation: "Painting + sculpture + plastic dynamism + words-in-freedom + composed tone noises + architecture + synthetic theatre = Futurist cinema."[48] This is almost a precursor to what Lev Manovich and Andreas Kratky called a "montage of simultaneity" for their *soft cinema* database, where different media are used simultaneously to create films without regard for the development of a narrative storyline.[49]

The intrinsic drive toward realism as expressed in the moving image predates television and the reality TV format.[50] A few realist film traditions can be seen as milestones for contemporary reality television. Tsiga Vertov's audacious experimental *kino pravda* of the 1920s Soviet film era analyzed the audience's role in the process of the construction of "truth." The French New Wave redefined classic cinematic narration by turning the screen actor into a person with Brechtian self-awareness of her own actions (as in Jean-Luc Godard's 1962 *Vivre sa vie*). The French *cinema vérité* movement in the 1960s brought attention to the ethical dimension of the camera and the filmmaker as witness of a political moment, as in Jean Rouch's *Chronique d'un été* (1960).[51] Finally, "putting reality on the screen" was the goal of the Italian neorealist filmmakers of the 1940s. In the years following World War II, Roberto Rossellini, Vittorio de Sica, and Luchino Visconti developed and applied techniques that are common in today's reality-TV productions—real locations; possibly authentic, on-location interviews; a subjective hand-held camera; synchronized sound; and the mixing of amateur and professional actors. Italian *neorealismo*[52] was influenced by the European realist and naturalist literary tradition that emerged in the middle of the nineteenth century, with authors like Honoré de Balzac and Giovanni Verga.

Like these authors, Italian neorealism filmmakers used ordinary people's lives as metaphors for such master narratives as Christianity (as with the Christ metaphor in Rossellini's *Rome, Open City*). Reality television also focuses on simple lives. Without the political critiques of *cinéma vérité* or the sociohistorical critiques of the neorealists, the reality television narrative capitalizes entirely on the mise-en-scène and consumption of the "simple life." This is what Marc Andrejevic finds in interviews with reality TV fans: "I like the fact that it's real people—people I can identify with, instead of superstars and Olympians."[53] Reality television seems to be looking at the lives and deeds of "real people," not the kings and Olympians. But these people are made into celebrities via the power of a format that can turn anything and anybody into somebody by putting them in a film or on a television program. In a global media economy, being watched means coming to life and being someone. As the executive producer of the reality makeover show *Dr. 90210* said: "if you are on television, you are someone."[54] Neorealism, *cinema vérité,* and reality television hold a similar contract with the audience: it could be me. I could have been interviewed. I could have had my bicycle stolen on the first day of work and could have considered stealing another person's bicycle to keep my job. In 1964, Marshall McLuhan called television a "cold" medium, but TV has warmed up to its audience with interactive strategies such as telephoning to vote for a favorite cast member, thereby influencing a show's narrative structure (or providing that illusion) and applying to become a cast member and potential winner.

André Bazin, a French film critic in the 1940s and 1950s, foresaw that the fascination with reality would revolutionize the image culture. Bazin coined the expression "thirst for reality." Long before the age of ubiquitous computing and full-immersion media and even before basic immersive technologies like synchronized sound and hand-held cameras (invented in the early 1960s), Bazin dreamed of a total cinema experience[55]—full immersion in screen reality. For Bazin, cinema was a phenomenological experience that was no different from experiences in the real world. He felt that seeing a neorealist film was an experience of witnessing truth. As Sam Dilorio puts it: "In moving film nearer to the world, each technological development better satisfied what he [Bazin] saw as an instinctive (and fundamentally insatiable) thirst for representation."[56] Representations of real life can provide insights into life or can be an escape from it. The media philosopher Jean Baudrillard suggests that our subjectivity vanishes in a world order where only the real persists. In his video *Marlene Redux: A True Hollywood Story!* (2006),[57] the media artist Francesco Vezzoli satirizes his own suicide in the celebrity-driven Hollywood environment he inhabits.[58] The video's format is an ironic critique of the TV reality genre and uses an enhanced reality-show rhythm and an over-the-top glimmer and glitter editing-style.

For Baudrillard, "we have murdered the real."[59] The Bazinian dream (of experiencing the real via convincing and truthful images that replace the "real real") leaves us in a desert of subjectivity—the "desert of the real," as Morpheus says in *The Matrix* (1999). It is no longer a symbolic murder, as

Figure 3.3
Film still from *John* (2005) by Ian Charlesworth. Courtesy of the artist.

with the Nietzschean murder of God in the nineteenth century, but is now an extermination of the real, where nothing is supposed to be left behind, not even a corpse.[60] But who is the murderer? In the logic of the virtual, as Baudrillard points out in many writings, no subject can be identified and held responsible. The subject becomes a useless function. Baudrillard's prophecy that the subject will become both a useless function and also the only "protagonist" of himself within the logic of the virtual is illustrated in Ian Charlesworth's video art installation *John* (2005) (figure 3.3).

In this video,[61] a working-class kid, John, from Northern Ireland "plays" himself while a male voice asks him to "play" the "spidey" (i.e., the working-class kid from Northern Ireland) that he, the director, not just envisions him to play but to *be*. As Anne Ellegood points out, John represents the disconnection from self that Baudrillard talks about. He refers not to himself in a real economy but to his type in a global economy—which floats in the logic of the hyperreal: "Caught between the knowledge that the director is looking for some kind of (false) authenticity rooted in the notion that he can just 'play himself' and the actuality of being isolated on a stage, decontextualized from the world, and asked to re-create an experience or event, there is a profound disconnection from self."[62] This exhibition and appropriation of John's culture—of his type as Northern Irish "spidey"—can be seen as an example of the media's cannibalism and of what Elliott calls the commodification of a look on the global electronic market.

Cannibalism suggests another of Baudrillard's points concerning the exhibition and reappropriation of the real within the logic of the virtual—the violence of the image. The images encountered in this global electronic market are "violent" in that they are fully transparent, as Baudrillard puts it. He contrasts this violence to the "classical violence" that was hidden or even invisible. This violence lies not in the content of the image but in the fact that we must see it. Seeing is not the only act of violence but also the fact that we are forced into perception. In the Baudrillardian paradigm, the violence lies not in the message but in the media and in our unconditional exposure to them. The rise of this image violence is reflected in the cases of Susan, Pat, and "Richard," who experienced their "before" appearance as offensive and their "after" appearance as comfortable and nonaggressive, despite the violent nature of surgery.

As with the examples of Susan, Pat, and "Richard," Charlesworth's video installation reveals the machinic suture itself—the way that the technology of media and our media-saturated culture integrate themselves into the core identity that we seek when we wish to express, reveal, or retrieve the true selves we believe to lie hidden behind our appearances. Although the Baudrillardian idiom tends toward the dramatically catastrophic, in a more sober and dispassionate sense we can conclude that subjects who place their faith in such an identity will find a corpse, for the real they seek there remains inescapably virtual—the retroactive projection of the standards and categories that are embodied in the technology they use to pursue it. Susan and Pat are celebrating their own "death" in newer and better approximations of their "true selves," and the video art installation is ironically trying to capture John's performance of his own "death" as the inability to escape the status quo of inborn social status in Northern Ireland—before and after.

The current media economy provides access to three images at all times—our old or current self, our improved or future self, and our ego ideal (the self that we project onto others, such as in the realm of reality television onto the celebrities). But as Mark Hansen points out, all reality is a "mixed reality"[63] for which the dream of total immersion has to be abandoned. The new media revolution has made it possible to move more and more seamlessly and ever so simultaneously from one media reality to another—leaving Facebook and other third-screen identities (such as smart phones) "open" and receiving at all times. Reality television and its subgenre the makeover show contribute to the emergence of this movement, coupling what Elliott calls the "global electronic economy of looking good" with a willingness to replace our identities with market-driven, slightly altered, and improved ideals of ourselves. Because makeover shows are about change, which they perform and stage, they also include what Brian Massumi has called affect or intensity, a basic ingredient of a late capitalist information- and image-based culture.[64] Affect no longer has subjective content (such as emotion). It is an evasive concept that Massumi describes as "unqualified" and "resistant to critique." As one of the main strategies in literature's and film's realist tradition, it is present in reality television if not its main ingredient. (I return to this concept in chapter 4 in the discussion of the *reveal*, the moment of "truth" when the makeover show participants are turned into new selves during a televised event.)

As Meredith Jones points out in her cultural analysis of the practice of watching such shows,[65] the consumption of screen bodies is essential to the event of reality television. Jones suggests that we read cosmetic surgery reality television as a platform to present these "media bodies" to the viewer as "real bodies" that come about via screen births: "I suggest that our own body images are connected to and are sometimes dependent upon and interchangeable with the 'media-bodies' that cosmetic surgery reality television presents."[66] In Jones's Baudrillardian reading of the conquest by the virtual over the real, the audience of reality television makeover shows walks out into the real world with a "media body" that it has consumed and assimilated into its own.[67] In other words, thanks to reality television, particularly makeover television, we don't need "real surgery" to experience it. The "continuum of reality,"[68] as Bazin described it for Italian neorealism, extends from the real world to the screen world and has now turned and transferred the ontological screen life to the real life of real bodies, from media to flesh. To return to Baudrillard, "the virtual takes over the real as it appears, and then replicates it without any modification, in a prêt-à-porter (ready-to-wear) fashion."[69] One of the most extreme television reality makeover shows is *The Swan*.

The Swan: You Must Surrender

In 2004, 11,855,013 cosmetic surgeries were done in the United States. Procedures decreased to 11.3 and 11.4 million in 2005 and 2006 but increased to 11,701,310 in 2007. ASAPS president Peter Fodor attributes this growth to media coverage, including the new makeover and cosmetic surgery shows: "I believe at least some of this upward trend may be attributable to increased media coverage of plastic surgery in 2004. . . . People have had many more opportunities to see, first hand, what plastic surgery is like and what it can do for others. That can be a strong incentive for them to seek the same benefits by having cosmetic procedures themselves."[70] These reality television makeover shows started in 2002 with ABC's *Extreme Makeover*, which was followed by FX's (fictional) *Nip/Tuck* (2003), Fox Broadcasting's *The Swan* (2004), E! channel's *Dr. 90210* (2004), and MTV's *I Want a Famous Face* (2004). They have influenced the overall consumption of cosmetic surgeries. In 2003 (8.3 million cosmetic procedures), surgical procedures increased 12 percent and nonsurgical procedures increased 22 percent from 2002. In 2004 (11.9 million procedures, up 44 percent from 2003), surgical procedures increased by 17 percent, and nonsurgical by 51 percent. In 2005 and 2006, surgical procedures increased by only 1 percent, and in 2005 nonsurgical procedures declined by 4 percent (9.3 million). In 2007, there were 11.7 million cosmetic procedures. These elective procedures are not imposed by eugenics programs (discussed in chapter 1), and their large numbers suggest that U.S. culture has incorporated the standards of makeover television into its cultural imaginary and practice.

One question that arises in the context of cosmetic surgery reality TV is who is watching these shows. In general, the main demographic for reality TV is women ages eighteen to twenty-five.[71] The prime viewers of *The Swan* were eighteen- to twenty-four-year-old white women with a parental household income of $60,000 to $100,000 and some college education.[72] The men who watched *The Swan* reported feeling more enjoyment while watching it than the women did. As the data from cosmetic surgery procedures show, women are the main consumers of these procedures and thus of makeover discourse. Unlike men, who experience these show as pure entertainment and do not feel they have anything to do with them personally, women feel invoked personally.

In 2004, 2005, and 2006, I directed an in-depth study on the viewing habits and demographics of college students in Buffalo, New York, and Los Angeles, California.[73] In a survey of students' viewing of the shows *The Swan* and *I Want a Famous Face*, 662 undergraduates in sociology courses at the University at Buffalo and at the University at Southern California filled out a questionnaire that included questions about their own body image and their perception of the shows. The questionnaire was approved by an institutional review board and excluded the possibility of body dysmorphic disorder. As Heyes argues, in some ways the term *body dysmorphic disorder* and its use to distinguish participants who are too "sick" to participate deploys disciplinary power in a "crystalization of culture."[74]

The survey results revealed some interesting regional and socioeconomical differences in these viewers. For instance, the Los Angeles men felt less attractive than the Buffalo men, probably as a result of their exposure to the beauty and celebrity culture in Los Angeles. But the Buffalo students, who were surrounded by less makeover culture than the L.A. students, watched more shows and showed more beauty anxiety than the L.A. students. The Buffalo students also tended to come from less educated and less wealthy families, which may be a class-related reason[75] for why they were more drawn to the shows. As Albright explains:

The fact that many of these plastic-surgery reality shows are set in high-class environs like Beverly Hills is likely to amplify class consciousness among the Buffalo, New York, viewers. Thus the beauty anxiety felt by the Buffalo sample may really be a manifestation of a deeper class anxiety, with these shows serving to heighten the awareness of the differences between their bodies and those that inhabit places like Beverly Hills, and the implication of those differences.[76]

Women, who in general were much more likely than men to watch the shows, also reported that the more they watched the shows, they more they felt increased body anxiety about their own appearance.[77] Conversely, the more body anxiety the women showed, the more likely they were to watch makeover shows. The reality television market is aware of this vicious circle and therefore creates various wish-fulfillment shows that sell body and beauty anxiety.

At one point, Fox Reality Channel (launched in mid-2005 and discontinued in mid-2010) was the most prolific purveyor of such wish-fulfillment reality programs in the United States. On October 14, 2008, the network was broadcasting 144 different programs.[78] Following the debut of *Extreme Makeover* on ABC in the fall of 2002, a flood of reality TV shows tried to emulate its success with various approaches to the makeover, some more extreme than others. One hotly debated reality show, *The Swan* (2004–2005),[79] was created and produced by Nely Galán, who was born in Cuba, was the president of entertainment at Telemundo, and lives—as she puts it—"a self-confident businesswoman's life in Hollywood."[80] Galán, whose mantra is "if something bothers you . . . , why wait and suffer? Go fix it," herself underwent a total makeover after her separation from the father of her son to boost her self-confidence as a single mother raising her son alone (figure 3.4).

In her reality-television version of Hans Christian Andersen's fairy tale "The Ugly Duckling," beauty pageant contestants undergo major surgery and noninvasive procedures (such as hair and clothing styling, dieting,

Figure 3.4
Nely Galán: "Go fix it!" Film still from *Made Over in America: A Voyage to the Land of Makeover* (Bernadette Wegenstein and Geoffrey Alan Rhodes, 2007). Courtesy Icarusfilms.

exercise, and psychological therapy) to be transformed into current female beauty ideals. In her role as a "life coach," Galán watches over her "swans" over the three-month period that they live away from their families and habitual lives, undergo these external and internal transformations, and pass into a new life. Galán can be aggressively straightforward: "no more candy, ice-cream. Say good-bye to your old life and habits. Look into the future and into feeling good." For seven weeks in each episode, two contestants compete against each other, and the winner of the final competition (the first-season finale was watched by more than 10 million Americans on May 24, 2004) is crowned "the Swan" and walks away with $50,000 and a new self.[81] According to Galán, to be a successful contestant, a woman must be willing to surrender to beauty culture and thus to the advice given by the show's experts, including surgeons, personal trainers, stylists, psychologists, and the life coach herself. Rachel Love-Fraser and Elisa Stiles won the first and second seasons, respectively, because apparently they "gave in" the best or the most.

Nearly all contestants who appeared on two seasons of *The Swan* were obsessively unhappy with a particular body feature[82] but seem to look just fine. The first season's sixteen white[83] contestants were tested for body dysmorphic disorder—which they were perhaps predisposed toward but did not clinically suffer—and were chosen for being "normal" while at the same time being willing to "surrender" to something that would come "upon" them. Their "before" photos on the show and in beauty magazines and tabloid newspapers were taken from bad angles and showed them wearing unattractive clothing and with sad and at times desperate faces, but nothing dramatic was wrong with them. The photos could not show, however, the way that they felt about themselves and the kind of fragile relationship they had with their own body image. Rachel Love-Fraser, for instance, winner of the first season, wanted to leave everything behind and focus on "who she really was."[84]

Galán's goal was not to change culture but to get to the "truth" within these women's psychic spheres and help them find out who they really were. In a reinterpretation of the concept of *kalókagatheia*, Galán claims that only by matching outside to inside will these women be able to fit in and pass. Galán sees herself as a therapist and shaman, someone who knows more about the truth than do her patients themselves. Like a therapist, she wants to help these women to be comfortable in their own skin, and her idea is that by fixing a body part, the entire body self will be fixed too. This includes the "inside," which is the "place" where—according to Nely Galán and the show's psychotherapist, Dr. Lynn Ianni—a woman who wants to undergo a body transformation should start. This frail inner place that the patient wishes to "heal" via a surgical intervention has long been identified by clinical psychologists. Sanford Gifford, for instance, interprets the desire for cosmetic surgery as externalization of inner conflicts onto a particular body part.[85] Virginia L. Blum puts this clinical diagnosis in a cultural-theoretical context. For her, "the reason plastic surgery can relieve emotional suffering is that, for the modern subject, the surface of the body and the body image are where object relations, both good and bad, are transacted, not only in the formative moments or our identity, but throughout the life circle."[86]

In her many interviews with cosmetic surgery patients in the early 1990s, Kathy Davis found that the body and the body image have become the location or even fixation for social struggle, shame, and a certain inability to go on with regular life—especially in the public realm. Davis notes that women want to use surgery not to become "more beautiful" but to become normal-looking people, "just everyone else."[87] They want to blend in, become "normal," and not stick out. In their field research on women's motivations for undergoing cosmetic surgery, Kathy Davis and Virginia L. Blum have both shown that most women are doing it "for themselves." This argument is also part of the discourse of *The Swan* and many other makeover shows, which seek to "excuse" the candidate and to "absolve" her from the "sin of wanting to please." In fact, Susan Bordo calls the "for-me-argument" the "mantra of the television talk show"[88] and claims that this phrase is usually produced to refute the supposition that women are giving in to cultural or societal expectations of the body beautiful. "In these constructions," Bordo argues, the "'me' is imagined as a pure and precious inner space, an 'authentic' and personal reference point untouched by external values and demands. A place where we live free and won't be pushed around."[89] The question thus arises "whether women can be said to choose cosmetic surgery, or whether that 'choice' is overdetermined by a larger patriarchical structure that makes cosmetic surgery seem like the only option for psychological survival in a world hostile to women's bodies."[90]

In its belief in such an "authentic inner space" and its attempt to match outside to inside, reality TV makeover culture connects a beautiful body with a beautiful soul and with a moral duty to reveal this connection as a civilian duty. But what does it mean to have a beautiful "soul" in the era of makeover culture? What does a properly twenty-first-century *kalókagath-eia* look like? Physiognomy always reads the body against the backdrop of an era's most desired type of character. Johann Kasper Lavater's physiognomic tradition was inspired by a face that expressed closeness to God, and today's makeover body claims to do something similar. Cosmetic makeovers claim that the goal is not to look like anyone else but to find oneself and how one was really meant to be and look. This self has moved beyond its a limited reality as a flesh body into the mixed realities of the various ways it can be envisioned, with or without technologies of enhancement, and improved according to the laws of the cosmetic gaze. This self is now capable of relentless transformation. The belief in the authenticity of this transformation does not contradict this notion of fluid or transformative self. Transformation is the imperative as well as the true nature of the makeover self. In fact, its nature lies in the surrender to the imperative, as Galán puts it. The "authentic" self is not a given but lies out there to be discovered. It has to be achieved, which is a by-product of the actual moral virtue of the made-over self—hard work. The body is no longer a given but a platform to invest in, and the act of resisting a bettering of the body (and soul) is taken as an expression of bad morals. In *The Swan Curriculum*, the book that accompanied Fox's makeover show *The Swan*, for instance, Nely Galán sets up a contract for the makeover-prone reader about what she owes her own self. The contract is framed by this moral reminder: "When you're ready to begin the program, sign the final contract with yourself."[91] The contract includes the following: "I promise to allow myself the time and attention necessary to make real changes happen in my life. I understand that certain exercises may be uncomfortable and challenging, but I will resign myself to the process because I deserve to the best woman I can be."[92] Breaking this contract would mean not trying to be your very best—an offense to yourself and others.

Cindy Ingle, second runner up to the second *Swan* season (2005), deserved to be one of these best women. Cindy, a housewife from San Diego, started her hard work by leaving her two young sons behind for

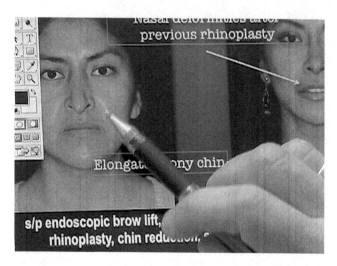

Figure 3.5

Production still of Cindy Ingle's "before" and "after" at Dr. Randall Haworth's office. The surgeon points to her "droopy" nose and "pointy" chin. From unused footage from *Made Over in America: A Voyage to the Land of Makeover* (Bernadette Wegenstein and Geoffrey Alan Rhodes, 2007). Courtesy Waystone Productions.

three months and moving with the *Swan* dream team to a clinic in Hollywood with no mirrors on the walls (figure 3.5). Cindy was one of the girls described by Kathy Davis for whom "their appearance began to represent 'everything that was wrong' in their lives."[93] As a young girl in junior high school, Cindy felt like the token "ugly girl" and the "natural Halloween witch" because of her large nose.[94] As Davis notes in her research on women undergoing cosmetic surgery in the 1990s, some people suffer from a degree of body image disorder as they become more and more fixated on one body part that represents for them the entirety of their appearance. They cannot look into a mirror without seeing only the one part that "ruins the rest."[95]

Cindy's husband, Ken, works for the U.S. Navy but does not earn enough to realize his wife's "dreams she always wished for."[96] For producer Nely Galán, Cindy is an appealing contestant (out of half a million applicants to the show). She is positive, is active, and has a strong sense of self, which suggests that she is not too risky a contestant to expose to a "new you" and a televised media spectacle.[97] (Cindy's cosmetic makeover is discussed in detail in the final section of chapter 4.) Cindy reports that she has researched cosmetic surgery (as Susan and Pat from Newport Beach reportedly had). She came to the show prepared with an inner picture of what her outer transformation should look like and with many addresses and Web sites of the best surgeons in her area (San Diego and Los Angeles). Cindy applied to the show primarily to change her pointed chin and her bent nose, which had already been surgically transformed before in an army hospital but not to her satisfaction. *The Swan* celebrity surgeon, Dr. Randall Haworth, addressed these areas and added a few more procedures as part of Cindy's "contract" with *The Swan*.[98] He, too, thought she was the "ideal plastic surgical patient,"[99] as "there was a lot to work with."[100] Haworth, a well-spoken man who emphasizes his artistic eye and touch, is a "world renowned leader, innovator and expert surgeon in the field of plastic surgery."[101] He is an artist: "I just feel what's right, what looks good. I am a very instinctual surgeon, and come from a very artistic background; and then I know how to translate the vision that I have for the patient surgically into a reality."[102] To draw a connection between his work and sculpture, he quotes the French sculptor Auguste Rodin: "the form is in the block, you need to just expose it." Cindy and Randall sustained their friendly relationship, even a few years after the show when I visited them during the production of the documentary film *Made Over in America: A Voyage into the Land of Makeover* that I made with Geoffrey Alan Rhodes (2007). In their relationship, we see what Virginia L. Blum has found in many of the cosmetic surgery patients she interviewed: the surgeon identifies with the surface narcissism of the patient. How he sees her becomes how she wants to be seen.[103] As Sander L. Gilman has it, surgeons are not operating on the material body but are "reshaping our fantasies of ourselves."[104] The extent to which Cindy's fantasy entered Randall's mind frame can be seen in an experiment we suggested during our film shoot. We asked the two to reverse their roles and remember what they said to each other during her first visit to his office (figure 3.6):

Randall as Cindy: Do you think I need a facelift, doctor?

Cindy as Randall: I think you could use a little one [puts her hands on his face].

Randall as Cindy: Oh, I like that, doctor [with a flirtatious voice].

Randall as Cindy: I was told my lips were thin. Can we make them more sexy looking?

[Cindy as Randall confirms that all of her patient's wishes can be realized.]

Figure 3.6
Film still of Dr. Randall Haworth and Cindy Ingle in reverse roles examining each
other and having a good time remembering Cindy's first visit to Randall's office.
From unused footage from *Made Over in America: A Voyage to the Land of Makeover*
(Bernadette Wegenstein and Geoffrey Alan Rhodes, 2007). Courtesy Bernadette
Wegenstein and Geoffrey Alan Rhodes.

Randall as Cindy: I am really excited! When can we start? I can't wait! I have been looking for this my whole life. I have one more question about anesthesia: is it safe?

[Cindy as Randall confirms that it is safe and that it will probably affect Randall as Cindy the same way that it did during previous anesthesias.]

Randall as Cindy: Doctor, when I had anesthesia before, I woke up and ran around naked.

Cindy as Randall: Oh, that's not a problem. There is only a few of us here in the office. In fact, would you like to have some [anesthesia] now?[105]

Many surgeons say that patients usually step into their office without a concrete plan for change. They want to hear what the surgeon will suggest because the doctor's cosmetic gaze is the one that will give them beauty and will restore them to the "way they were meant to look." What Lavater would refer to as his physiognomic intuitions, Haworth and many aesthetic surgeons explain with their sense of symmetry, scale, and art at large. Because doctors are on the other end of the spectrum and operate on patients, a transference needs to take place between the wish or fantasy of the patient and that of the surgeon. Both are connecting via an interiorized image of a better self, and together they create something new—the patient's new face or body and hence world and the doctor's fantasy of a better body and hence world. It is outside the scope of this section to dig deeper into this patient and surgeon universe of transference and countertransference, which is often a place that is hypercharged with emotionality and even love. Women falling in love with their plastic surgeon and men falling for their creations are common in literature and life. (In chapter 4, I look at some film examples from the history of cosmetic surgery and film.)

For the patient, who has an "investment" in change, giving in to makeover transformation does not allow her to lay back passively and just let it happen under the surgeon's knife. As Cindy's case shows, letting change happen requires relentless self-discipline. This is also what the audience wants to hear. One of the major concerns of young people[106] who watch reality television makeovers shows is that the contestants may not deserve this beautiful new body because they did not "work hard enough" for it. In other words, what we are supposed to see on these new bodies is labor.

In his book *Better Than Well: American Medicine Meets the American Dream*, bioethicist Carl Elliott finds a connection between taking Prozac and anabolic steroids and undergoing cosmetic surgery. All of these current "strategies of the self" are ultimately in the service of looking "the way we were meant to look."[107] Elliott approaches the theme of enhancement technologies in search of the "true authentic self" from both medical and bioethical perspectives. In one of his approaches to makeover culture, Elliott interprets the 1939 Hollywood film, *The Wizard of Oz*: "Here is a key to understanding the place of enhancement technologies in contemporary America. The Scarecrow, the Tin Man, and the Lion do not go to the Wizard because they want to be 'enhanced.' They go because the want to be *themselves*. In *The Wizard of Oz*, as in contemporary America, the search for the good life is an inward search for authenticity. As Dorothy says, 'If I ever go looking for my heart's desire again, I won't look any further than my own backyard. If I don't find it there, I never really lost it to begin with.'"[108] Finding this utopian space presumes two indispensable steps for a successful makeover—to surrender as Nely Galán dictates and to be changed.

For Gilman, a physical makeover means the ultimate "passing" into a visibly marked invisibility, to give in to that "desire to return to that ideal state in which we had control of the world."[109] In this state, everybody will ultimately look better but the same—"ugly ducklings" who ended up looking like their "mama-swan," Nely Galán. Joanna Zylinska takes this thought further by reading this desire to possess the face from the time "before the world was made" as a deeper fantasy for a "world without alterity, for the annihilation of difference and return to a fantasy moment when the self was a master of time, space and language."[110] In this provocative reading (which I agree with), makeover is a utopian attempt at the "escape from the biopolitical regime that marks some bodies as different— racially, erotically, or in terms of their ability to perform well in the labor market."[111] To function on the TV show *The Swan*, in what Zylinska depicts as an "army training camp," contestants/soldiers need to learn the rules and regulations of the regime, or the master and commander-in-chief Nely Galán will publicly humiliate them, punish them, or expel them from the show (an occurrence that the producer reminisces about with pleasure). Zylinska's conclusion:

The training camp (if we are prepared to call it this) becomes here a zone of exception ruled by martial law, where the lives of the contestants are placed outside the politico-ethical normativity of the democratic *polis*. In the camp, their bodies can be cut open, abused and remoulded beyond recognition so that they can be returned to the "normal world," the eschatological space "after the transformation."[112]

Zylinska's reading, which is inspired by Giorgio Agamben's notion of the "zone of exception,"[113] can be related back to Nely Galán's mantra "you must surrender." The surrender is the necessary step of depriving oneself of identity, emotionality, and will for the purpose of a restructuring the self on the basis of an original machinic suture. The next section examines how the machinic suture is informed by facial identification technology, gaming, and Internet pornography as they interact in today's global electronic media market.

E-FIT, or How to Draw a Suspect

The first example concerns a software program called E-FIT (electronic facial identification technique, but also "evolutionary fit") that was developed in Edinborough, Scotland, by VisionMetric Ltd. E-FIT is based on Victor S. Johnston and M. Franklin's evolutionary faces (discussed in chapter 2). Rather than looking for an average (as in the research of Judith Langlois based on the facial composite; also discussed in chapter 2), E-FIT and its enhanced version, EFIT-V, enable the creation of a unique face that exists only in the memory of an eyewitness to a crime. Chris Solomon, software engineer at E-FIT, explains: "the system is trained on about 2500 images of men and women of various ethnicities.[114] The processing we do enables us to understand the dominant or key ways in which faces differ from the average face, i.e., an average of all those that are used in the database. We are then able to produce new faces, which are a random combination of all these key components. As such, the system no longer needs the original pictures. It has learned how to create faces belonging to a given group and can in fact produce a near infinite number of 'new' faces. All the faces you create are 'virtual' in the sense that they are not made from individual elements of real faces but nonetheless look real."[115]

The first choice to make within E-FIT's logic is that of gender (male and female) and ethnicity. The pool of ethnic images is limited to the categories of Hispanic, Indian, Middle Eastern, eastern European, Oriental, black, and white for men and to Hispanic, Indian, Oriental, black, and white for women. The system can deal only with ethnicities that it was "trained" on, as Solomon says. It does not have eastern European women

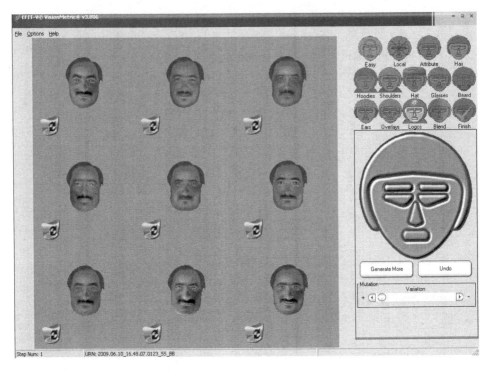

Figure 3.7
E-FIT screen shot. Courtesy VisionMetrics.

as a category because VisionMetrics did not have sufficient sources for such images and eastern European women did not constitute a risk category for crime in the United Kingdom. In this first step, the system has "learned" to use stereotypical judgment of what, for instance, a Middle Eastern criminal may look like (figure 3.7).

A software user chooses an age that starts with a range from fifteen to twenty and ends with a range of fifty-five to sixty, chooses an approximate face shape, and initiates the creation process by "writing" a face into E-FIT's evolutionary mode. This is where, as Solomon has it, the system takes over just like the "beautification engine." The witness to a crime views groups of computer-generated faces, rejects the worst matches, and selects the best groups. As the program itself says, it "takes account of these decisions and gradually evolves the face closer to the target." A mutation glider controls the amount of variation among the faces displayed. When the witness recognizes a facial template, he or she freezes it (figure 3.8).

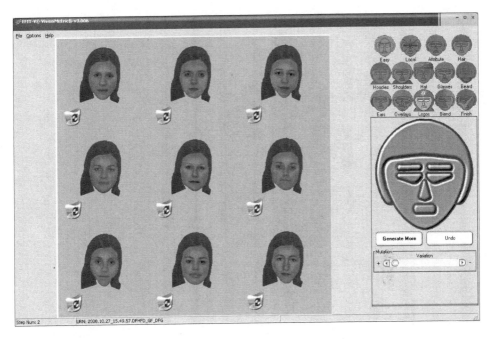

Figure 3.8
E-FIT screen shot. Courtesy VisionMetrics.

The next steps involve the application of "local tools" that narrow the facial accessories and other accessories, such as the choice of hats. The categories for hat, for example, include ethnical descriptions, materials, and functions as they appear in the cultural imaginary—African, bandanas, Indian, helmet, woolen, and so on. Finally, the dynamic overlay tool enables the use to insert realistic effects, such as aging lines, wrinkles, eyebags, prominent cheekbones, and double chins. In the overlay tool, the user can also adjust age and create an "aging video."

John and Jessica, two twenty-six-year-old students attending my Cosmetic Gaze seminar at Johns Hopkins University in the fall of 2008, had their appearances approximated by other students with the help of E-FIT. We found that it was easier to create John's criminal suspect avatar than Jessica's, which did not really look much like her. Because males are statistically more likely than females to commit crimes, the system was trained better on male images (figures 3.9 and 3.10).

E-FIT presupposes that there is a "real image pool" out there. According to software designer Chris Solomon, the software is designed to learn on

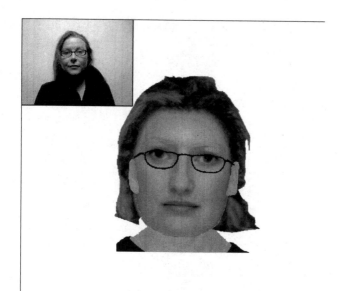

THIS IS AN EFIT-V FACIAL COMPOSITE. IT IS NOT A PHOTOGRAPH.

2008.11.03_13.58.11.GREG_GETRG4E_JESSICA

Figure 3.9
Jessica's E-FIT composite and picture taken in 2008. Courtesy Jessica and VisionMetrics.

the basis of these character, gender, and ethnic types but creates completely new virtual faces. But the real pool from which the data are drawn is a result or retroactive projection of the technological interventions themselves.

These interventions can be called machinic sutures insofar as they act to sew together a real body's process of becoming with an ideal whole whose existence is presupposed by the technology's deployment in the first place. In this sense, disparation, transduction, mixed reality, and now machinic suture achieve full theoretical operativity. Gilbert Simondon explains the conceptual pair of disparation and transduction in the following terms: "There is disparation when two twin sets that cannot be entirely superimposed, such as the left retinal image and the right retinal image, are grasped together as a system, allowing for the formation of a single set of a higher degree which integrates their elements thanks to a new dimension."[116] Adrian Mackenzie develops this line of reasoning, stipulating that

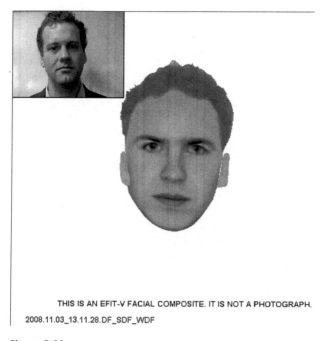

THIS IS AN EFIT-V FACIAL COMPOSITE. IT IS NOT A PHOTOGRAPH.
2008.11.03_13.11.28.DF_SDF_WDF

Figure 3.10
John's E-FIT composite and picture taken in 2008. Courtesy John and Vision Metrics.

transduction "is a process whereby a disparity or a difference is topologically and temporally restructured across some interface."[117]

The essential point is that disparate images exist as components in a preindividual stage. Individual subjects then come into being as results of transductive processes. Machinic sutures are operative when, rather than a transduction involving two purely biological instances (like that of a left and right retina), one or both of the disparate poles depends on a technological intervention or nonarbitrary intervention. These machinic sutures or renderings of Jessica and John act to sew together an ideal whole whose existence is somehow presupposed by the technology's deployment in the first place. Similarly, Richard, Susan, Pat, and other players discussed in this chapter refer to an idealized version of themselves that is created by the globalized application of the cosmetic gaze. In the case of E-FIT's facial composites, the disparation and transduction process is operative at multiple levels. Facial samples are chosen on the basis of stereotypical categorizations of real population pools and in turn are digitized and morphed into virtual models that in turn inform the expectations and judgments of real perceptions. Chris Solomon's image pool is nothing other than a retroactive construction from the perspective of the machinic sutures that create, through innumerable image morphings, the admittedly virtual individuals of the E-FIT facial recognition software. Even the "reality" that Solomon claims to have trained the system on is informed by a moral judgment and a cosmetic gaze that knows, for instance, how to distinguish eastern Europeans from other Europeans. It is not surprising that VisionMetrics is waiting for input from around the world, just as Cesare Lombroso collected photographs of criminals that people sent him from around the world. Says Solomon, "If you know of any potential sources for such pictures of Eastern European women, let me know."[118]

The Sims: Build, Buy, Live

Another example of an application of the cosmetic gaze has been developed by the entertainment industry. The videogame called *The Sims*, a computerized-dollhouse-turned-community that was first produced in 2000, is currently in its third edition. *The Sims 1* and *2* and their expansion and stuff packages sold more than 100 million copies by 2008.[119] By 2005, over 52 million users had become part of the international Sims community,[120] a community of seventeen different languages and a variety of fan Web sites including Sims exchange sites such as *modthesims*. The premise of the game is simple: "Build, buy, live." As Charles Paulk has it, "a home is built, a family moves in, and Sim life takes its course."[121] Originally designed as a "home renovation" game, *The Sims* came on the market at the same time as the first home makeover show *Trading Spaces*, which aired from 2000 to 2008 on the cable channels TLC and Discovery Home. The expansion stuff packages of *The Sims 2* 2004 edition included "IKEA Home Stuff" and "H&M Fashion Stuff Packages." Two years before the release of *The Sims 2*, Celia Pearce noticed that Sims furnishings appeared in a catalog-style menu and dubbed it "the IKEA game."[122] Paulk notes that on the global electronic market, both body parts and any consumer good with a sign exchange value are exchanged: "A century back, the dining room table really meant something. It spoke of tradition and patriarchal morality, and it brought everyone accordingly into line. What, by comparison, does that $79 IKEA where you eat your toaster pastry signify?"[123]

The Sims 3 is no longer confined to a home with an IKEA dining room or one-street neighborhood. The environment has now become a community, and you can look at it from a "Google earth prospective." *The Sims 3* added a more complex creation mode to the interior design component. In Sims language, it provided the *Create a Sim* (CAS) feature. The mode is more limited than a similar feature in *The Sims 2*, which allowed noses and eyes to be enlarged to an eerie and crazy extent. In *The Sims 3*, the art of *kalókagatheia* has been introduced so that in the process of customizing a Sim in *The Sims 3*, the player chooses a mood for a character, and the mood will determine his or her facial expression, as well as his or her success. What matters in *The Sims 3* is personality, not bodily appearance. Within the Create a Sim feature, the player customizes a Sim within five main categories—Basics, Looks, Hair, Clothing, and Personality. The Basics category includes such "basic" information as a name, a gender, an age, and a skin tone—similar to E-FIT's gender and ethnicity category. One important feature is a "makeover feature." In Sim language, the "body modifier" customizes body weight and muscle size along a sliding scale (figure 3.11).

The cosmetic gaze underlying this feature is also informed by gender specificity: increasing the body muscles for men enhances their arm muscles; increasing the muscles for women makes their stomach flatter and enhances their calf muscles and thighs. This feature is in line with focus-group findings for girls' wishes. In one of the focus groups about body modification and reality television we conducted at the University at Buffalo, twenty-two-year-old Cathy said that she would consider liposuction to obtain the six-pack implied on *The Sims 3* muscle-size scale for women: "Ok, I'm trying to get a six pack and (laughter) and, like, I have a definite two-pack, and I have a four-pack coming. But I guess (laughter), I guess I am doing crunches every night, and I kind of want the head start with a little liposuction just to, like, build on muscle. And, and that's why I would get it because I've been doing crunches since . . .—it was my New Year's resolution. Like, OK, this time I going to have the six pack and 'cause I have the definition and everything. But, yeah, that's what I would get."[124]

The next main category in Create a Sim mode is Looks. Here, the player can determine the position and configuration for head, ears, eyes,[125] nose;

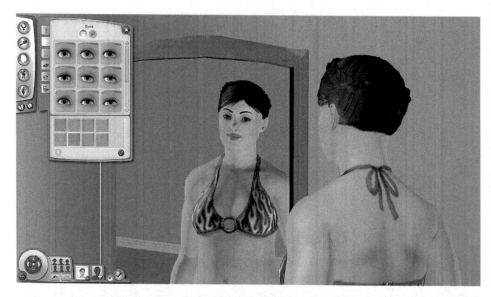

Figure 3.11
Screen shot of "body modifiers" from *The Sims 3*.

"topical details" such as freckles and beauty marks; and "make-up."[126] In Create a Sim mode, there is no difference between make-up and body features, such as muscle size and body weight. They all belong to the realm of what we see and the category of "looks." The third category is Hair (including eyebrows and eyelashes) and offers a wide variety of styles and colors. Clothing is the fourth category and includes subcategories like everyday, formal, sleepwear, athletic, and swimwear (especially needed for the "never nude Sim"). The fifth and final category—Personality—is the most innovative change from the world of *The Sims 1*, created by Will Wright, to the world of *The Sims 3*. Over sixty personality traits can be chosen to customize a Sim along four psychological categories—mental (such as absent-minded, can't stand art, natural cook, and virtuoso), physical (such as clumsy, neat, never nude, and unlucky), social (such as charismatic, great kisser, commitment issues, and schmoozer), and lifestyle (such as hot-headed, kleptomaniac, vegetarian, and daredevil). After choosing a Sim's favorite food, music, and color, the player has constructed a creature with five personality traits that are at times mutually exclusive. If a Sim, for instance, is family oriented, he cannot "dislike children." Or if a Sim is "never nude," he will have to shower with his bathing costume. Finally, a player can select a lifetime wish for a Sim, such as "future leader for the free world." If the Sim fulfills this wish in her Sim life, you can gain a lifetime happiness award, such as a "steel bladder," so the Sim no longer has to go to the bathroom. The Sims, as Paulk has it, are "hard-wired social climbers."[127] They are like us (figure 3.12).

The Sims became a cultural phenomenon immediately after being introduced in 2000, not least because it broke the gender dynamic of video games that attracted mostly boys and young men: "*The Sims* has pulled the neat trick of building a player base evenly split along gender lines, drawing in women without alienating male gamers."[128] Up to this point, males were playing only escapist games such as *Bioshock 2*, a first-person shooter game that lets the player travel as Big Daddy through the fallen undersea city of Rapture, where a monster has been snatching little girls.[129] *The Sims* lets players into the fantasy realm of their own normal lives. There are no monsters, but there are ghosts, who are resurrected dead Sims and can be played like any other Sim. As Ben Bell, executive producer of *The Sims 3*, explains: "if somebody passes away in the game, which happens,

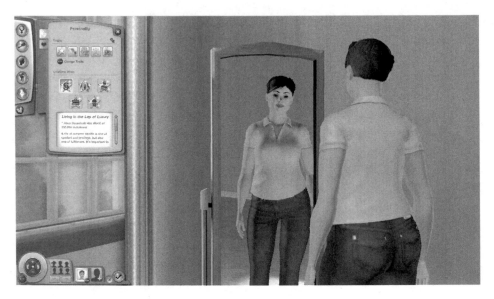

Figure 3.12
Olivia (age fourteen) creates Berna in *The Sims 3* and her lifetime wish. Courtesy of
Olivia W.

unfortunately, you can take them over as a playable character and they'll
be this fun, interesting thing to play with."[130]

The Sims uniquely combines the operations of the machinic suture. On
the one hand, it gives players a variety of possibilities for customizing,
creating, and controlling the Sims' lives and deciding what they do as
slightly better or *sim*ilar versions of ourselves. In this sense, they can resu-
ture together those areas of our lives that have been scarred or damaged—
with the help of a pop-up menu that gives the machinic suture a variety
of possibilities. As executive producer Bell notes, the game appeals to
people because it "immediately reflects who you are as a person when
you're playing it. . . . you can recreate situations from your own life with
the game. So immediately as you start to play with it, it becomes a reflection of you, and I think that's really appealing to people. It inspires creativity as you're playing, so it's a piece of entertainment, but it also becomes
like a diary."[131] On the other hand (as in any other type of reality TV show
situation), players can also watch their Sims on television, and from this
dysphoric point of view, they can simply sit back and watch themselves
living in this euphoric alternative to their real life. The improvements in

The Sims 3 let players more fully enjoy this reality-driven perspective thanks to the Sims' enhanced intelligence: "so the traits determine not only what the Sims want from life, but how they relate to other people, how they use things in the world, what they're capable of in life, and so on. It's really rich, it's really deep, and it's very believable."[132] This increased independence leads the Sims to the ability to take care of themselves. They are less in need of the creators and voyeurs who set them up. In fact, there is a certain *Schadenfreude* and irony built into the game, as Bell emphasizes: "when something bad happens to the characters, first of all you're an observer. It's kind of like it didn't really happen to you, it happened to them, and you probably made it happen to them."[133]

With both *The Sims* and reality television, viewers watch what happens to someone else but could happen to themselves. The Sims player might have built a Sim to be a hot-headed politician, which will involve him in discussions with his neighbors and maybe even physical fights. The Sim player becomes all at once producer, casting director, participant, and viewer of her own reality show. Olivia W., fourteen years old, has played all three versions of *The Sims*. In an interview, she described herself more as a producer-casting director than a player-viewer of her Sims: "I like to create pretend people—completely made-up ones. If I make someone everybody knows and I say at dinner 'I created my friend . . . ,' then everybody will want to look at my Sim and go, 'That doesn't look like her at all!' So I like to create my own Sims."[134] Olivia draws on her own life experiences as the youngest daughter of a family with six children. She keeps her Sims to herself to protect her own territory and is aware of her psychological motivation: "I like to control my Sims. I am the youngest in my family and never got to control my sisters. So now I like to do that in the game."[135] Just like in old doll games, the girl extends her social realm into the realm of the game—smoothly mixing realities.

Self-ploitation, or When the Gaze Strikes Back

These examples of how the cosmetic gaze is at work within our consumer culture on the global electronic market show that there is a strong connection between our real lives and the ways in which we can enhance our reality in our screen lives. With all of the examples—the cosmetic transformation of ugly ducklings to swans, E-FIT's criminal suspects, and *The*

Sims video characters—the platform and content of these transformations are the self. These operations point us back to an original "authentic" or "sacred" inner place, but that place is constantly being produced by the machinic suture in a way that our deepest and most intrinsic "originality" is touched by the intervention of technology. We cannot escape from this place. We are bound to look at ourselves in what has been called a gaze that looks at itself in "self-ploitation."[136]

This movement of the gaze is apparent at Internet porn sites like Ishotmyself.com or Beautifulagony.com.[137] These "self-ploitation" sites represent a new configuration of maker, screen, and audience. As Rhodes has it, "they are closing the circuit between maker and audience, gaze and object, camera and screen.[138] According to the site Ishotmyself.com, "Project_ISM is a public art apparatus. Each day we exhibit a new folio in which the artist presents herself in a bold statement about nudity, fame and the Internet. This is Selfploitation. It can make you look, make you think, make you jelly-kneed, and if you want, it can even make you famous."[139] Contributors to Ishotmyself, who are called "artists," are invited to upload still nude shots of themselves. The "exhibitor" must be eighteen years of age, appear on camera solo, show full-frontal nudity, and always keep one hand on the camera. The site is presented as an art project, and its visitors are compared to visitors to the Guggenheim Museum. It asks for a member fee of $24.95 per month and awards a monthly ISM art prize of $250.

What is interesting about this site and other similar sites is the question of the gaze they construct and the "place" of the screen. As Rhodes observes, "the performer, alone, is locked in a narcissistic circuit, both observer (or herself), and object, subject and object of the gaze, their hand holding, erotically, the eye, their body arousing and performing for this eye."[140] From Slavoj Žižek's perspective, the self may strive to resist this otherness, but it always returns to the central question of the other's desire: "che vuoi da me?" (what do you want from me?).[141] In the logic of "self-ploitation," though, the question of the other's desire has been turned around. Now the self asks itself, "What do I want from me?" In this "completion of exposure, where every member is removed from the capture, but the self,"[142] a circuit is generated that wishes to erase the self as other. This phenomenology of self-erasure can be compared or related to a "perspectiveless" point of view that is organized in a 360-degree manner, with a gaze indebted to the realm of the cinematic. As Lev Manovich has it, this realm was produced from the outset as a loop: "A loop, a repetition, created by the circular movement of the handle, gives birth to a progression of events—a very basic narrative which is also quintessentially modern: a camera moving through space recording whatever is in its way."[143] The loop also gave rise to computer programming, as most programs are based on repetition and feedback. In digital environments such as the Ishotmyself.com interactive Web site, the loop becomes an engine that sets a narrative in motion.[144] The images produced in this circularity can no longer be read with a structural and linear gaze in mind (as, for instance, in Laura Mulvey's "male gaze"). Instead, the gaze in such online narratives claims to come from within, from a self that has sutured itself machinically at its "origin." This perspectiveless image of the bettered self can also be read as an implosion of the ancient rules of *kalókagatheia* in that appearance is no longer a sign for a character trait. Rather, as in the world order of *The Sims 3*, personality is just one aspect of the individual, along with looks and hair. In the logic of the loop, everything has depths and surface at the same time.

According to Jean Baudrillard,

the worst alienation is not to be dispossessed by the other but to be dispossessed of the other, that is to say to have to produce the other in his absence, and thus be continuously referred back to oneself and to one's image. If we are today condemned to our own image . . . , this is not because of an alienation, but because of the end of alienation and because of the virtual disappearance of the other, which is a much worse fatality.[145]

For Baudrillard, plastic surgery is merely a subgenre of the more radical surgery of otherness and destiny, as the examples of Cindy Ingle and the golden mask show us. In such an "economy of sameness,"[146] the gaze looks back at itself in a close circuit, and the body becomes the sole locus of identification. It implodes into a body that one is and leaves behind a body that one had. This economy of sameness can help explain Michael Jackson's "loss" of his nose and pigmentation. From a clinical perspective, Jackson's "problem" with his nose and skin color can be explained as the externalization of inner conflicts onto a particular body part. As with the logic of anorexia, Jackson's loss can be interpreted as the desire to leave his "old" body behind, along with the constraints of race, gender, and sex, and in its place create a "new" body, which in his case did not look subtly refreshed but harshly and violently altered into an otherworldly visage. Michael Jackson did not want to leave a trace of himself in his makeover process. His makeover emphasized this loss of self, but this radical departure was lived by him as an act of authenticity, of return to self. Thus, a physiognomic apparatus built within a moralizing *kalókagatheia* has run its logical course, and the digital and surgical tools of the twenty-first century have provided the cosmetic gaze with a plasticity and ubiquity that the past could only imagine. In the final chapter, I look at this history as registered in a medium that has served as one of the most effective means of transmission of the cosmetic gaze and that has been driven to thematize it as well—cinema.

4 Editing Women: The Cosmetic Gaze and Cinema

From a woman sin had its beginning, and because of her we all die.
—Ecclesiasticus, or the Wisdom of Jesus, Son of Sirach, 25.24 (New Oxford Annotated Bible)

He chose five [women] because he did not think all the qualities which he sought to combine in a portrayal of beauty could be found in one person, because in no single case has Nature made anything perfect and finished in every part.
—Cicero, "Zeuxis Selecting Models"[1]

A woman is more authentic the more she looks like what she has dreamed for herself.
—The transvestite Agrado, in the film *Todo sobre mi madre* (Pedro Almodóvar, 1999)

The cosmetic gaze is a way of perceiving our own and others' bodies as always requiring further modification to become complete. As it has developed in modernity, the cosmetic gaze has depended on a special relationship with women and with the female body. In the twentieth century, the cosmetic gaze incorporated both the traditional misogynistic fantasy that split woman's being into a duplicitous mask covering an abyss of death and a blank surface receptive to man's creative urge and also the avant-garde's aesthetic revolution, which required beauty to endure convulsive change. The dissemination of this beauty concept into the culture at large paved the way for a culture of makeover beauty, which embraces the imperative to alter the body through violent means and also accepts a certain aestheticization of the makeover process, such that abnormalities, deformities, and creative interventions can attain positive value as modes of self-expression. The cosmetic gaze, in other words, valorizes socially conforming end products and opens up a space of acceptability for beauty's dark side.

In this final chapter, I return to the dual valence of the cosmetic gaze by exploring its manifestation in one of the most powerful media of its dissemination—the cinema. A long tradition of psychoanalytically oriented film theory has focused on the "male gaze" as structuring the cinematic image and propagating patriarchic values. One argument made in this chapter is that it may be time to replace the notion of the male gaze with that of the cosmetic gaze, and for this reason the starting point of much of the analysis that follows is psychoanalytic in nature. Although the male gaze captures the misogynistic and conformist aspects of the cosmetic gaze, it is less adept at understanding an aesthetic current in the cinema that specializes in exploring and even celebrating the liberating gestures of beauty's dark side. Cinema has played a powerful role in transmitting the gaze that binds us and in creating a language for conceptualizing, criticizing, and ultimately contesting that very gaze.

To this end, the first section briefly looks at how cosmetic surgery has been thematized in a series of films from the 1940s to the first decade of the twenty-first century. Anxieties about surgical interventions in cinema have changed toward increasing normalization, but an unspoken assumption about the desire structure underlying these interventions has not changed. In these films (all made by men), a woman's willingness to undergo the cut is motivated by the love of a man—whether a lover or a surgeon or both in one person—and the fantasy underlying each film's vision is that a woman's whole, original, and true self is what the man loves.

The notion of the cosmetic gaze is more expansive and subtle than that of the male gaze, and it permits an understanding of cinema and art that reveals the machinic sutures on which the cosmetic gaze is built. The chapter's next sections look at two films by women auteurs that disrupt and trouble the romantic myth of female wholeness[2] at the heart of the cinematic transmission of the cosmetic gaze. In these films by Marina de Van and Jane Campion, the disturbing and contradictory desires of the female protagonists are oriented along the fissures in the self that the cosmetic gaze seeks to hide. In them, women enter into erotic relations with images of cut-up, disarticulated bodies. In other words, the sutures underlying the cosmetic gaze (and not the women) are laid bare and experienced as beautiful.

I then look at how this revelatory ability of cinema has expanded beyond cinema to performance art and reality TV. And in the final section, which also serves as a conclusion for the book, I take up the moment of "the reveal" in reality makeover TV as the ultimate model for how different media have resuscitated a nineteenth-century physiognomy intent on reading the good behind the surface of the beautiful, retooled and repackaged in the form of a twenty-first-century cosmetic gaze.

Cinematic Anesthesia: Cosmetic Surgery and Film

I selected these films, all made by men, because they showcase the female myth of wholeness (described above) while emphasizing different subthemes, from the creation of woman by the hands of men to the idea of refreshing a marriage or love through a face change. These films range historically from the 1940s to 2006 and include an original superimposition of the "ugly woman" with the "bad woman" (to use Lavater's terminology) to a more complex and subtle application of the cosmetic gaze's investment in the modern beauty myth of woman's wholeness in Ki-duk Kim's *Time*. The films are all examples of a Western gaze. Even *Time*, which was made by a South Korean director, was intended for an international audience and assumes a certain fluency in the principles of the cosmetic gaze, which also explains why the DVD version was released in Italy.

My anecdotal history of cosmetic surgery and film starts in the late 1930s and early 1940s with two films based on the 1933 French play *Il était une fois* (Once upon a time) by Francis de Croisset. The 1938 Swedish film by Gustaf Molander (*Kvinna Ansikte En*) starred Ingrid Bergman (its English title is *A Woman's Face*), and the 1941 U.S. remake was directed by George Cukor and starred Joan Crawford (also titled *A Woman's Face*). In the following discussion, I restrict my reading to the 1941 U.S. version of this classic cosmetic surgery tale.

Told in flashback from the vantage point of a murder trial, the story concerns a beautiful female criminal whose face is partly disfigured by a hideous scar. The woman, Anna Holm (Joan Crawford), wears a hat pulled down to cover her scars during the first half of the film and avoids the contact with the mirror (figure 4.1). Following the rules of *kalókagatheia*, the film presents Anna as a woman whose disfigurement makes her into a criminal, or is her face disfigured because she is a criminal, as Lombroso would have it? During one of her burglaries, Anna runs into Dr. Gustaf Segert (Melvyn Douglas), a cosmetic surgeon, whose wife Vera plays the

Figure 4.1
Film still from *A Woman's Face* (1941). Courtesy of Warner Brothers.

part of the antiheroine in the film, cheating on her husband by conducting love-letter relationships with other men (which, according to 1940s values, is a worse offense than burglary).

Having "gotten rid" of the integrity of wife Vera, the story proceeds with a predictable love story between Anna and Gustaf, who offers the disfigured woman a free procedure because he is interested in her type of disfigurement. After her surgery, Anna changes from "cold-blooded" to "sentimental," as Gustaf notices right before revealing her new face to her and us viewers. The "reveal" brings forth Anna's "better self" and also is a moment highly charged with eroticism between the doctor and the criminal. The mise-en-scène is a classical love scene with the man elevated above the woman, who has her eyes closed as if expecting to be kissed. The doctor, who looks directly onto his passive object of creation, takes off her facial bandage like taking off an intimate piece of women's clothing, while she clearly enjoys his gesture (figure 4.2).

The male gaze in this shot is typical of the traditional cinematic treatment. Soon the two marry. The last scene returns to the trial, and not surprisingly the new Anna is acquitted. Gustaf stands to speak about her character, and when Anna disputes him by recalling that he labeled her

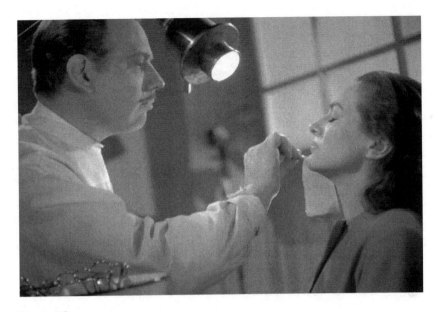

Figure 4.2
Film still from *A Woman's Face* (1941). Courtesy of Warner Brothers.

"this most terrifying, ruthless creature," he interrupts her: "It wasn't you. It never has been you!" At this moment, Anna finds her new self—a woman who has always wanted to marry, as she confesses, so she could "belong to the human race." Anna's makeover satisfies the moralistic predicaments of the cosmetic gaze: she is now whole, not just partly beautiful. Becoming beautiful made her a good human being and a woman—that is, no longer a monster or otherwise excluded from the human race. Finally, this makeover could not have happened on its own. A man was needed to facilitate it, and the man will now love his creation forever.

The male surgical power to make woman whole does not always result in romance in literature and film. In the horror film *Gritos en la noche* (*The Awful Dr. Orlof*) (Jesus Franco, 1962), Dr. Orlof wants to restore the disfigured beauty of his daughter, Melissa (another of his creations), and therefore abducts beautiful women to a castle with the help of his blind henchman, Morpho (whose name reflects the fact that Orlof has disfigured him). The former physician experiments on the women by taking off their skin to reuse on his daughter. Orlof operates on innocent beautiful women, whom he treats with a certain necrophilic devotion in his operating room, which is reachable only by boat (Figure 4.3).

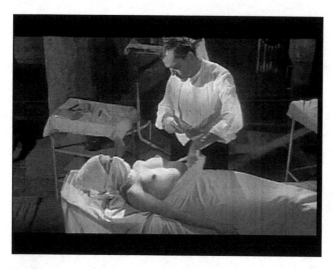

Figure 4.3
Film still from *The Awful Dr. Orlof* (1962). Courtesy of Eurocine.

In many ways, Dr. Segert and Dr. Orlof are similar. They both are (or believe they are) capable of making women whole, they both are erotically invested in their objects of creation, and they both engage the viewer in a scopophilic spectacle of a woman's body being cut open to be made "whole" (even if its purpose is to make another woman whole at the expense of the beautiful abducted women). Neither film, however, attempts to enter the perspective of the woman who is cut open.

An early attempt o do so was made in the French cosmetic surgery psychodrama *Les yeux sans visage* (*Eyes without a Face*) (Georges Franju, 1960), which was a follow-up to *The Awful Dr. Orlof*. This film, which was released in the United States in 1962 with the title *The Horror Chamber of Dr. Faustus*, is more subtle and cinematic than its precursors in its attempts to enter the psychic sphere of the disfigured woman. In this story written by Jean Redon, the disfiguring and irreparable facial damage happens to Christiane Génessier in a car accident (already a step away from Anna, whose disfigurement was caused by "nature"). Christiane, like Dr. Orlof's daughter, Melissa, is "lucky" to be the daughter of a surgeon, who will attempt to repair his daughter's face in an experimental surgical intervention. For this purpose, Dr. Génessier needs the flesh of beautiful women (as does Dr. Orlof) so that he can experiment on their faces. His helper is not a disfigured and blind Morpho but his beautiful young girlfriend, Louise (not Christiane's biological mother but her stepmother), whom he has operated on as well and who helps him lure young women, sedate them, remove their faces in a hidden underground laboratory, and dispose of their corpses. But the story is different from the previous films in that viewers experience it from the point of view of Christiane, who has been wearing a mask since her accident and is desperate for a new face. The camera shows us only Christiane's back until she finally looks at us through a horrifying white facial mask, which shows that her beautiful eyes are shimmering with tears. Christiane feels guilt for the women who are sacrificed to restore her face, but her desire for a new face is stronger. This is told in a revealing sequence that starts when Christiane secretly encounters one of the sedated and soon-to-be-operated-on victims in her father's underground lab, takes off her mask in front of the mirror, and sees the victim's horrified reaction. In *Eyes without a Face*, the source of horror is both the evil surgeon and Christiane herself, whose ugliness is stylized through an absent face behind a mask and whom we are supposed to feel compassion for because we now have a sense of what it means to have no face.

Dr. Génessier's attempt to restore his daughter's appearance fails. After the final skin graft operation, he notices that the new tissue is being rejected, and Christiane must wear her mask again. Ultimately, Christiane realizes that she will never be made "whole" again, frees the last victim, and kills Louise.

This tale from the early 1960s provides a glimpse into the possibility of a feminist reading of Christiane's action. She decides to have no face. However, this "choice" is not entirely feminist, since Christiane is not really applying her own definition of beauty to her appearance. Nor is the mask an example of the machinic suture whose traces have been erased— far from it. Christiane never receives a new face because it was medically impossible at the time, but the cosmetic gaze is still fully operative, looking for Christiane's true and beautiful self.

The mask as signifier of the construction of femininity also appears in the experimental cult film *La Montaña Sagrada* (*The Holy Mountain*) (Alejandro Jodorowsky, 1973). This science-fiction, psychedelic tale about man's impossible desire to achieve immortality and control beauty (among many other themes) takes place on the planet Venus. Facial masks are

Figure 4.4
Film still from *La Montaña sagrada* (1973). Courtesy of ABKCO Music and Records.

being mass produced, and they are living organisms that will adapt to any purpose (figure 4.4):

We know that people want to be loved not for what they are but what they want to appear to be. So we have created a line of masks that have the texture, warmth, and smell of living human beings. The customer can have any face she wants. . . . Every face is unique and lasts a lifetime. She can wear her artificial face to the grave. Our make-up department for corpses eliminates the appearance of death. Not only do we beautify cadavers; we also equip them with electronic devices. They can kiss their family good-bye, participate in their own last rights, or give a live show.

Although Jodorovsky's avant-garde film discusses and parodies the impossibility of changing your face through the metaphor of the life-long mask, it does not question the centrality of the female face or the importance of its eternal beauty premise from the perspective of a male gaze. In fact, all of these films, whether they are critical or uncritical of the romantic myth of female wholeness, presuppose in one way or another that men decide a woman's appearance or a woman's face by inscribing their own vision onto it.

In my discussion of the next set of films, I turn to this problem of lack of feminine agency. In the previous films, men have made over women after disfiguring events occurred in these women's lives, whether the damage was done before birth or in a car accident. In the French film *Le miroir à deux faces* (*The Mirror Has Two Faces*) (André Cayatte, 1958), a housewife (Michèle Morgan) decides that she wants to have cosmetic surgery to refresh her marriage with a "normal schoolteacher." But the outcome is not what she hopes for, and her transformation from ugly duckling to beautiful wife ultimately ruins her marriage. Not accepting your "originality" becomes indicative of a cursed existence—the opposite message from what the first films show, that beauty is a survival strategy. The U.S. remake of this film, *The Mirror Has Two Faces* with Barbra Streisand as Rose Morgan (1996), tells the same makeover story but without the cosmetic surgery. Instead, Rose diets, exercises, changes her hairstyle, learns to use makeup, and chooses flattering clothes, which are all "natural" and "independent" makeover strategies. She even makes this point to her husband, Gregory (Jeff Bridges), who is a professor at Columbia University and says that he prefers the "old Rose": "I just made a few changes. It's not like I had surgery," Rose responds.[3] The Barbra Streisand remake emphasizes that Rose's makeover is independent from male expertise, unlike the original *Le miroir à deux faces*, where Michele Morgan goes from wanting to please her husband to falling in love with her surgeon (figure 4.5). Nevertheless, the plot change raises a question that was raised in chapter 3: is there really such a thing as a makeover for oneself?

The Mirror Has Two Faces can be seen as a precursor to the Korean film *Shi gan* (*Time*) (2006) by South Korean director Ki-Duk Kim, which was released on DVD in Korean with Italian subtitles. Although outside the

Figure 4.5
Film still from *Le miroir à deux faces* (1958). © 1958 Gaumont/Celincom SPA (Italy).

Western cultural norm established thus far, Ki-Duk Kim intended his film for international distribution and was reflecting on a cinematic tradition and an international obsession with cosmetic surgery that have been disseminated with little regard for borders or cultural distinctions. The film opens with an eyelid operation: a Korean woman is undergoing blepharopasty to look "less Asian." Like the films discussed thus far, *Time* was made by a man and activates a male, heterosexual gaze in its organization of its female characters' desires. One difference is that in this makeover thriller from 2006, the surgical act is almost an afterthought. The technology of intervention has become so normalized that it can be easily subsumed into the flow of the plot without leaving a trace of the stitches behind.

Time tells the story of a troubled love between a young man, Ji-woo, and woman named See-hee. See-hee is worried that she is not good (looking) enough for Ji-woo and decides to leave him out of fear that their love could one day end. But she decides to have cosmetic surgery so that she can reappear into Ji-woo's life as a new woman who is unrecognizable to him. Her hope is that Ji-woo will experience her as a "new" woman in his life. This renewed self is reminiscent of the four-years-younger version of oneself that the new beauty industry is promoting (discussed in chapter 2). But this myth is also an expression of the belief that *anything* is renewable—not just beauty but love itself. As the director points out in an interview: "In the oriental culture there isn't this clear distinction between body and soul. The point is that a woman wants to be touched in a certain way by her lover, but often in a relationship the caresses lose their power of passion after a certain while."[4] *Time* is thus a story about the impossible desire of stopping time from progressing and bringing changes. It is about an attempt to freeze the initial moment of love forever. In this sense, the film is an extrapolation of what makeover discourse promotes—the idea that you can and must renew your soul, your body, your love by hitting the Refresh button.

Cosmetic surgery does not play any role other than the technological facilitator to this fantasy. It is not presented as anything to be afraid of or critical of. To the contrary, the surgeon is turned into the "helper." His "surgery" is no longer presented as a violent "cut" into the flesh of beautiful women, as in the other films analyzed thus far, but rather as an aestheticized experience. Fittingly, the opening scene in *Time* is a montage of highly aesthetic images of a surgical intervention. It starts with a woman's eye opening one last time before falling into an anesthetized sleep. Dr. Segert and Dr. Orlof were invested in the beauty of their female patients, whom they dare to uncover in the operating room, but this nameless young Korean plastic surgeon would never do anything like that. His eroticism, captured by a highly aestheticized cinematography, is here invested in the surgery and the surgery utensils, which like the intravenous tubes, are depicted in an almost phallic relation to the patient's body. The extreme closeup of her pupil reflects the symmetrical lights in an operating room. Romantic piano music evokes expectation. The surgeon is starting his work. His pencil marks are presented as beautiful drawings (figures 4.6 and 4.7).

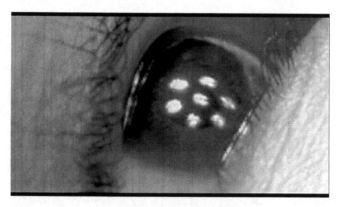

Figure 4.6
Film still from *Time* (2006). Courtesy of Lifesize Entertainment.

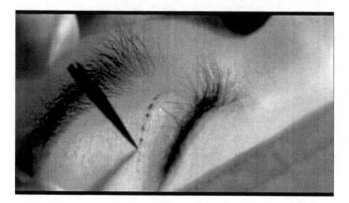

Figure 4.7
Film still from *Time* (2006). Courtesy of Lifesize Entertainment.

The opening montage ends with an erotic juxtaposition of a bloody breast procedure with an erect nipple. This surgery is "not scary" but is "magical" in that it compresses a three-month recovery period from a surgically scarred breast into a "whole." This opening is a first glimpse into a "sedated" or "slow" cosmetic surgery environment. At the doctor's door, there is an "after" picture with the question "Do you want a new life?" See-hee explains to her surgeon: "I don't want to be more beautiful. I want a new, different face." The doctor appears intelligent and competent. He shows his patient a film about the risks of surgery and emphasizes that her decision will not be reversible. The surgeon adopts the role of the warning fairy in this modern beauty myth when he says, "Do not change!" This gentlemanly gesture would have been unthinkable for the lustful surgeons of the 1940s and 1960s. The film thus situates the desire for cosmetic surgery beyond the beauty discourse. Indeed, the surgeon admits that he will most likely not be able to make See-hee "more beautiful." He admits the limits of artificial beauty, while he alters his patient on the computer screen before going into real surgery (figure 4.8).

But See-hee does not want beauty. She wants the love that she felt at the beginning of her relationship with Ji-woo. With her makeover, she wants to go back in history to the time when she felt their love was perfect

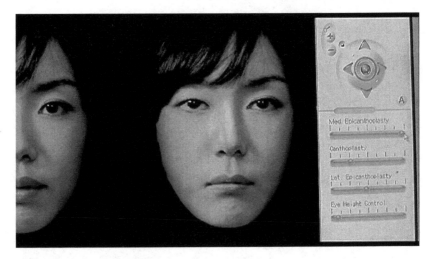

Figure 4.8
Film still from *Time* (2006). Courtesy of Lifesize Entertainment.

and fresh—and for this experience she gives up her face and becomes alien to herself.

See-hee's plan works at first. She meets Ji-woo again, and he is attracted to the "new" See-hee. After they have sex for the "first" time, Ji-woo says, "I have never felt this way before," but he wonders who she is. He plays with the photos he took at their first encounter. He tries to grasp her identity but remains perplexed. See-hee becomes sad and is overtaken by strange feelings. Does he love her new identity, or is he still attracted to her old self? The "old" See-hee starts leaving Ji-woo phone messages about wanting to go back to him. He is torn and admits to still love the "old" See-hee. The "new" See-hee fiercely confronts her lover about the "old" girlfriend: "I will find her, and I will stop her."

Time is about a woman's desire, but this desire is described from a male point of view. See-hee wants to be desired as she was when love was new, but when she recreates this feeling, she cannot help but wonder whether the new love is authentic. Since an unbridgeable span of time separates "real, existing" love from love in its fresh, new, and somehow always past form, See-hee's use of cosmetic surgery to erase that time fails. See-hee cannot be a new person and also be a person who can experience herself as new. This failure plays itself out in *Time* as a love triangle with two characters. Insofar as this is the film's goal, it is both successful and entertaining. But *Time* fails to question the same desire structure that informs all of the films discussed to this point, particularly the two versions of *The Mirror Has Two Faces*.

As in all of these films, a woman seeks surgery (or surgery is imposed on her by an evil antihero surgeon) in the service of an image of herself as the object of a man's desire. Whether surgery is successful or not, what is never questioned is the idea that an original, whole, feminine identity is the proper and ultimate complement to the male desire structure underlying the cinematic gaze. As in all functioning of the cosmetic gaze, this cinematic gaze convinces women that they are incomplete but only temporarily so. Interventions and procedures succeed or fail based on how well their final product approximates that ideal female identity. But as shown in chapter 2, female identity, as the most powerful element of the cosmetic gaze, is both the foundation of traditional notions of beauty and the source of beauty's convulsive dark side. Female identity can be both of these things because it is a contradictory construction that resists totalization.

Lacan referred to the position of woman as not-all, and one of his most famous and scandalous utterances was "La femme n'existe pas."[5] The following section looks at two films by women that explore the dangers of a feminine desire that orients itself around a fragmented identity that the cosmetic gaze covers. These films invite a psychoanalytic approach, and that approach leads viewers from the presumptions of a male gaze to the analysis of the cosmetic gaze.

In My Skin and *In the Cut*: Two Accounts of Femininity

Marina de Van's feature film debut, *Dans ma peau* (*In My Skin*) (2002), could have been based on a case of hysteria described by Lacanian psychoanalyst Joël Dor.[6] In Dor's case, Ms. X is a woman who suffers from severe body dysmorphic disorder. She seeks the help of a psychoanalyst because her compulsion to mutilate her arms, legs, stomach, and breasts causes an infection that needs to be treated in the hospital. During psychoanalytic therapy sessions, the woman lets her body speak through her inscriptions or markers of narcissistic bodily violence. This strategy is a characteristic of the hysteric, who desires something by making it desirable for and visible for the other.

For de Van's character Esther, the first encounter with self-mutilation is apparently an accident. Esther (played by Marina de Van herself) does not realize that her leg is cut when she walks in the dark through a backyard full of rusty metal waste. Later, she sees blood streaming from under her pants, realizes what has happened, and visits a doctor. When the doctor asks her if the wound hurt at first, she says that it did not. Dor's Ms. X inflicted her first self-mutilation purposely, albeit with no apparent motivation. She recounts that at age seventeen, after a panic attack in high school, she slashed her right breast with a razor. Like de Van's Esther, in this "state of dissociation" Ms. X did not feel any pain at the moment of making the self-inflicted wounds: rather, "when the blood began to flow, she felt an unaccustomed effect of well-being that lasted until the end of this brief hemorrhage."[7] In psychoanalysis, one of the favorite roles taken by the hysterical subject is that of suffering. Ms. X has several traits that are typical for hysteria, and pain and blood are relevant for those traits. Through the combined processes of repression and condensation and with the help of the analyst's detailed associative investigation, Ms. X reworks "how certain signifiers had been selectively elaborated by the unconscious in a combination of successive metaphoric and metonymic substitutions that crystallized the pathological symptom of self-mutilation."[8] There is not space here to explore Ms. X's floating signifiers, but the color/word *red* became one trigger for the associative signifying chain that was responsible for her engagement in self-mutilation: the color/word *red* "became an unconscious metaphor for having sexual pleasure with a man, and was, furthermore, associated with the experience of something streaming down the body."[9] The desire for streaming red blood, which Ms. X experienced from self-inflicted mutilation by cutting, was, in this psychoanalytical reading, a result of a chain of sexual encounters during Ms. X's adolescence, which she had repressed and which were metonymically displaced in her unconscious. Her body language brought out the signifiers in this form of narcissistic bodily mutilation.

Despite the similarity of the symptoms manifested in Ms. X and Esther, Marina de Van's *Dans ma peau* resists a psychoanalytical approach (explicitly in the director's commentary on the film's DVD special features). De Van's account does not "blame" Esther's self-mutilation on her sexual incapacitation or adolescent trauma. The film shows that Esther lives in a "normal and healthy" sexual relation with her partner, Vincent. This does not necessarily contradict her hysterical self-destructive outbreak, but the film does not show any psychological motivations behind it. The first scene that reveals the main character's body disorder takes place at work, when Esther is suddenly overcome with the desire to cut into the already healing wounds from the earlier accident.[10] About this incident, she later tells Vincent: "I did it without thinking. It came over me."

The sequence that is most provocative for an analysis of self-mutilation as a female identity strategy is the business dinner during which we can witness Esther's hallucination of being physically detached from her body. This literally fragmented body experience involves her seeing her arm as a detached entity lying on the dinner table (figure 4.9).

Esther's detachment is further emphasized in a dinner conversation about Japan (a "detached" culture from the diners' Western point of view, as is pointed out in the conversation), which she is not able to follow or engage in. The words uttered during the dinner literally surround her without touching or reaching her, just as her arm sits next to her as if entirely dissociated from her. In the director's commentary on this scene,

I go there on vacation.
I like the feel,

Figure 4.9
Film still from *Dans ma peau* (2002). Courtesy of Marina de Van.

de Van asks: "and if my arm was something I can simply place on the table like a fork?" Esther's alienation and disassociation from her own body is presented as a necessary condition for the self-mutilation she engages in. As de Van explains in the director's commentary, "by focusing only on one's own body and one's relation to one's body, all other social relations cannot but fail." Her intention is to show the transformation of a body fragment (such as a leg or an arm) into an object of self-mutilation. De Van is after the transformation of a subject into an object—a female tale.

The fragmented body has been of interest since early modernity, when new insights and technologies emerged that were concerned with viewing the body anatomically. What interests me in *Dans ma peau*, however, are not the visual or narrative strategies of getting under the skin but rather issues of the female gaze and female spectatorship. In other words, what interests me most are the configurations of a female body in disorder and the strategies of recuperation that gain or regain an image that is capable of holding that female body together. The first crucial question that I ask is: does *Dans ma peau* address and construct the spectator as female? The answer is both yes and no. On the one hand, the female protagonist Esther's body image is what is at stake in this film, although it is not in the Hollywood tradition of a passive body that we are merely invited to look at and take pleasure from. Rather, viewers are invited to witness Esther's "boundary-disorder" from her perspective, which at times is highly aesthetic and even eroticized but still is (as E. Ann Kaplan has argued) a masculine position.[11] The position is "masculine" (as is pointed out by many feminist film theorists) in that it is capable of activating the gaze, while the feminine identification with the image is of a passive nature, a reason for Teresa de Lauretis to call female subjectivity a "nonsubjectivity."[12] On the other hand, *Dans ma peau* does not offer a feminist (or any other) solution to the problem of the construction of the female body image. The film has a traditional way of addressing and representing the female body, so Esther's body becomes a problem for viewers. In that sense, this is a film in which femininity is at stake in excess. As Anneke Smelik puts it,

One of the functions of narrative, de Lauretis argues, is to 'seduce' women into femininity with or without their consent. . . . the female subject is made to desire femininity. Here de Lauretis turns Mulvey's famous phrase around: not only does a story demand sadism, sadism demands a story. Desire in narrative is intimately bound up with violence against women and the techniques of cinematic narration both reflect and sustain social forms of oppression of women. Representation is a power by another name.[13]

Physical violence executed on the female body is the theme of Marina de Van's nonpsychological account of a female body disorder. The disorder becomes visibly most relevant and drastic in the ending sequence of the film, when Esther—determinedly on her way to work—is once more overwhelmed with an irresistible urge to engage in self-mutilation. We see the world as perceived through her eyes, a disorientated isolated viewpoint that brings us to another hotel room, where she literally cuts herself into pieces (figure 4.10). The result is a blood bath, a climactic ending to Esther's body disorder tale.

Femininity, body disorder, and representation are closely connected in *Dans ma peau*. De Van's film does not offer a therapeutic solution to her female character's troubled body, but she touches on what seems to be at the core of the problem—the female body and its unstable image or, in Jacqueline Rose's words, the "impossibility of the feminine outside of representation."[14]

Jane Campion's feature film *In the Cut* (2003) lends itself even more than *Dans ma peau* to an exemplification of the paradoxes of representing femininity and female sexuality. The novel on which this film is based—*In the Cut* (1995) by Susanna Moore—sets up a strong relationship from the outset between the appearance of a female body-in-pieces (the murdered body of a twenty-six-year-old red-haired woman named Angela Sands) and

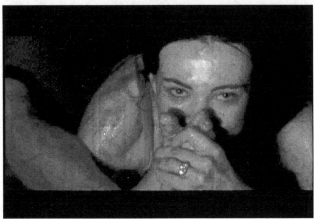

Figure 4.10
Film still sequence from *Dans ma peau* (2002). Courtesy of Marina de Van.

erotic desire (the attraction of the first-person narrator, Frannie,[15] for Detective James A. Malloy, who investigates this murder case in Manhattan's Washington Square neighborhood):

"How was she killed?"

"Her throat was cut." He paused. "And then she was disarticulated."

What a good word, I thought. Disarticulated.

He slid the notebook back into his pocket and took two cuff links from another pocket and turned down the sleeves of his shirt, and I remembered that it was masculine gestures that aroused me.[16]

The word "disarticulation" sticks to the English teacher, Frannie, who in her leisure time writes a slang dictionary in which she records such ambivalent and indicative words as "*skins*, n., sex from a female (as in 'getting some skins from the pretties'); or, *to do*, v., to fuck; *to do*, v., to kill."[17] Frannie experiences both threat and disgust from the word "disarticulation," but at the same time it triggers her arousal.

In fact, the ambivalent desire structure of the novel *In the Cut* is the driving force behind its narration. This is a story about a serial killer who engages in cutting techniques on his female victims (for instance, by carefully dismembering a woman's head between the fifth and sixth cervical vertebrae), but it is equally a story about the linguistic cutting that nearly all characters engage in when talking about femininity. For example, Frannie listens to this conversation between Detective Malloy and his colleague Detective Rodriguez: "Rodriguez looked away from the girl and said, 'You know, all you really need is two tits, a hole and a heartbeat.' Malloy said mildly, 'You don't really need the tits.' Rodriguez said, 'You don't even need the heartbeat.'"[18]

Adapting a similarly aggressive language, the victim Pauline, a nightclub dancer who lives in New York's red light district and Frannie's friend (in the film she becomes her stepsister, Pauline Avery), says to Frannie: "There are some people . . .usually women, whom you can fuck only if you have permission to kill them immediately afterward."[19]

In these and many other examples in the novel, femininity is disarticulated by the sharp knife of words at the same time as the serial killer's razor blade is literally cutting up female bodies. In *Dans ma peau*, a woman desires self-mutilation and hence is in a position of fragmentation. *In the Cut* is the counterpart to this experience, in that the female narrator experiences her own femininity through a desire structure that is aroused by the idea of being the object of the cut. In the novel, this desire ultimately devours her own body, delivering it in bits and pieces into the hands of her killer. The novel's death-driven ending differs from the film's more Hollywood-style happy ending:

I did not feel the razor when he cut me, only knew it an instant later with the sudden rush of heat and pain, the sting of it, the warm blood slaking down my arms and over my hands. It didn't hurt that much after I got used to it. It wasn't a bad cut. Not too bad.

He didn't mean to cut me, he said. But he couldn't help it.[20]

Cutting does not take place only in a literal sense. The misogynist (and racist) language delivered mostly by Detective Malloy "cuts" into Frannie's and the reader's consciousness. These linguistic cuts attract her, stimulate her, and intrigue her, as is shown by Frannie's linguistic dictionary, in which she collects misogynist and racist phrases from the New York streets. Frannie clearly desires the cut. She needs it for her own identification as a woman. In the film version, Malloy's linguistic cuts are complemented by the editing technique and other cinematographic measurements. When Frannie has sex with Detective Malloy in the novel, the language continues to be of a fragmented nature. Their bodies and particular body parts are interplaying here: "He let his arm fall from my neck, down across my chest, until his hand was on my breast, his fingers finding the nipple. He pulled me back against him. He had an erection. I could feel it."[21] Frannie's first sexual experience with Malloy is about his expertise with female genitalia (which he learned in his early years from an older woman), not about her body image, entire appearance, or even persona.

Like in *Dans ma peau* and even more expressively so, the particularized, "disarticulated" female body becomes the place from which femininity is spoken. In fact, femininity itself resides "in the cut." Toward the end of the novel, when Frannie is already under the serial killer's knife, she says the following revealing sentences: "Cutting me. He doesn't like it. I don't like it, either. I have a new word for the dictionary. Malloy told it to me. A street word. A word used by gamblers for when you be peepin', he said. In the cut. From the vagina. A place to hide. To hedge your bet. But some-place safe, someplace free from harm."[22]

It is "in the cut"—this dangerously safe place—that Frannie identifies her sexual drive. It is the position from which she peeped on a woman who in turn will become the first victim of the novel. This experience is what turns the novel on, quite literally. Not coincidentally, the woman and Frannie (in the novel) share the same destiny of being cut to death by a serial killer. But they also share, as Frannie informs the reader, "a secret that was exciting because it was dangerous to both of us: A woman with red hair had been on her knees with his red cock in her red mouth a few hours before having her throat cut and her arms and legs pulled from their sockets."[23]

The question I pose here is, what is cinema's relation to the skin of *Dans ma peau* and the cut of *In the Cut*? If activating the male gaze is a "masculine position," are women auteurs like Marina de Van and Jane Campion capable of telling a different story? My answer is yes. There is something different here, and it can be explained by the cinematic languages employed in these films.

From a technical, camera perspective, the "in" of either a "cut" or the "skin" represents an impossible position. One cannot inhabit the "cut" of *In the Cut* or the border designated by the skin in *Dans ma peau*. Both films deploy a viewing technique that undermines the essential duality of inner and outer that metaphors for the skin as border of the body have always required. Both films deal with the question of female fragmentation by editing woman. These directors are able to provide some answers to the question of the desire for cutting women by drawing our attention more to the cosmetic gaze than to the male gaze.

In *Dans ma peau*, fragmentation is rendered in the cinematographic layout of the film's end sequence. The screen is split in half, and the double frames suggest cut, isolation, break, the abyss. Fragments of Esther's cut-open skin are superimposed with fragments of her meticulous preparation for this "surgical intervention"—a knife, a marker, and a camera that documents her work. But there also is a mirror, which serves as an almost literal metaphor for her entering the precoherent fragmentation of the mirror stage. Esther looks at herself in the mirror, and we look at her from the fourth wall (from behind the mirror), helping her to create a body image. Viewers reconstitute the fragmented wounded body into the entire image of Esther that we have created in our minds throughout the film. This is a visual account of Lacan's mirror stage and the idea of the lack of an "original" bodily identity. Esther's fractal or dispersed body is waiting on the viewer's account for inscription and semantization from the outside world. Her wounded and bloody female identity lies—once again—in our hands.

In the case of *In the Cut*, one of the strongest elements for activating a female point of view is the cinematographer Dion Beebe's camera technique. The camera is often hand-held, and scenes are often shot with a primitive lens, which lends itself to the hand-held camera because the focus can be manually adjusted by the operator.[24] Campion's choice of a camera that speaks the language of fragmented femininity has been misrecognized by the popular press, however. For instance: "It's not just the opening shots here that are blurry and unsteady: the point and perspective of the whole film remain unfocused throughout."[25]

In the first scene of sexual arousal in the book as it appears in the film, Malloy speaks with Frannie, who is a potential witness of the murder of Angela Sands, in Frannie's apartment in lower Manhattan: "You don't remember seeing anything, hearing anything?" Frannie looks at his tattoo and says: "Can you tell me how it happened?" Malloy: "The throat was cut and then she was disarticulated." When he says the word "cut," the camera moves to Frannie. When Malloy says "disarticulated," the camera goes back to the detective, who in Campion's version is called Giovanni instead of James.[26] Frannie writes down the word "disarticulated," and the camera closes up on the handwritten word, ending the first quasi-erotic sequence. Much later in the narration, after having been mugged on the street and right before her first sexual encounter with Malloy, Frannie asks the detective again: "How was that girl killed?"

Malloy and Frannie's intimacy shortly follows this question and is linked with talking about the murders of a serial killer and the female body in pieces. Adding to this suspense—inherent to the figure of the "lady killer," whose power regime oscillates between "murdering a woman" and "arousing a woman"—the film version presents an even more ambiguous detective who, for the film audience, could be the killer.[27] Near the end of the film, the viewer is drawn into the diegetic film space, within which Malloy is only a detective.

The word "disarticulation" still resonates between them from their first encounter and inaugurates the first sexual encounter between Frannie and Malloy: "What exactly does disarticulation mean?" Frannie asks. Malloy tries to calm her down and explains: "He is trying to dismember the female body." In the same breath, he continues: "Show me. How did he [the mugger] hold you?" Malloy touches Frannie to reenact the attack. He takes her from behind, like the mugger, touching her breast. At this point, the camera loses its objective focus and zooms into the erotic act. Details are shown of their bodies: Malloy's (ambiguous) tattoo. Frannie brings a condom from the other room. She takes off her dress. Malloy gives her orders: "Take those [panties] off." Then he touches her buttocks and starts licking her genitals, giving her sexual pleasure. The connection between female sexuality and the "cut up" female identity is expressed explicitly.

While at a crime scene involving another dismembered female body (this one at a laundromat), Malloy gets a call from Frannie. Again, dismemberment and eroticism are combined into one scene. Malloy explains:

"Another girl has been murdered." Frannie: "What happened?" Malloy: "She has been cut up. We can't find her head. The fucking press is all over." Malloy quickly changes subjects: "Can you do something for me, will you?" He now gives her instructions to give herself pleasure. The red lights from the crime scene are cut against Frannie following Malloy's orders. "Slip your middle finger in that pussy that I like."

The next crime scene enters more invasively into Frannie's private story. The camera caresses her sexualized body, and in the next scene, Frannie finds the body parts of her stepsister, Pauline. At the police station, she wants to know exactly how her sister died, and Malloy, who she suspects of being the murderer, explains it to her:

This guy, this guy must have known her. He strangled her until she lost consciousness probably in the bedroom, then he dragged her to the bathroom, cut her throat, cut through the windpipe, the jugular, the epiglottis, the hyoid, the tongue, he held her by the hair and cut all around. This guy likes blood. When he got to the vertebrae, he needed a bigger knife to cut through that and he had one. He pulled the drain in the sink before he left, so he left us nothing that could help us. It scares me that this guy knows about drains.[28]

Malloy's aggressive language affects Frannie. When she asks him suspiciously where he was when Pauline was murdered, he responds, "Working." Frannie challenges him: "You mean getting blow jobs?" Malloy challenges her back, engaging her in a conversation about whether there can be a "bad blow job." This time, however, Malloy's competence about the crime does not arouse Frannie sexually but increases her suspicion that he is the murderer. She ends their conversation by asking, "Did you kill her?" Malloy does not answer the question but has his female colleague accompany her home, expressing his feelings of humiliation with the words: "Get the fuck out of here."

The scene that probably best explains the relationship between Frannie and Malloy is in one of the book's last chapters, called "Frannie Is in Control." Frannie handcuffs the detective to a pipe in her apartment and begins giving herself pleasure using Malloy's body like a sex toy. This scene in the film follows the novel exactly. Here Malloy utters the phrase "in the cut" in connection with their shared predilection for watching: "You like watching," I [Frannie] said. "Yeah," he said, "I like it in the cut."[29]

Malloy is "in the cut" of Frannie's femininity, of a woman taking pleasure. Frannie is in the cut of her own openness. The camera follows with a sensitive eye, at times even slightly out of focus, as if it were almost too close to the scene. The characters are both shown in pieces—Frannie's shoulder, mouth and nose, Malloy's hair from behind.

Activating the Female Gaze

As in other filmic tales and literary adaptations by Jane Campion (such as *An Angel at My Table, The Piano*, and *Portrait of a Lady*), *In the Cut* undermines the romantic myth of woman played out for the male gaze by centering on a woman's experience of the world and her point of view.[30] Frannie's private myth is alluded to near the beginning of the film in a black-and-white dream sequence of how her father, an elegant ice skater, proposed to her mother by kneeling down on the ice and offering her a sparkling engagement ring. The problem is that he proposes to her impulsively after seeing her for the first time on the ice while he was skating with his girlfriend. By grasping for love at first sight, the father sacrifices a previous relationship and hurts a woman who loves him. This romantic myth comes at the cost of great pain. This metaphor is not far from the story of *In the Cut*. Romanticism and sexuality are presented as interrelated with murder and tragedy.

The father's marriage proposal and his departure from his previous relationship takes place on ice, a surface that is white (tabula rasa), hard, and frictionless until the skates engrave and curve their weight into it. In the film, this inscription is rendered loudly and aggressively. We hear the skates cutting into the ice. It is "in the cuts" on the ice that the myth reveals itself. As Campion states in the director's commentary, Frannie is caught in the paradox of glorifying her parents' romance, which emanated from and is intrinsically related to the disappointment of another person. Later in the film, the destiny of Frannie's stepsister, Pauline, stands exactly in this tradition. The father left Frannie's mother and had Pauline with another woman, whom he never married. As Frannie says in a conversation with her sister, this disappointment literally killed Frannie's mother.

Unlike Esther's antipsychologism in *Dans ma peau*, Frannie alludes to many possible explanations for her psychological instability and ultimately for the tragedy of being a woman. After Pauline's death, when Frannie is at the police station, she tells Malloy a key story of her past: "When I was thirteen, my father left me in Geneva. He was called away to Washington for five days. He said later that it never occurred to him that I wouldn't be all right. Pauline said later that I failed to take advantage of the situation, that I should have ordered 100 boxes of chocolate and made a snowman."[31] Another place in the film where Campion's undercutting of romantic mythology resonates is a conversation between Frannie and her mentally disturbed former boyfriend, John Graham, who asks her: "Did I ever tell you that my mother used to dress me in girls' blouses?" John explains his difficulties and craziness by making his mother responsible for pushing him into being different.

The film's final sequence can be seen as an allegory for Frannie's female tragedy. We see Frannie, who has defeated the "monster" (the actual perpetrator, Detective Rodriguez), walking back from the lighthouse. As she approaches lower Manhattan, the camera looks at her from her own apartment. Frannie walks through her backyard, which is covered with white blossoms. She walks up to the apartment and lies down next to the handcuffed Malloy. The door closes. This sequence recalls images from the film's beginning, such as those of lower Manhattan. In the beginning, those images were juxtaposed with Pauline walking the same blossoming garden to visit her stepsister, Frannie. For Campion, this opening sequence has a special meaning:

It really is in a nutshell the whole film because it talks about the girl looking lost. The blossoms come down and it's a beautiful transcendent moment in their own little Manhattan garden. Frannie looks out the window and mistakes the blossoms for snow. It's all a series of mistaken identity. We think we have seen something and then we find out we haven't. Most human knowing is faulty and most of the time wrong. Everyone is in a private dream, a private mythology. The dream Frannie is trying to free herself from, she inherits from her mother. It's the romantic mythology from her mother's childhood. The romance is attractive to Frannie, but on the other hand, she saw the mother die because she was so betrayed by the father.[32]

Campion's filmic narration brings viewers into the mythic realm of romance, a realm within which the desire for a "happy ending" is presupposed and passively omnipresent: the myth is that the father marries the woman of his dreams (Frannie's mother), has a child with her, and stays with her until death separates them. In Campion's film, however, the cut superimposes itself on the myth. Paradoxically, the romance between Frannie and Malloy is activated only because of the cut and played out in the cut, the disturbance and injury of the myth. In other words, the myth can be established only on the abyssal foundation of the cut and as such is always threatened by its own undoing. The destiny of feminine subjectivity is to desire both, although they are mutually exclusive—the mythical whole of romance and its dissolution in the cut. If the conscious ego is drawn to the former, the latter is the realm of the unconscious and of sexual desire. In the case of *Dans ma peau*, however, the myth is never activated. We do not know why Esther engages in her self-mutilation. What remains the same is that she, too, cannot access femininity in any other way than by cutting into the female—her own—body.

What Campion means by "we think we have seen something and then we find out we haven't" is beautifully adaptable to this myth of broken family happiness. The characters she portrays are thrown into their worlds. They know something of their past, as is revealed in Frannie's dreams, but they follow a path that is marked by contingency. Frannie looks for clues in the world of the language poetry that she ardently collects. She looks for meaning and determinacy. What she gets back, however, is nothing but contingency. She walks down those steps at the bar and witnesses a sexual encounter between a female victim and her killer. She thinks she recognizes the tattoo on Malloy's arm, but eventually it is revealed as belonging to Detective Rodriguez. In other words, the cutting can also be read as castration, where castration is understood philosophically as the acceptance of contingency. The castrated mother gave life to Frannie and exposed her to the radical contingency of her own existence. It is not a coincidence that *In the Cut* ends with an eerie-sounding rearrangement of Jay Livingston and Ray Evans's song "Que Sera Sera" (1956):

When I grew up and fell in love, I asked my sweetheart what lies ahead. Will there be rainbows day after the day? Here is what my sweetheart said: Que sera sera, whatever will be will be. The future's not ours to see. Que sera sera. Now I have children of my own. They ask their mother what will I be. Will I be pretty, will I be rich? I tell them tenderly: Que sera sera, whatever will be will be. The future's not ours to see. Que sera sera.[33]

In both filmic tales, the female body is not left whole. In *Dans ma peau*, Esther cannot stop cutting herself; she carries the signs of a female body in pieces in her very skin. Indeed, the expresssion "in my skin" (*dans ma peau*) plays off and ironically contorts a common saying ("*Je suis bien dans ma peau*," I feel all right) to express the intricate relationship between violence, femininity, and sexuality. However, the female subjects of these films are no longer just made to simply desire femininity, as de Lauretis argues. Instead, femininity is addressed in both films as a position that is caught within the cosmetic gaze itself. There is no outside to this position but only an "in" the skin or the cut. We are presented with the status quo of a femininity that consists of fragmentation. There is no whole female body; there never has been. In these emblematic and artistic films, femininity has to be narrated and visualized in bloody bits and pieces to stress the impossibility of an outside gaze onto femininity.

The Spectator as Cocreator

According to the Freudian notion of the symptom as a form of wish fulfillment, Esther and Frannie both fulfill their desire for femininity by playing out their intense relationship with their own fragmented body images. Both characters manifest the problem that feminine subjectivity is always, to an extent, someone else's, although in different ways. For Esther, this is a desire to put all her "body cards" on the table: "Here is my body. It is not mine entirely. In fact, it may be yours. But I am going to take it back, even if it means cutting it and eating it." For Frannie, this desire is more unconscious. She is situated in the realm of mythical behavior that is not innate but learned and assumed through culture and her own family history. For Frannie, to be desired as a woman means running the risk of being cut. Similarly to Esther's abrupt outbreaks of self-mutilation, Frannie's sexual drive overcomes her in moments of linguistic or actual encounters with cut-up female bodies (the triggering word is *disarticulation*), and the construction of femininity as parceled feeds her sexual desire for Detective Malloy, whom she desires despite and because of suspecting him of murder. Frannie's vision of the female body always combines danger and sexuality. Her unconscious sexual desire is to be cut, but she notices the paradox that is inherent in this desire structure: "Those two girls sitting across from me on the bench, holding hands, smoking and arguing, are not going to keep their bodies intact and whole simply by locking their apartment doors at night."[34] As she explains to her stepsister, Pauline, there is no protection for the female body from falling into pieces. The danger is on them and on femininity.

Esther carries the dilemma of feminine, cut-up identity literally on her body. She shares her desire to exhibit her body and its vulnerability with a variety of female artists and performers, who have been in search of the female body's own space—a space that defines itself neither through lack of castration nor through the imitation of phallic power—since the actionist body art and the body performances of the 1960s and 1970s.[35]

The Austrian performance artist Elke Krystufek—one in a long list of female body performance artists, including Gina Pane, Yoko Ono, Valie Export, Orlan, and Cindy Sherman in the 1970s and the Abject Art movement of the 1990s—expresses the dilemma of severed subjectivity and the representational trap of femininity. In one of her collages that thematize self-mutilation through cutting, she writes: "Far from being suicidal, far from indicating a desire for self-annihilation, cutting is a radical attempt to (re)gain a hold on reality, or (another aspect of the same phenomenon) to ground the ego firmly in bodily reality, against the unbearable anxiety of perceiving oneself as nonexistent."[36]

Just as Esther in the ending sequence of *Dans ma peau* looks at herself in the hotel room mirror, Elke Krystufek looks at herself from the outside, often making use of mirrors. In Krystufek's work, the abused female body is displayed as abusive (of the viewer's cooperation). To avoid the trap of female representationalist paradigms (as pointed out by Jacqueline Rose, Teresa de Lauretis, and many others), "The artistic treatment of female subjectivity has to invest a great deal of irony, mockery and distance in order to ward off the danger of equating the vulva with the phallus in the hierarchical order of the sexes. [Krystufek's] collages, which could just as fittingly be called decollages, achieve just this."[37] In Krystufek's collages, sexual difference as well as the shifting difference in such viewer positions as display and observation, voyeurism and exhibitionism, are deconstructed as the artist performs both as victim and perpetrator, abuser and abused. Peter Gorsen theorizes about the reason that Krystufek—among other feminist artists—was able to create such a new space for female representation: "Only when feminism introduced a review of traditional gender relations did the change of perspective from the phallic to the vulva display of the obscene and abject body make it possible for women to switch from an objective and victimized status to assertive aggression and active self-defense."[38]

Esther's self-mutilation is not far from Krystufek's self-defense. Krystufek notes on the question of self-induced pain: "I don't see myself as a masochist. I see my work as an attempt to get away from it."[39] In *Suture* (1994), Krystufek touches on the female body's boundaries, its fractal

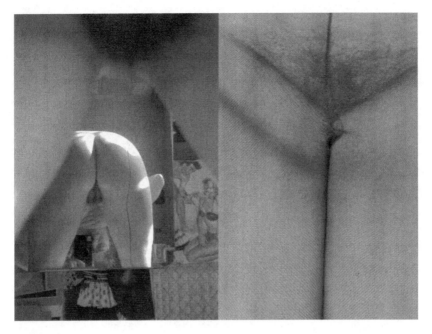

Figure 4.11
Elke Krystufek, *Suture*, 1994. Courtesy of the artist.

construction in the mirror and gaze of others, and its dependence on the outside perspective. This collage has a split frame: on one side, the artist looks at herself through her own legs (construction of self), and on the other side, there is an image of the "sutured vagina" in the other's gaze (figure 4.11).

The image can be compared to the ending sequence in *Dans ma peau*, in which Esther's self-mutilation performance is inaugurated with an image of her eye split by the reflective mirror (figure 4.12). The complexity of female representation, the union between the female subject's body and her environment (suture), and the violence of the viewership (eye) are here under investigation and accusation.

Using Jacques Lacan's terms, in *Dans ma peau*, Esther identifies with the symbolic *je* (*I*), the place from which I identify myself as the other sees me. The subject builds its ego under the auspices of the other's gaze, a place from which its fragmented bodily experience may be seen as whole and as "sutured" together. Lacan has depicted this process with the diagram of the inverted vase (figure 4.13).[40]

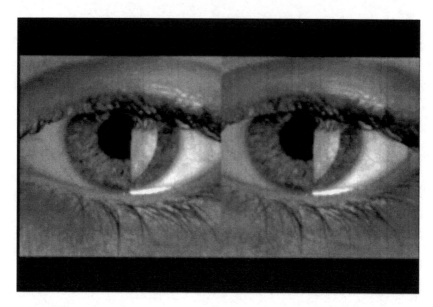

Figure 4.12
Film still from *Dans ma peau* (2002). Courtesy of Marina de Van.

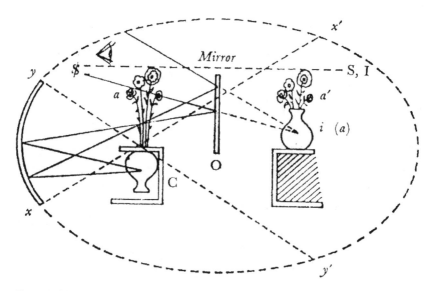

Figure 4.13
Jaques Lacan, "The Inverted Vase Diagram," from seminar 11, "The Four Fundamental Concepts of Psychoanalysis" (1973). Courtesy W.W. Norton.

Lacan's diagram, as William Egginton writes,

reproduces a parlor trick cum experiment in optics in which an observer can be made to see a vase with some flowers in a mirror where such an object, at least so arranged, does in fact not exist. What exists, on the side of the observer's body, is something else: a box, with the back side open and a vase suspended upside down inside it. Behind the box, about where the observer should be standing, there is a concave mirror. In front of the vase, and in the observer's line of sight, a flat mirror. If the observer is correctly positioned within the cone of light emanating from the concave mirror and converging on his or her visual cortex, he or she will see, reflected in the flat mirror, a virtual vase containing an equally virtual bouquet. The scenario is Lacan's metaphor for the constitution of the ideal ego. This image (the vase) attains its coherence in a virtual world, what Lacan calls the space of the Other. It is where the Other sees us, and where we see ourselves as seen by the Other.[41]

What unites the films of Marina de Van and Jane Campion with the art of Elke Krystufek can be seen, in its simplest form, as a view into the box, a gaze that sees the incoherence of a body's self-identification prior to the retroactive suturing that make its whole. Since this suturing in the case of women's bodies and identities is particularly violent, the female gaze as activated by these women artists can produce violent, disturbing representations. Unlike most media productions, their work reveals the underbelly of the romantic myths propagated by the cosmetic gaze.

In the reality makeover television format discussed in chapter 3, contestants are not allowed to see their mirror images during the months of their surgical, psychological, and dietary makeover. Viewers, however, have a global view of the entire process, from graphic depictions of surgery to intimate interviews and candid digital footage. Viewers are in the position of the people who are taking the pictures, the producers of Fox Reality TV. Viewers "help" the contestants find their new body image in the show's last scenes, when the participants look at the mirror—that is, the camera and the viewer's gaze pushing through the fourth wall. The audience literally occupies the place of the other and becomes the screen on which the contestants' fragmented identities are suddenly and drastically sutured together again.

As Lisa Dickson notes in her analysis of Tarsem Singh's *The Cell* (2000), the penetrating gaze of an audience-witness into a violent act on the screen opens up an array of problems.[42] In such cases, the spectators' "bodies and minds are violently opened by the gaze." As a result, she continues, their reception of the spectacle vacillates between such opposed poles as "art/science, beauty/grotesqueness, sympathy/repulsion, evil/ illness, living/dead, subject/object, self/other."[43] Likewise, the identities of the contestants on *The Swan* are displayed for the consuming gaze of spectators, who are also split by Dickson's boundary zones. The "new selves" are the outcome of an artistic intervention by a "team of experts" who have suggested a makeover for each woman based on "scientific knowledge." The viewer often cannot decide whether to look at the "new self" as beautiful or grotesque, whether to feel sympathy or repulsion, whether the women in question are being naïve or suffering from body dysmorphic disorder. Thus, what Dickson concludes for *The Cell* is equally valid for a reading of *The Swan*: "The penetrating gaze puts such categories into flux, deconstructing and challenging boundaries on which identity is based and through which social power is produced and maintained."[44] That said, the strategic intent of the show—the reveal that occurs before the loving eyes of family and with the supportive embraces of the team of experts—is to resolve the unsettling thrust of this gaze as quickly and positively as possible. We thrill at the sensational nature of the change that the contestants have undergone and quickly accept that the new self is really the old, authentic self they have been looking for all along.

There is a different contract at stake between television spectators and the "women under the knife" in *The Swan* and between film viewers and the performance examples in *Dans ma peau* and *Suture*. But these spectatorships are nevertheless related. In all of these representations, women undergo self-induced torture, and both kinds of spectatorships presuppose a constructed and literally sculptured female identity. But whereas the construction of Esther's identity and a new body image in her self-mutilating practices remains an open question, *The Swan* turns the spectator into a cocreator of the contestant's new self. When the contestants stand in front of the mirror and "discover" their makeover, they ask, "Is that really me?" and their question is affirmatively answered by a spectator whose gaze helps the contestant gain a new identity. This violation or transformation of the spectator into an interactive mirror that actively reshapes the women's identity fills most intellectuals with disgust, repulsion, or a sense of the uncanny.

By engaging the viewer in a masochistic gaze, Campion, de Van, and Krystufek point to the same problem of the inscription of meaning onto the female body, its trap of representation, and its dependency on the other's gaze. But they linger on the border terrain they are investigating, refusing to institutionalize the place of the spectator in its suturing function, whereas the body makeover show *The Swan* and its contestants construct a femininity that is based entirely on the usurpation of the gaze. *The Swan* is the romantic myth of the sutured femininity, which is disarticulated in Campion's film. This reality television spectacle had its crude genesis in how the female body had to be put together to fit the myth. The gaze activated in *The Swan* knows no other language than that of the homogenization of late capitalism. No markers of difference (such as ethnic traits, motherhood, or sexual difference) are permitted. This "economy of sameness" values only markers of U.S. middle-class normalcy, such as white teeth and small, symmetrical Caucasian noses.

The contestant's question in front of the mirror ("Is that really me?") can now be answered: "Yes, this is the real you! The you that you've always desired to be." In *The Swan*'s version, the real "you" of the contestants is a sutured and then sewn-up version of their original "self." From the feminist point of view proposed in this final chapter, *The Swan* is simply the vulgarized and popularized version of the problem that is inherent in the representation of female subjectivity and sexuality. The "swans" do not exist outside of the realm of the gaze; they exist for the camera's eye of reality television viewers. Unlike the characters in *Dans ma peau* and *In the Cut*, however, these women have given their bodies consciously and contractually to the publicly displayed performance of female tragedy, and contestants on *The Swan* have been chosen for their social value in the U.S. market. Although de Van, Campion, and Krystufek offer sophisticated views into the intricacy of the problem of displaying the female body, these swans have been given the answer—beauty as therapy.

Conclusion: From the Male Gaze to the Cosmetic Gaze

Modern makeover culture, as I show throughout this book, is about what Meredith Jones calls "the display of ongoing change and labour."[45] It requires a self-willing and able person to translate a mental picture into reality. In this way, the natural and implicit *kalókagatheia* of eighteenth-century physiognomy is coopted by a more instrumental culture: beauty is still the best indicator of virtue, but now this is the case because of the work you've put into it. Cosmetic surgery, in other words, figures within the realm of what Michel Foucault calls "technologies of the self," a self-care,[46] but it does so in the service of the cosmetic gaze. The cosmetic gaze is not a new way of being in the world and of looking. As is shown in chapter 1, different technologies convey and permit new possibilities for the cosmetic gaze to structure how bodies are perceived and lived. What is new about modern makeover culture are the technologies that facilitate looking at and construing the body as a screen. These body screens are simultaneously recipients and producers of a makeover self that tries to "carve out" an improved version of itself with the help of invasive and noninvasive makeover practices. The gaze at use in this process is circular. It looks at itself, projecting from inside out, but it uses the imagery of "ideals" that the culture craves and sells. This self projects onto its body screen neither what was nor what will be but what is "supposed to be." With the projection comes the imperative to see something new that has to be discovered. What it projects thus is a desire for change and improvement.

Modern makeover culture inherited the physiognomic predisposition of Johann Kaspar Lavater and the ethic of self-improvement that animated eugenics. That ethic remains, even as the horrors of the eugenicists' concentration camps decoupled it from openly racist and genocidal politics. Although the cosmetic gaze once expressed itself in the politics of racial cleansing, it has now been repackaged by technology into a socially acceptable care of the self.

This move has not gone unnoticed by culture. The possibilities offered by technology to re-envision and revise the physical body have been incorporated into our beauty ideals, but aesthetic and erotic impulses have pushed back, turning the artistic gaze on the violence of the cosmetic gaze and exploring—in literature, art, and film—beauty's dark side. Like any visual medium, cinema has not been immune to the cosmetic gaze. But acknowledging the operativity of the cosmetic gaze reveals another potential in cinema that parallels and undermines what has been called the male gaze. The male gaze objectifies the female body by totalizing it in a kind of corporatist fantasy as whole, fulfilled, ideal. The male gaze of traditional representations of the female body thus hides the violence of the cosmetic gaze. This violence, which is inherent to the act of *kosmein* (arranging and adorning) has been revealed in a feminist film, *Dans ma peau*, by a female auteur who is troubled by its destructive power.[47] These violent images undo the romantic myth of an original nature by revealing the convulsive beauty of the cosmetic gaze.

Notes

Introduction

1. As the chapters that follow make clear, this book is more technological critique than cultural-theoretical or political critique and thus complements in this regard the important contributions that Meredith Jones has made.

Chapter 1

The plates analyzed in this chapter are from The Sheridan Libraries at Johns Hopkins University's Special Collection. The 280 pen and ink drawings mounted on cardboard are some of the original drawings that Lavater drew for his *Essays on Physiognomy* (*Physiognomische Fragmente, zur Beförderung der Menschenkenntnis und Menschenliebe* [Leipzig: Weidmanns Ergen und Reich, 1775–1778]). Each drawing bears a date between 1775 and 1777 and a description in Lavater's handwriting. The translations of these captions from German are by Bernadette Wegenstein and Nora Ruck, unless otherwise referenced.

1. Plato, *Phaedrus*, trans. B. Jowett, http://www9.georgetown.edu/faculty/jod/texts/phaedrus.html, last accessed July 21, 2011.

2. I am following Kaja Silverman's reading of Jacques Lacan's *Four Fundamental Concepts of Psycho-Analysis*, in Kaja Silverman, *The Threshold of the Visible World* (London: Routledge, 1996), 133.

3. Silverman, *The Threshold of the Visible World*, 135.

4. The Lacanian notion continues to be operative here: the gaze is one of the fundamental *objets petit a*—a surplus piece of the real. I feel it looking at me and desire to occupy its place; it marks the disjuncture between how I see myself and how I want to be seen by others. In Lacan's words, "In the scopic relation, the object on which depends the phantasy from which the subject is suspended in an essential vacillation is the gaze." Jacques Lacan, *The Four Fundamental Concepts of Psychoanalysis*, ed. Jacques-Alain Miller, trans. Alan Sheridan (New York: Norton, 1977), 83.

5. *The Swan*, the collected DVD series, 2004–2006, Galán Entertainment, distributed by Xenon Pictures, Santa Monica, CA.

6. The ground was thus laid for the images of the "perfect body" that have been propagated by the twenty-first-century television makeover industry, which is analyzed in detail in chapter 3.

7. Norbert Elias, *The Society of Individuals* (Oxford: Blackwell, 1991).

8. Bernadette Wegenstein, *Getting under the Skin: Body and Media Theory* (Cambridge: MIT Press, 2006), 4.

9. Michel Foucault, *The Birth of the Clinic: An Archeology of Medical Perception*, trans. A. M. Sheridan Smith (New York: Vintage Books, 1973), xii (originally published in 1963).

10. Barbara Duden, *The Woman beneath the Skin: A Doctor's Patients in Eighteenth-Century Germany*, trans. Thomas Dunlap (Cambridge: Harvard University Press, 1991), 3.

11. Ibid., 4.

12. Carsten Zelle, "Soul Semiology: On Lavater's Physiognomic Principles," in *The Faces of Physiognomy: Interdisciplinary Approaches to Johann Caspar Lavater*, ed. Ellis Shookman (Columbia, SC: Camden House, 1993), 44.

13. Patrizia Magli, "The Face and the Soul," in *Fragments of the History of the Human Body*, part 2, ed. Michel Feher (New York: Zone, 1989), 89.

14. Ibid.

15. Plato, "The Republic," 402d, in *Plato: Complete Works*, ed. John M. Cooper, associate ed. D. S. Hutchinson (Indianapolis: Hackett, 1997), 1039.

16. The term was not invented by Plato. The notion of *agathoi* (the good) has been in circulation since Homer. In Athenian society, the *agathoi* were the most virtuous, best educated, and best equipped (by birth and through acquired skills) to rule next to the king and also as a group (*aristoi*) over the people (*demos*). This aristocracy was replaced in the sixth and seventh centuries by dictatorships, and the aristocracy became part of the *demos*. At the end of this development, the noble and "best" start to be labeled good (*agathoi*) and beautiful (*kaloi*). According to Julius Jüthner, this conjunction was an expression of a new social class of nobility that was identified not only by birth but also by merit and money. This class consisted in all types of deserving people from chevaliers to normal civilians. Julius Jüthner, "Kalogathia," in *Charisteria. Alois Rzach zum achtzigsten Geburtstag dargebracht* (Reichenberg: Verlag von Gebrüder Stiepel, 1930), 114–115.

17. *Liddle and Scott's Greek-English Lexicon* (New York: Oxford University Press), 1961, references *kalókagatheia* as "nobleness and goodness" and the original denotation

of *kalós kagathós* as the "perfect gentleman" and in a second denotation the "perfect character in a moral sense."

18. The compound noun was used only in the apocryphal *Definitions*. Plato referred only to *kaloi kagathoi* or alluded to the concept.

19. Robert E. Norton, "The Eighteenth Century and the Hellenic Ideal of *Kalokagathia*," *The Beautiful Soul: Aesthetic Morality in the Eighteenth Century* (Ithaca: Cornell University Press, 1995), 100–136.

20. An "Edelmensch" in Jüthner's words. Jüthner, "Kalogathia," 115.

21. Norton, "The Eighteenth Century and the Hellenic Ideal of *Kalokagathia*," 122.

22. Jüthner, "Kalogathia," 103, refers to Xenophon's *Symposion*, trans H. G. Dakyns, online at http://www.fordham.edu/halsall/ancient/xenophon-sym.html, last accessed July 21, 2011.

23. Xenophon, *Memorabilia*, 3.10.8, trans H. G. Dakyns, online at http://www.classicreader.com/book/1792/27, last accessed July 21, 2011.

24. Aristotle, *Metaphysics*, 1078a31, trans W. D. Ross, online at http://classics.mit.edu/Aristotle/metaphysics.html, last accessed July 21, 2011.

25. Norton, "The Eighteenth Century and the Hellenic Ideal of *Kalokagathia*," 133.

26. Jüthner, "Kalogathia," 107.

27. The use of the word *Neoplatonic* is evidently anachronistic, as the term was coined in the nineteenth century.

28. Plotinus, *The Enneads*, trans. Stephen MacKenna (New York: Larsons, 1992), 71–72.

29. Johann Gottfried Herder, "Ist die Schönheit des Körpers ein Bote von der Schönheit der Seele?" (1766), in *Sämtliche Werke I*, ed. Bernhard Suphan (Hildesheim: Georg Olms Verlag, 1877), 43.

30. Ibid., 56 (my translation from the German).

31. Norton, "The Eighteenth Century and the Hellenic Ideal of *Kalokagathia*," 101.

32. The French Enlightenment philosopher Voltaire was among Plato's sharpest critics.

33. Norton, "The Eighteenth Century and the Hellenic Ideal of *Kalokagathia*," 107.

34. From Brucker, *Critical History of Philosophy* (1767), quoted in Christopher S. Celenza, "The Revival of Platonic Philosophy," in *The Cambridge Companion to Renaissance Philosophy*, ed. James Hankins (Cambridge: Cambridge University Press, 2007), 93.

35. Norton, "The Eighteenth Century and the Hellenic Ideal of *Kalokagathia*," 113, characterizes Hölderlin as a "graecomaniac" in the context of his poem on Griechenland: "Ach! Es sei die letzte meiner Thränen, Die dem lieben Griechenlande rann, Laßt, o Parzen, laßt die Scheere tönen, Denn mein Herz gehört den Todten an! "Griechenland. An St.," in Friedrich Hölderlin, *Sämtliche Werke*, ed. Friedrich Beissner and Adolf Beck (Stuttgart: Cottasche Buchhandlung, 1946), 1:180.

36. Christoph Martin Wieland, *Sämmtliche Werke*, ed. by the Hamburger Stiftung zur Förderung von Wissenschaft und Kultur in Zusammenarbeit mit dem Wieland-Archiv, Biberach/Riss und Dr. Hans Radspieler, Neu-Ulm (Hamburg: Hamburger Stiftung zur Förderung von Wissenschaft und Kultur [Hamburg Foundation for Science and Culture], 1984), 4:183.

37. John Caspar Lavater, *Essays in Physiognomy Designed to Promote the Knowledge and Love of Mankind*, vol. 1, ed. Thomas Holloway, trans. Henry Hunter (London: Murray and Highley, 1789), 135. This is the sixteenth fragment "Of the Harmony between Moral Beauty and Physical Beauty," which is a translation from the German fragment nine.

38. Lavater supports himself with classical rhetoric by quoting book XI.3.72 of Quintilian's *Institutio Oratoria* (trans. by Christopher Celenza): "The face is the most dominant part of the head. It is by means of it that we are submissive, threatening, charming, sad, funny, proud, and humble. . . . Even before we speak, by it we express love and hatred from it we understand many things. Often enough, the face is equivalent to all the words we could possibly use." Quoted in Johann Kaspar Lavater, "Von der Harmonie der moralischen und körperlichen Schönheit" (fragment), *Physiognomische Fragmente zur Beförderung der Menschenkenntnis und Menschenliebe* (Leipzig: Weidmanns Ergen und Reich, 1775–1778), 59.

39. The German original uses the verbs *verekeln* (to make something disgusting), *verschlimmern* (to worsen), and *verschönern* (to beautify).

40. John Caspar Lavater, *Essays on Physiognomy for the Promotion of the Knowledge and the Love of Mankind*, trans. Thomas Holcroft, 4 vols. (London: C. Wittingham, 1804), 1:147–148.

41. Sander L. Gilman references the "great chain of being" in regard to the innate difference of the black and white races in nineteenth-century iconography: "in this view of mankind, the black occupied the antithetical position to the white on the scale of humanity. This polygenetic view was applied to all aspects of mankind, including sexuality and beauty." Sander L. Gilman, "Black Bodies, White Bodies: Toward an Iconography of Female Sexuality in Late Nineteenth-Century Art, Medicine, and Literature," *Critical Inquiry* 12.1 (1985): 212.

42. Lavater, *Essays*, 2:7.

43. Ibid., 12.

44. Lavater, *Essays* 1:7ff.

45. Lavater, 1:xiv.

46. Lavater, *Essays*, 4:131.

47. Lavater, *Essays on Physiognomy* 2:22.

48. Ibid., 28.

49. The Sheridan Libraries at Johns Hopkins University's Special Collection.

50. Lavater, *Essays*, 3:198.

51. Antisyphilis campaigns of the early nineteenth century are just one of many examples in which a public medical discourse drew on this type of parallelism. The French campaign *L'ennemi dans le sang* (the enemy in the blood), for instance, featured a seductive woman, presumably a prostitute, whose appearance is demonized by this caption: "while the woman looks pretty on the outside, she nevertheless has bad blood that could transmit the deadly disease of syphilis."

52. Plotinus, *Enneads*, 1.6.5.

53. Lavater, *Essays*, 3:202.

54. For a more elaborate discussion of the monster and its history, see chapter 2.

55. Lavater, *Essays*, 3:208.

56. Lavater, whose anti-Enlightenment sentiments were famous for being antagonistic to Jesuit rationalism, seems to have used this portrait and description as an outlet to his own feelings of resentment.

57. Lavater, *Essays*, 3:77–78.

58. Lavater, *Essays*, 2:209.

59. Lavater, *Essays*, 2:185. A beautiful Lavaterian nose is not small but is long and prominent and is symmetrically positioned in the face.

60. See, for instance, the words of Jesus, Son of Sirach, from around the second century BCE: "A woman's wickedness changes her appearance, and darkens her face like that of a bear. . . . A bad wife is chafing yoke; taking hold of her is like grasping a scorpion." Ecclesiasticus, or the Wisdom of Jesus, Son of Sirach, 25.24, The New Oxford Annotated Bible (Oxford: Oxford University Press, 2001), 136–137.

61. Nora Ruck, "Die Schöne und das Biest. Weibliche und 'monströse' Schönheit in Physiognomik und Schönheitschirurgie," *Koryphäe. Medium fürfeministische Naturwissenschaft und Technik* 45 (2009): 40–45.

62. Lavater, *Essays*, 2:31.

63. On the other hand, not too much of a focus. In a portrait entitled *Odd and Dumb Beauty*, we see a female face that is totally symmetrical, but her gaze is too still, so Lavater interprets her as staring dumbly.

64. Lavater, *Essays*, 2:43.

65. Ibid., 210–211.

66. Ibid., 209.

67. Charles Darwin, *The Descent of Man and Selection in Relation to Sex* (New York: Appleton, 1909), 568.

68. Francis Galton, *Inquiries into Human Faculty and Its Development* (London: Macmillan, 1883), 39.

69. Melissa Percival, "Introduction," in *Physiognomy in Profile: Lavater's Impact on European Culture*, ed. Melissa Percival and Graeme Tytler (Newark: University of Delaware Press, 2005), 18–20.

70. Ibid., 15.

71. Michel de Montaigne, *Essais*, book 3, chapter 12, "De la Physiognomie," ed. Pierre Villey, rev. Verdun L. Saulnier (Paris: Presses Universitaires de France, 1965), 1059.

72. Lucy Hartley, *Physiognomy and the Meaning of Expression in Nineteenth-Century Culture* (Cambridge: Cambridge University Press, 2001), 7.

73. Claudia Schmoelders, *Hitlers Gesicht. Eine physiognomische Biographie* (Munich: Beck, 2000), 23.

74. See the section on "Deviant Bodies: Criminals and Women = Monsters."

75. Schmoelders, *Hitlers Gesicht*, 28.

76. Marcel Proust, *Swann's Way* (New York: Penguin Books, 1984), 152 (originally published in 1913).

77. I return to the Darwinian notions of sexual selection and the evolutionary value of ornamentation and the resulting question of the connection between morality and aesthetics (Kant) in chapter 2.

78. "Eugenics is the science which deals with all influences that improve and develop the inborn qualities of a race." Francis Galton, "Eugenics: Its Definition, Scope and Aims," *Nature* 70 (1904): 82.

79. Galton, *Inquiries into Human Faculty*, 3–4.

80. For a critical discussion of the concept of objectivity inherent in Sir Francis Galton's physiognomy, see Peter Galison and Lorraine Daston, "The Image of Objectivity," *Representations* 40 (special issue titled "Seeing Science") (Autumn 1992): 81–128.

81. Kaja Silverman reminds us that, "the camera has been installed ever since the early nineteenth century as the primary trope through which the Western subject apprehends the gaze." Silverman, *The Threshold of the Visible World*, 135. The camera, originally operated by mainly male photographers, has therefore historically aligned itself with the "male gaze." I return to this point in chapter 4.

82. Silverman summarizes Lacan's point as follows: "The camera, like God and master, represents one of the persistent screens through which we have traditionally apprehended the screen." Ibid., 168.

83. Galton, *Inquiries into Human Faculty*, 6.

84. Ibid., 7.

85. Francis Galton, "Composite Portraits Made by Combining Those of Many Different Persons into a Single Figure," *Nature* 18 (1878): 97–100.

86. Galton, *Inquiries into Human Faculty*, 10.

87. Ibid., 11.

88. Ruck, "Die Schöne und das Biest," 40–45.

89. Galton, *Inquiries into Human Faculty*, 118.

90. Ibid., 118.

91. Galton, "Eugenics," 82.

92. In Galton's time, genetics was in its infancy. Around 1900, scientists knew that genes were transported on chromosomes, but the actual structure of the gene as consisting of a DNA strand with a coded sequence was discovered in the 1950s by James Watson, Francis Crick, and Maurice Wilkin.

93. Sharrona Pearl, *About Faces: Physiognomy in Nineteenth-Century Britain* (Cambridge: Harvard University Press, 2010).

94. I thank Nora Ruck for finding this subtitle.

95. As he writes, "During the classical period, there was a rapid development of various disciplines—university, secondary schools, barracks, workshops; there was also the emergence, in the field of political practice and economic observation, of the problem of birthrate; longevity, public health, housing, and migration. Hence there was an explosion of numerous and diverse techniques for achieving the subjugation of bodies and the control of populations, marking the beginning of an era of 'bio-power.'" Michel Foucault, *The History of Sexuality*, vol. 1, trans. Robert Hurley (New York: Vintage, 1990), 140.

96. Michel Foucault, *Discipline and Punish: The Birth of the Prison*, trans. Alan Sheridan (New York: Vintage, 1979), 277.

97. "Editors' Introduction," in Cesare Lombroso and Guglielmo Ferrero, *Criminal Man*, trans. and with an introduction by Mary Gibson and Nicole Hahn Rafter (Durham: Duke University Press, 2006), 15.

98. Ibid., 48.

99. Some of these are similar to the physical traits that Lavater lists by quoting the Storm and Stress poet J. M. R. Lenz (1751–1792): "It is evident to me that the Jews bear the sign of their fatherland, the orient, throughout the world. I mean their short, black, curly hair, their brown skin color. Their rapid speech, their brusque and precipitous actions also come from this source." Quoted in Lavater, *Physiognomische Fragmente*, 3:98. Those same traits later were described by racial theorists of the Third Reich. Paradoxically, Lombroso was a Jew and was featured by the main racial theorist of the Nazis, Hans F. K. Günther, as a prototypical Jew from Italy with oriental and other influences.

100. Philip K. Wilson, "Eighteenth-Century 'Monsters' and Nineteenth-Century 'Freaks': Reading the Maternally Marked Child," *Literature and Medicine* 21.1 (Spring 2002): 12.

101. Samuel R. Wells, *How to Read Character: A New Illustrated Handbook of Phrenology and Physiognomy for Students and Examiners with a Descriptive Chart* (Rutland, VT: Tuttle, 1971), 5 (originally published in 1895). For Lavater, the forehead had been of utmost importance. In "On Certain Individual Parts of the Human Body," he praises the forehead as "the most important of all the things presented to a physiognomical observation" (164).

102. Ibid., 6.

103. Ibid., 5.

104. Ibid., 124–125.

105. See chapter 3 for more details on twenty first-century before and after representations.

106. Cesare Lombroso, Enrico Ferri, Rafaele Garofalo, and Giulio Fioretti, *Polemica in difesa della scuola criminale positiva* (Bologna: Zanichelli, 1886), 5, quoted in David G. Horn, *The Criminal Body: Lombroso and the Anatomy of Deviance* (London: Routledge, 2003), 47.

107. The discipline of anthropometry, a discipline that studies the human measurements comparatively, was cofounded by Adolphe Quetelet, a Belgian criminologist. See his *Anthropométrie, ou Mesure des différentes facultés de l'homme* (Brussels: C. Muquardt, 1871).

108. Cesare Lombroso and Guglielmo Ferrero, *Criminal Woman, the Prostitute, and the Normal Woman*, trans. and with a new introduction by Mary Gibson and Nicole Hahn Rafter (Durham: Duke University Press, 2004), 107.

109. Horn, *The Criminal Body*, 13.

110. Lombroso and Ferrero, *Criminal Woman*, 107.

111. Ibid., 20.

112. Horn, *The Criminal Body*, 146.

113. Lombroso and Ferrero, *Criminal Woman*, 4.

114. Ibid., 37.

115. Ibid., 35–36.

116. Ibid., 43.

117. Ibid., 76.

118. Ibid., 76. For Darwin, it was exactly the other way round: the attractiveness of the male in the animal world is more important to ensure reproduction than the female. Hence, sexual selection is ensured when females are attracted by the voices or appearances of males.

119. For example, woman is rarely wicked, but when she is, she is worse than man.

120. Ibid., 142–143.

121. Ibid., 77.

122. Ibid., 78.

123. Ibid., 37.

124. Ibid., 37.

125. Horn, *The Criminal Body*, 23.

126. Lombroso, *Criminal Man*, 202.

127. Ibid., 205.

128. Ibid., 205.

129. Alphonse Bertillon, *La photographie judiciaire: avec un appendice sur la classification et l'identification anthropométriques* (Paris: Gauthiers-Villars, 1890).

130. Horn, *The Criminal Body*, 23.

131. Horn points this out, challenging the Enlightenment notion of the child as innocent. Ibid., 40.

132. I return to the discussion of photography and the cosmetic gaze in detail in chapter 3.

133. Lombroso, *Criminal Man*, 300.

134. On the relation between the visual media of the time and physiognomic theories, see Martin Blankenburg, "Der Seele auf den Leib gerückt. Die Physiognomik im Streit der Fakultäten," in *Gesichter der Weimarer Republik. Eine physiognomische Kulturgeschichte*, ed. Claudia Schmoelders and Sander Gilman (Cologne: Dumont, 2000), 280–301.

135. Erna Lendvai-Dircksen, *Flandern. Das Germanische Volksgesicht* (Berlin: Meisenbach Riffarth, 1942), 1 (my translation).

136. Hellpach does not compare southerners with northerners but southerners with Germans.

137. Willy Hellpach, "Erblehre und Rassenpflege. Der völkische Aufbau des Antlitzes," *Die medizinische Welt* 8.43 (1933): 1547.

138. Although DNA analysis is now able to assign individuals to racial groups, most scientists today agree that what we call race corresponds to a confluence of biological and social factors.

139. Hellpach, "Erblehre und Rassenpflege," 1548.

140. For a discussion of the opposition of modernists and antimodernists of the time (both of them sharing, however, the desire for a "new man," a "new body," and a "new image of man"), see Paula Diehl, "Körperbilder und Körperpraxen im Nationalsozialismus," in *Körper im Nationalsozialismus. Bilder und Praxen*, ed. Paula Diehl (Munich: Fink, 2006), 9–32.

141. Willy Hellpach, "Erblehre und Rassenpflege," 1549 (my translation) (the original: "[D]as stärkste und feinste Ausdrucksorgan des Menschen, eben sein Antlitz, ist auch ein Spiegel, der uns, Wohlbildung oder Fehlbildung der Menschenseele ablesen lässt. In erschütterndem Grade kann ein Gesicht dem Kundigen offenbaren, dass sein Träger weder ein eugenes noch ein euplastos ist! Zeugende Wohlartung (Eugenik) und führende Wohlbildung (Euplastik) verleihen uns erst die Herrschaft über die Natur, die noch wichtiger sein wird als die sachtechnische der Maschine: die Herrschaft über die Menschennatur!").

142. Ibid.

143. Jennifer Michael Hecht, "Vacher de Lapouge and the Rise of Nazi Science," *Journal of the History of Ideas* 61.2 (April 2000): 285–304.

144. As Sander L. Gilman notes in various places in his work—for instance, in "Die Rasse ist nicht schön—Nein, wir Juden sind keine hübsche Rasse," in *Der Schejne Jid: Das Bild des "jüdischen Körpers" in Mythos und Ritual*, ed. Sander L. Gilman, Robert Jütte, and Gabriele Kohlbauer-Fritz (Vienna: Picus Verlag, 1999)—the Jewish "ugliness" becomes the measure for their "bad character" inscribed into their body. In fact, in the Yiddish language, *beauty* refers to a character trait of the soul rather than of physical beauty (57–58).

145. According to Jack Zipes, Oskar Panizza borrowed the name of his protagonist in *The Operated Jew* from Friedrich Freiherr von Holzschuh's parody, *Die Manzipaziuhn der houchloebliche kienigliche bayrische Juedenschaft. En Edress an die houchverehrliche Herren Lanstaend, ousgestudiert von Itzig Faitel Stern* (1834). Jack Zipes, *The Operated Jew: Two Tales of Anti-Semitism*, trans. with commentary by Jack Zipes (New York: Routledge, 1991), 97.

146. The stations of anti-Semitism in the Christian West are many and intricate. The New Testament claims that "Jesus was killed by the Jews" (1 Thessalonians 2: 14–15), but at the same time the Bible is largely authored by Jews. The Jew as enemy figure in the late nineteenth century is built on a long history. There were anti-Jewish riots in Alexandria in the third century BCE, persecutions of the Jews in early medieval times, and an 1752 Austrian law that required Jewish families to limit their offspring to one son. In the nineteenth century, anti-Semitism was active in all areas of culture (for example, Richard Wagner's *Jewishness in Music* from 1850). At the time Panizza wrote his comedy about the inner and outer ugliness of the Jew Itzig Faitel Stern, Wilhelm Marr had already founded the Antisemitic League (1879). Fifty years later, on November 12, 1938, after *Kristallnacht*, Goebbels announced that "the Germans are an anti-Semitic people."

147. Panizza, *The Operated Jew*, quoted in Zipes, *The Operated Jew: Two Tales of Anti-Semitism*, 96.

148. Oscar Panizza, *Prolegomena to the Contest: Improvement of our Race*, in *Die Gesellschaft* 9 (1893): 275–289, quoted in Zipes, *The Operated Jew: Two Tales of Anti-Semitism*, 98.

149. Ibid.

150. Ibid., 100.

151. Panizza, *The Operated Jew*, quoted in Zipes, *The Operated Jew: Two Tales of Anti-Semitism*, 48.

152. Ibid., 68.

153. Ibid., 105.

154. The susceptibility for illness was interpreted as a result of Jewish life in the ghetto, "a place where illness cultivates itself and thrives." This was one of many truisms of the time spread by the French historian Anatole Leroy-Beaulieu, quoted in Gilman, "Die Rasse is nicht Schon," 60. The U.S. eugenicist Albert Wiggam was afraid that, by letting Jews into the country, the American race would be uglified (as he states ironically, "we want ugly women in America"). He therefore recommended that Americans marry only beautiful people and non-Jews to ensure a "race that is tumbling with physical and mental vitality." Albert Wiggam, *The Fruit of the Family Tree* (Indianapolis: Bobbs Merrill, 1924), 262–279.

155. Lavater had a different reading of color: "I find more strength, manhood, and thought, combined with brown than with blue [eyes]." Lavater, *Essays*, 2:171.

156. Hans F. K. Günther, "Die Blonden und Helläugigen unter den Juden," *Rassenkunde des jüdischen Volkes* (Munich: Lehmanns Verlag, 1930), 225–239.

157. Ibid., 229.

158. Ibid., 231. Günther quotes the famous German pathologist Rudolf Virchov (1821–1902) and a study of 10 million school children and their racial inheritance. Virchov, whose research in cell analysis was influential in later theories of the Aryan race, however, was the author of *Against Anti-Semitism* (1880).

159. Günther features the picture of Cesare Lombroso as a prototypically Jewish-looking face. The caption reads: "Jew from Italy. C. Lombroso, psychiatrist, 1856–1909. Southwest Asian [Vorderasien], oriental and other influences." Günther, *Rassenkunde*, 233.

160. Ibid., 1.

161. Ibid., 1.

162. Hecht, "Vacher de la Pouge and the Rise of Nazi Science," 299ff.

163. Allgemeine, SS-ärztliche Untersuchung für Verlobungs- und Heirats-Genehmigung, document no. B 37 o 10/18. 5. 37, National Archives, Genealogies of Waffen SS party members.

164. As summarized by Silverman, Lacan anthropomorphizes the gaze encouraging us to think of it more as the "symbolical third term, or Other, than as an imaginary rival." Silverman, *The Threshold of the Visible World*, 175.

165. Willy Hellpach, *Der deutsche Charakter* (Bonn: Athaeneum Verlag, 1954), 136.

166. The Holocaust is just one example of genocide in the twentieth and twenty-first centuries. In 1994, 500,000 Rwandan Tutsis were killed by the Hutu majority in Rwanda, and in the early twenty-first century, 400,000 Darfur-Sudanese were killed by the Sudanese government and the Arabic Janjaweed militia group. The basis for both African genocides were racial, ethnic, and religious differences, such as the non-Arabic lineage of the Darfurians, also called "blacks" by the Sudanese. The scope of this book cannot include the physiognomic principles underlying the racist roots of these African genocides, but in both of these cases, appearance is used as an explanation for the creation of the other and ultimately for mass murder.

167. Schmoelders, *Hitlers Gesicht*, 23.

168. For example, Jacques Lacan, Roland Barthes, Philippe Dubois, and Susan Sontag.

169. Christian Metz, "Photography and Fetish," in *The Critical Image: Essays on Contemporary Photography*, ed. Carol Squiers (Seattle: Bay Press, 1990), 158.

170. Silverman, *The Threshold of the Visible*, 149.

171. Roland Barthes, *Camera Lucida: Reflections on Photography*, trans. Richard Howard (New York: Hill and Wang, 1981), 10–12.

172. Craig Owens describes the action of a person who is about to be photographed as follows: "I freeze . . . as if anticipating the still I am about to become; mimicking its opacity, its stillness inscribing, across the surface of my body, photography's mortification of the flesh." Craig Owens, *Beyond Recognition: Representation, Power and Culture* (Berkeley: University of California Press, 1994), 210.

173. Susan Sontag, *On Photography* (New York: Strauss, Farrar & Giroux, 1977), 85.

174. Freud considered this schism of beliefs to be the true nature of fetishism.

175. Meredith Jones, "Media-Bodies and Screen-Births: Cosmetic Surgery Reality Television," *Continuum: Journal of Media & Cultural Studies* 22.4 (2008): 517.

176. For an in-depth discussion of today's morphing culture, see Vivian Sobchack, ed., *Meta-Morphing: Visual Transformations and the Culture of the Quick-Change* (Minneapolis: University of Minnesota Press, 2000).

177. See Jürgen Link, *Versuch über den Normalizmus. Wie Normalität produziert wird* (Opladen: Westdeutscher Verlag, 1997).

178. Suzanne Lipsky, "Internalized Racism," *Black Re-emergence* 2, http://www .rc.org/publications/journals/black_reemergence/br2/br2_5_sl.html.

179. Jennifer Fero, quoted in Barb Lee's documentary *Adopted*, Point Made Films, 2008. See also Cressida Heyes's argument about ethnic surgery as the perpetuation of the invisibility of whiteness. Cressida J. Heyes, "All Cosmetic Surgery Is 'Ethnic': Asian Eyelids, Feminist Indignation, and the Politics of Whiteness," in *Cosmetic Surgery: A Feminist Primer*, ed. Cressida J. Heyes and Meredith Jones (Surrey, UK: Ashgate, 2009).

180. William Egginton, "The Best or the Worst of Our Nature: Reality TV and the Desire for Limitless Change," *Configurations* 15.1–2 (special issue "Reality Made Over: The Culture of Reality Makeover Shows," ed. Bernadette Wegenstein) (2008): 177–191.

181. Silverman, *The Threshold of the Visible World*, 174.

182. Lacan, *The Four Fundamental Concepts of Psycho-Analysis*, 72.

183. Lorraine Daston and Peter Galison, *The Image of Objectivity* (New York: Zone, 2007), 117.

184. Joanna Zylinska, "Of Swans and Ugly Ducklings: Bioethics between Humans, Animals and Machines," *Configurations* 15.1–2 (special issue "Reality Made Over: The Culture of Reality Makeover Shows," ed. Bernadette Wegenstein) (2008): 125–150; Joanna Zylinska, *Bioethics in the Age of New Media* (Cambridge: MIT Press, 2009), 101–124.

Chapter 2

1. Plato, *Phaedo*, trans. Benjamin Jowett, http://www.classicallibrary.org/plato/dialogues/14_phaedo.htm, last accessed July 22, 2011.

2. Ibid.

3. Ibid.

4. Robert E. Norton, "The Eighteenth Century and the Hellenic Ideal of *Kalokagathia*," *The Beautiful Soul: Aesthetic Morality in the Eighteenth Century* (Ithaca: Cornell University Press, 1995), 129.

5. Plato, *Phaedrus*, 250d, as quoted in ibid., 128.

6. Plato, *Symposium*, trans. Benjamin Jowett, http://classics.mit.edu/Plato/symposium.html, last accessed July 22, 2011.

7. Plato, *Hippias*, trans. Benjamin Jowett, http://www.ellopos.net/elpenor/greek-texts/ancient-greece/plato/plato-hippias-major.asp?pg=9, last accessed July 22, 2011.

8. Ibid.

9. Konrad Paul Liessmann, *Schönheit* (Vienna: Facultas UTB, 2009).

10. Konrad Paul Liessman, "Vom Zauber des Schönen," in *Vom Zauber des Schönen: Reiz, Begehren und Zerstörung*, ed. Konrad Paul Liessman, Philosophicum Lech (Vienna: Paul Zsolnay Verlag, 2010), 8.

11. See William Egginton, *Perversity and Ethics* (Stanford: Stanford University Press, 2004), chap. 2.

12. As Woody Allen remarked after working with Penelope Cruz on his movie *Vicky Cristina Barcelona*, "I don't like to look at Penelope directly; it can be too overwhelming." Quoted in Ingrid Sischy, "The Passions of Penelope," *Vanity Fair*, November 2009, http://www.vanityfair.com/culture/features/2009/11/penelope-cruz200911, last accessed 7/22/11.

13. "The Moon," at http://www.br-online.de/br-alpha/koehlmeiers-maerchen/maerchen-michael-koehlmeier-mond-ID1209484217661.xml.

14. Howard Bloch, *Medieval Misogyny and the Invention of Western Romantic Love* (Chicago: University of Chicago Press, 1991), 65–92.

15. See Egginton, *Perversity and Ethics*, chap. 4.

16. Arthur C. Danto, *The Abuse of Beauty: Aesthetics and the Concept of Art* (Chicago: Open Court, 2003), xiv.

17. Ibid.

18. Ibid., xv.

19. David Hume, "Of the Standard of Taste" (1757), http://www.csulb.edu/~jvancamp/361r15.html, last accessed July 22, 2011.

20. Immanuel Kant, *Critique of the Aesthetic Power of Judgment*, ed. Paul Guyer, trans. Paul Guyer and Eric Matthews (Cambridge: Cambridge University Press, 2000), esp. 87–127.

21. Danto, *The Abuse of Beauty*, 68.

22. Ibid., 15.

23. Sharla Hutchison, "Convulsive Beauty: Images of Hysteria and Transgressive Sexuality: Claude Cahun and Djuna Barnes," *symplokē* 11.1–2 (2003): 212.

24. André Breton, *Nadja* (London: Penguin Books, 1999), 160.

25. André Breton, *Segundo manifiesto del surrealismo* (Madrid: Guardarrama, 1969), 164.

26. Breton, *Nadja*, 66–67.

27. Ibid., 101.

28. Ibid., 116.

29. Ibid., 112–113.

30. Ibid., 115–116.

31. Ibid., 159–160.

32. Nathaniel Hawthorne, "The Birthmark," at http://www.online-literature.com/hawthorne/125.

33. Virginia Blum, *Flesh Wounds: The Culture of Cosmetic Surgery* (Berkeley: University of California Press, 2003), 94.

34. Ibid., 96.

35. Hawthorne, "The Birthmark."

36. Blum, *Flesh Wounds*, 96. Blum notes that Daguerre fixed his first imprint in 1839, four years before Hawthorne's story.

37. Ibid., 96.

38. Alice Munro, "Face," *The New Yorker*, September 8, 2008, 59–67.

39. Ibid., 66.

40. Ibid., 66.

41. Ibid., 67.

42. Lucy Grealy, *Autobiography of a Face* (New York: Harper Perennial, 2003) (originally published in 1994).

43. Ibid., 5.

44. Ibid., 152.

45. Ibid., 127.

46. Ibid., 112.

47. Ibid., 7.

48. Ibid., 101.

49. Ibid., 157.

50. Ibid., 175–175.

51. Ibid., 176.

52. Ibid.

53. Ibid., "Afterword" by Ann Patchett, 232–233.

54. Jessica Queller, *Pretty Is What Changes* (New York: Spiegel and Grau, 2009), 92.

55. Ibid., 109.

56. Ibid., 113.

57. Ibid., 124.

58. Ibid., 133.

59. Ibid., 195.

60. Jessica's birth name was Tiffany, which she changed, as she says, as an explicit rejection of her mother.

61. Queller, *Pretty Is What Changes*, 239.

62. From *New Beauty* (Winter-Spring 2010): 194.

63. Marquard Smith, "The Vulnerable Articulate: James Gillingham, Aimee Mullins, and Matthew Barney," in *The Prosthetic Impulse: From a Posthuman Present to a Biocultural Future*, ed. Marquard Smith and Joanne Morra (Cambridge: MIT Press, 2006), 43–72, 59.

64. Lee Bul, interview with Seung-duk Kim, *art press* (Paris) 279 (May 2002): 2.

65. Rosi Braidotti, *Madri, mostri e macchine* (Milano: Manifestolibri, 2005), 83.

66. Ulisse Aldrovandi, *Ulyssis Aldrovandi patricii Bononiensis Monstrorum historia* (Bologna: Typsi Nicolai Tebaldini, 1642).

67. Braidotti, *Madri, mostri e machine*, 85.

68. K. E. Olsen and L. A. J. R. Houwen, *Monsters and the Monstrous in Medieval Northwest Europe* (Leuven: Peeters, 2001).

69. Ibid.

70. Barabara Duden, *The Woman beneath the Skin: A Doctor's Patients in Eighteenth-Century Germany*, trans. Thomas Dunlap (Cambridge: Harvard University Press, 1991), 4.

71. Nicolas Andry, *Orthopaedia*, facsimile reproduction of the first edition in English, London, 1743 (Philadelphia: Lippincott, 1961) (French original: *L'orthopédie ou l'art de prévenir et de corriger dans les enfants les difformités du corps; le tout par des moyens à la portée des pères et mères et toutes les personnes qui ont des enfants à élever*, 1741).

72. In today's makeover culture, the tree would not need to be rectified because surgical technology is always available as a way of returning it to its natural state (see chapter 3). This is a natural extension of the normalization of deviance discussed in chapter 1. The monsters who were displayed and gawked and marveled at have been replaced with bodies that have "gone wrong"—deviant bodies with "out"-growths and hence with parts that are not meant to be or were not meant to have grown.

73. Nora Ruck, "Die Schöne und das Biest. Weibliche und 'monströse' Schönheit in Physiognomik und Schönheitschirurgie," *Koryphäe. Medium fürfeministische Naturwissenschaft und Technik* 45 (2009): 40–45; John Caspar Lavater, *Essays on Physiognomy for the Promotion of the Knowledge and the Love of Mankind*, trans. Thomas Holcroft, 4 vols. (London: C. Wittingham, 1804), 3:188.

74. Philip K. Wilson, "Eighteenth-Century 'Monsters' and Nineteenth-Century 'Freaks': Reading the Maternally Marked Child," *Literature and Medicine* 21.1 (2002): 11.

75. Such normalization is symptomatic of what Foucault terms *productive* as opposed to *repressive power*: "What the eighteenth century established through the 'discipline of normalization' seems to me to be a power that is not in fact repressive but productive." See Michel Foucault, *Abnormal: Lectures at the Collège de France 1974–1975* (New York: Picador, 1999), 52.

76. See Lorraine Daston and Katharine Park, *Wonders and the Order of Nature 1150–1750* (New York: Zone Books, 1998), 205.

77. Lavater, *Essays on Physiognomy*, 3:156.

78. Ibid., 3:39.

79. Cesare Lombroso and Guglielmo Ferrero, *Criminal Woman, the Prostitute, and the Normal Woman*, trans. and with a new introduction by Mary Gibson and Nicole Hahn Rafter (Durham: Duke University Press, 2004), 183–184.

80. David G. Horn, *The Criminal Body and the Anatomy of Deviance* (London: Routledge, 2003), 16.

81. Chuck Palahniuk, *Invisible Monsters* (New York: Norton, 1999), 32.

82. Ibid., 45.

83. Ibid., 296–297.

84. Chuck Palahniuk, at http://chuckpalahniuk.net/books/invisible-monsters.

85. Palahniuk, *Invisible Monsters*, 31.

86. Joan Kron, "Michael Jackson's Dermatologist and Former Plastic Surgeon Talk," *Allure* (September 2009), at http://www.allure.com/celebrity-trends/2009/michael_jackson#intro, last accessed July 22, 2011.

87. Sander L. Gilman, *Making the Body Beautiful Beautiful: A Cultural History of Aesthetic Surgery* (Princeton, NJ: Princeton University Press, 1999), 333.

88. Michael Jackson, at http://www.everythingoprah.com/2009/06/michael-jackson-interview-with-oprah-winfrey-full-hour-at-the-neverland-ranch.html.

89. Meredith Jones, *Skintight: An Anatomy of Cosmetic Surgery* (Oxford: Berg, 2008), 161–164.

90. Michael Eric Dyson, "Black Superhero," *Rolling Stone*, special commemorative issue "Michael Jackson 1958–2009," July 2009, 73.

91. See the documentary film *This Is It* (HBO, 2010).

92. Blog entries at http://www.awfulplasticsurgery.com/2009/06/27/michael-jackson-the-plastic-surgery-years.

93. Email from Tara to Bernadette Wegenstein, June 22, 2010.

94. Ibid.

95. Jones, *Skintight: An Anatomy of Cosmetic Surgery*, 107.

96. Meredith Jones, "Makeover Culture's Dark Side: Breasts, Death and Lolo Ferarri," *Body & Society* 14.1 (2008): 87–102.

97. Jones calls her a feminist.

98. Nkrumah Shabazz Stewart, Kruma's Web blog, at http://www.8bm.com/?p=727, also quoted in Jones, "Makeover Culture's Dark Side," 88.

99. Parts of this section, originally titled "The New Attractivity," were written with Nora Ruck for "On Physiognomy, Reality Television, and the Cosmetic Gaze," *Body & Society* (forthcoming). Special thanks to Nora Ruck.

100. One exception is Ran Hassin and Yaacov Trope, "Facing Faces: Studies on the Cognitive Aspects of Physiognomy," *Journal of Personality and Social Psychology* 78 (2000): 837–852.

101. Michael R. Cunningham et al., "Their Ideals of Beauty Are, on the Whole, the Same as Ours: Consistency and Variability in the Cross-Cultural Perception of Female Physical Attractiveness," *Journal of Personality and Social Psychology* 68 (1995): 261.

102. Karen K. Dion, E. Berscheid, and E. Walster, "What Is Beautiful Is Good," *Journal of Personality and Social Psychology* 24 (1972): 285–290.

103. Randy Thornhill, "Darwinian Aesthetics," in *Handbook of Evolutionary Psychology*, ed. Charles B. Crawford and Dennis L. Krebs (Mahwah, NJ: Erlbaum, 1998), 543–572.

104. Victor S. Johnston, "Facial Beauty and Mate Choice Decisions," 2008, unpublished article.

105. Judith H. Langlois et al., "Maxims or Myths of Beauty? A Meta-analytic and Theoretical Review," *Psychological Bulletin* 126 (2000): 390.

106. Cunningham, "Their Ideals of Beauty Are, on the Whole, the Same as Ours," 261. With popular writers, the authors refer among others to Naomi Wolf, *The Beauty Myth: How Images of Beauty Are Used against Women* (New York: Morrow, 1991).

107. Karl Grammer, "Darwin'sche Ästhetik: Die evolutionspsychologischen Grundlagen der Schöenheit," in *Vom Zauber des Schönen: Reiz, Begehren und Zerstörung*, ed. Konrad Paul Liessmann (Vienna: Paul Zsolnay Verlag, 2010), 215–231, 222.

108. Winfried Menninghaus, *Das Versprechen der Schöenheit* (Frankfurt: Surhkamp, 2003), 159.

109. Grammer, "Darwin'sche Ästhetik," 221.

110. Ibid., 218.

111. Peter J. Brown and Melvin Konner, "An Anthropological Perspective on Obesity," *Annals of the New York Academy of Sciences* 449 (1987): 29–46, 42, quoted in Menninghaus, *Das Versprechen der Schöenheit*, 162.

112. Judith H. Langlois and Lori A. Roggman, "Attractive Faces Are Only Average," *Psychological Science* 1 (1990): 115–121.

113. Cunningham, "Their Ideals of Beauty," 263.

114. Johnston, "Facial Beauty and Mate Choice."

115. Ibid.

116. Jonathan Van Meter, "The New New Face," in "About-Face," *New York Magazine*, August 3, 2008, 86.

117. As Stephen Marquardt explains on his Web site: "The 'Golden Ratio' is a mathematical ratio of 1.618:1 that seems to appear recurrently in beautiful things in nature as well as in other things that are seen as 'Beautiful.' . . . Many things found in nature have parts that are in a ratio of 1.618:1." http://www.beautyanalysis.com/index2_mba.htm.

118. Marquardt is currently working on a full-body mask.

119. Interview with the author, April 23, 2009.

120. Tommer Leyvand, Daniel Cohen-Or, Gideon Dror, and Dani Lischinski, "Data-Driven Enhancement of Facial Attractiveness," *ACM Transaction on Graphics* 27.3 (August 2008): 1.

121. Telephone interview with Stephen Marquardt, June 10, 2009.

122. Danto, *The Abuse of Beauty*, 68.

123. Ibid., 69.

124. Ibid., 70–71.

125. July Albright, "TV Viewing Habits," *Configurations* 15.1–2 (special issue "Reality Made Over: The Culture of Reality Makeover Shows," ed. Berndette Wegenstein) (2008): 107.

126. Deborah L. Rhode, *The Beauty Bias: The Injustice of Appearance in Life and Law* (Oxford: Oxford University Press, 2010), 2.

127. Van Meter, "About Face," 28.

128. Telephone interview with Stephen Marquardt, June 10, 2009.

129. Interview with Tara, founder of Awfulplasticsurgery.com, June 3, 2010.

130. Ibid.

Chapter 3

1. Xenophon, *Memorabilia*, 3.10.4–7, trans H. G. Dakyns, online at http://www.classicreader.com/book/1792/27, last accessed July 21, 2011.

2. Jay David Bolter, Blair MacIntyre, Michael Nitsche, and Kathryn Farley, "Liveness, Presence, and Performance in Contemporary Digital Media," in *Throughout: Art and Culture Emerging with Ubiquitous Computing*, ed. Ulrik Ekman (Cambridge: MIT Press, 2012).

3. Carsten Zelle, "Soul Semiology: On Lavater's Physiognomic Principles," in *The Faces of Physiognomy: Interdisciplinary Approaches to Johann Caspar Lavater*, ed. Ellis Shookman (Columbia, SC: Camden House, 1993), 52.

4. Lucy Hartley, *Physiognomy and the Meaning of Expression in Nineteenth-Century Culture* (Cambridge: Cambridge University Press, 2001), 3.

5. C. U. M. Smith argues that visual thought is and has always been at the core of neurobiological science. C. U. M. Smith, "Visual Thinking and Neuroscience," *Journal of the History of the Neurosciences* 17.3 (July 2008): 260–273.

6. See an article on the beautification software program developed by Tommer Leyvand at Tel Aviv University. Sarah Kershaw, "The Sum of Your Facial Parts," *New York Times*, October 9, 2008, E1–E3.

7. The *Diagnostic and Statistical Manual of Mental Disorders (DSM-IV)* provides the following psychiatric diagnostic criteria for body dysmorphic disorder: "1. Preoccupation with some imagined defect in appearance. If a slight physical anomaly is present, the person's concern is markedly excessive. 2. The preoccupation causes clinically significant distress or impairment in social, occupational, or other important areas of functioning. 3. The preoccupation is not better accounted for by another mental disorder (e.g., dissatisfaction with body shape and size in anorexia nervosa)." As quoted in Katharine A. Phillips, *The Broken Mirror: Understanding and Treating Body Dysmorphic Disorder* (New York: Oxford University Press, 1996), 33.

8. Eric Wilson, "In a Light More Flattering," *New York Times*, August 13, 2009, E4.

9. Meredith Jones, *Skintight: An Anatomy of Cosmetic Surgery* (Oxford: Berg, 2008), 1.

10. Charles Miller, *The Correction of Featural Imperfections* (Chicago: Oak Printing, 1908), 3.

11. Elizabeth Haiken, *Venus Envy: A History of Cosmetic Surgery* (Baltimore: Johns Hopkins University Press, 1997), 94–95.

12. Cressida J. Heyes and Meredith Jones, "Cosmetic Surgery in the Age of Gender," in *Cosmetic Surgery: A Feminist Primer*, ed. Cressida J. Heyes and Meredith Jones (Surrey, UK: Ashgate, 2009), 5.

13. See http://www.surgery.org/media/news-releases. In 2008, there was a 12 percent decrease in the total number of over 10 million cosmetic procedures (15 percent for surgical and 12 percent for nonsurgical), and the numbers for 2009 decreased by 2 percent. As Anthony Elliott points out in his book *Making the Cut: How Cosmetic Surgery Is Transforming Our Lives* (London: Reaktion Books, 2008), "many patients seeing cosmetic and plastic surgeons in the U.S. consult experts from other organizations" (23), which means that these numbers are lower than the actuality. In the United Kingdom, as Elliott reports, estimates of how many procedures have been done in a given year are difficult to find because recent figures delivered by

the British Association of Aesthetic Plastic Surgeons did not include noninvasive procedures.

14. Procedures increased by 457 percent over one decade: in 1997, 176,863 liposuctions were performed, and in 2007, 456,828 were performed. Over the same period, breast augmentations increased by almost four times, and reductions increased by three times. Noninvasive procedures in the United States increased by an ever greater percentage. In 1997, 65,157 Botox injections were performed as the top nonsurgical intervention; in 2006, 3,181,592 injections were performed; and in 2007, 2,775,176 were performed.

15. Heyes and Jones, "Cosmetic Surgery in the Age of Gender," 3.

16. These data have to be read against the current U.S. demographics of a total of 298,757,310 Americans, of whom 74.1 percent are white, 12.4 percent black, 4.3 percent Asian, and 3.5 percent Hispanics. Data from the 2005–2007 American Community Survey three-year estimates, http://factfinder2.census.gov/faces/nav/jsf/pages/index.xhtml, last accessed July 22, 2011.

17. Elliott, *Making the Cut*, 7. Referenced is a survey conducted by *Grazia* magazine in 2005, quoted by Decca Aitkenhead in "Most British Women Now Expect to Have Cosmetic Surgery in Their Lifetime," *The Guardian*, September 14, 2005. Elliott also mentions Asia, particularly China, which spends more than $2.4 billion per year on cosmetic surgery (27), as new flourishing markets for cosmetic surgery procedures, both invasive and noninvasive.

18. Elliott, *Making the Cut*, 41.

19. See http://www.nbc.com/im-a-celebrity.

20. Jay David Bolter and Diane Gromala, *Windows and Mirrors: Design, Digital Art, and the Myth of Transparency* (Cambridge: MIT Press, 2003), 83.

21. On the first episode of the show that aired on June 1, 2009, the reality TV star Spencer Pratt (MTV's *The Hills*) reproaches the retired American professional wrestler, Torrie Wilson, for not being "famous" enough to be on the show with him.

22. Chris Rojek, *Celebrity* (London: Reaktion Books, 2002), 20.

23. Alan Riding calls this phenomenon *celebrityology*, which is the emptying of the self to make room for "whatever your neighbor is so cool about." See Alan Riding, "Entr'acte: The Lesson for Today Is: Study 'Celebrityology,'" *International Herald Tribune*, September 29, 2005, 2.

24. Virginia L. Blum, "Objects of Love: *I Want a Famous Face* and the Illusions of Star Culture," *Configurations* 15.1–2 (special issue "Reality Made Over: The Culture of Reality Makeover Shows," ed. Bernadette Wegenstein) (2008): 33–53. Blum's analysis is based on the television show *I Want a Famous Face*, season 2, episode 11, 2004.

25. See http://www.cindyjackson.com. But the attempt to look like someone is not restricted to a skin-deep assimilation. The fashion catalogs for H&M and similar brands document a global youth look that mimics Paris Hilton, Hannah Montana, and the characters on the Nickelodeon TV shows *iCarly*.

26. Elliott, *Making the Cut*, 43.

27. In prosperous economic times, people are more likely to engage in cosmetic surgery.

28. Alex Kuczynski, *Beauty Junkies: Inside our $15 Billion Obsession with Cosmetic Surgery* (New York: Doubleday, 2006), 196–198.

29. See Cressida Heyes's discussion of the relation between body dysmorphic disorder and cosmetic surgery and her problematization of the term. Cressida Heyes, "Diagnosing Culture: Body Dismorphic Disorder and Cosmetic Surgery," *Body & Society* 15.4 (2009): 73–93.

30. Kuczynski, *Beauty Junkies*, 196.

31. According to the Social Research Centre: "Among women over 18 looking at themselves in the mirror, research indicates that at least 80% are unhappy with what they see. . . . Research confirms what most of us already know: that the main focus of dissatisfaction for most women looking in the mirror is the size and shape of their bodies, particularly their hips, waists and thighs." Kate Fox, "Mirror, Mirror: A Summary of Research Findings on Body Image," http://www.sirc.org/publik/mirror.html.

32. Elliott, *Making the Cut*, 45.

33. Ibid., 46.

34. Kuczynski, *Beauty Junkies*, 18.

35. Dan Bilevsky, "If Plastic Surgery Won't Convince You, What Will?," *New York Times*, May 24, 2009, http://www.nytimes.com/2009/05/25/world/europe/25iht-nurses.html.

36. Elliott, *Making the Cut*, 109. "Richard Daley" is a pseudonym of a real person studied by Elliott.

37. Ibid., 111.

38. See the documentary film *Made Over in America: A Voyage to the Land of Makeover*, directed and produced by Bernadette Wegenstein and Geoffrey Alan Rhodes, Icarusfilms, 2007.

39. Kathy Davis, *Reshaping the Female Body: The Dilemma of Cosmetic Surgery* (New York: Routledge, 1995), 79.

40. For Susan, *French* and *Italian* often seem interchangeable with *good* and *beautiful*. She refers to the landscape around Newport Beach as Italian and to the houses in the area as looking like French castles.

41. Elaine Tyler May, *Homeward Bound: American Families in the Cold War Era* (New York: Basic Books, 1988).

42. Jonathan Van Meter, "The New New Face," *New York Magazine*, August 11, 2008, 87.

43. Ibid.

44. Rebecca Gardyn, "The Tribe Has Spoken: Reality TV Is Here to Stay," *American Demographics*, September 2001, 34–40.

45. Mark Andrejevic, *Reality TV: The Works of Being Watched* (Oxford: Rowman & Littlefield, 2004), 7.

46. The May 2009 finale of *American Idol* averaged 28.8 million viewers, drawing 40 million during the show's last seven minutes. http://tvbythenumbers.zap2it.com/2009/05/21/wednesday-ratings-american-idol-finale-surprise-draws-288-million/19222, last accessed July 22, 2011.

47. Chad Raphael, "The Political Economic Origins of Reali-TV," in *Reality TV: Remaking Television Culture*, ed. Susan Murray and Laurie Ouellette (New York: New York University Press, 2004), 119. For the term *reali-TV*, Raphael refers to an article by Ed Siegel, "It's Not Fiction. It's Not News. It's *Not* Reality. It's Reali-TV," *Boston Globe*, May 26, 1991, A1.

48. Filippo Tommaso Marinetti, *Teoria e invenzione futurista* (TIF), ed. Luciano de Maria (Milan: Arnoldo Mondadori Editore, 1968) (my translations from the Italian).

49. See http://softcinema.net.

50. The first commercially licensed television stations in the United States were established in the late 1940s and early 1950s.

51. See my discussion of recent realist film traditions—including the Scandinavian Dogme 95 films, the black American urban films of the 1990s, the Romanian New Wave's films of Cristi Puiu and Cristian Mungiu, and the recent Italian new realist films such as *Gomorra* (Cannes Palme d'Or, 2008)—in Bernadette Wegenstein, "Italien als zona grigia. Der italienischen Film des neuen Millenniums zeigt ein Land im Ausnahmezustand," *Maske & Kothurn* 56 (2010) (special issue "Das italienische Kino im neuen Millennium," ed. Birgit Wagner and Daniel Winkler), 15–35.

52. As David Bordwell points out, the European neorealist film tradition was labeled "art-cinema" in opposition to an already booming Hollywood studio film industry. David Bordwell, *Narration in the Fiction Film* (Madison: University of Wisconsin Press, 1987), 229–231.

53. Andrejevic, *Reality TV*, 9.

54. Wegenstein and Rhodes, *Made Over in America*.

55. André Bazin, "The Myth of Total Cinema" (1946), reprinted in André Bazin, *What Is Cinema?* (Los Angeles: University of California Press, 2005), 17–23 (originally published in 1958).

56. Sam Dilorio, "Total Cinema: *Chronique d'un été* and the End of Bazinian Film Theory," *Screen* 48.1 (Spring 2007): 29.

57. I saw Jean Baudrillard's video in the exhibition "The Cinema Effect: Illusion, Reality, and the Moving Image. Part II: Realism," Hirshhorn Museum and Sculpture Garden, Washington, DC, June 19–September 7, 2008.

58. Kristen Hileman, "Man and the Movie Camera," in *The Cinema Effect: Illusion, Reality, and the Moving Image*, Exhibition catalog (London: D. Giles, 2008), 104.

59. Lecture by Jean Baudrillard, "The Violence of the Image," European Graduate School, September 1, 2004, http://www.youtube.com/watch?v=9QF-eThkBOg&feature =related.

60. As Baudrillard points out, however, the perfect crime is never "perfect." Something always gets left behind, as we know from murder mysteries. In the case of the murder of the real, a "map"—a virtual abstraction of the real's territory—gets left behind, and on this "map" the fragments of the real are free floating, as he states.

61. I saw this installation in the exhibition "The Cinema Effect: Illusion, Reality, and the Moving Image."

62. Anne Ellegood, "Character Driven: Subjectivity and the Cinematic," in *The Cinema Effect*, 127.

63. Mark Hansen, *Bodies in Code: Interfaces with Digital Media* (New York: Routledge, 2006), 8.

64. Brian Massumi, *Parables of the Virtual: Movement, Affect, Sensation* (Durham, NC: Duke University Press, 2002), 27.

65. Meredith Jones, "Media-Bodies and Screen-Births: Cosmetic Surgery Reality Television," *Continuum: Journal of Media & Cultural Studies* 22.4 (August 2008): 515–524.

66. Ibid., 520.

67. Ibid., 522.

68. Bazin, *What Is Cinema?*, 37.

69. Jean Baudrillard, "Disneyworld Company," trans. F. Debris, *ctheory* (1996), http://ctheory.net/articles.aspx?id=158.

70. Peter Fodor, http://www.surgery.org/media/news-releases, last accessed July 22, 2011.

71. Andrejevic, *Reality TV*, 9.

72. Nielsen Media Research, 2004, provided by Jo LaVerde.

73. Four focus groups participated in this survey. It was performed from 2004 to 2006 in collaboration with Buffalo sociologist Mike Farrell from the University at Buffalo and Los Angeles sociologist July Albright from the University of Southern California. I directed the survey, which served as the basis for the documentary film *Made Over in America: A Voyage to the Land of Makeover* (2007), which I made with Geoffrey Alan Rhodes. For a sociological look at the survey, see July Albright, "Impossible Bodies: TV Viewing Habits, Body Image, and Plastic Surgery Attitudes among College Students in Los Angeles and Buffalo, New York," *Configurations*, 15.1–2 (special issue "Reality Made Over: The Culture of Reality Makeover Shows," ed. Bernadette Wegenstein) (2008): 103–123.

74. Heyes, "Diagnosing Culture," 77.

75. In his study on sports, Bourdieu showed that sport, like many other social practices, is an "object of struggles between the classes." Pierre Bourdieu, "Sport and Social Class," *Social Science Information* 17 (1978): 819–840.

76. Albright, "Impossible Bodies," 120.

77. Groups were surveyed using a sociological research scale based on the Tennessee Self-Concept Scale (TSCS). In a survey conducted at the University at Buffalo in April 2005, two hundred college students were asked to fill out a questionnaire in which a standardized body dysmorphic disorder scale was applied to assess the degree to which people are dissatisfied with some aspect of their bodies (James C. Rosen and Jeff Reiter, *Body Dysmorphic Disorder Examination—Self-Report* [BDDE-SR], 1995) and correlated with viewing practices and gender identification.

78. The Fox Reality Channel (started in 2005) was discontinued in mid-2010. Its Web site no longer exists.

79. The first season can be purchased on DVD. *The Swan, The Complete Series, First Season (2004)*, DVD edition, gaLAnEntertainment 2006.

80. Nely Galán, interview for Wegenstein and Rhodes, *Made Over in America*.

81. Galán stated: "On our show, you don't walk away with nothing, you walk away with $250,000 worth of services from day one." Michelle Green and Michael A. Lipton, "*The Swan* Controversy: Has TV Plastic Surgery Gone Too Far?," *People Magazine*, June 7, 2004, 61.

82. A certain portion of body dysmorphic disorder is necessary to satisfy Kyczinsky's and our own desire to watch people with problems on television. However, except

for the second season, where two episodes featured a handicapped person, there were hardly any other "real" problems detectable on the contestants' bodies at first encounter. Only two episodes featured ethnic diversity.

83. The second season featured two episodes that featured a handicapped woman, as well as some ethnic diversity.

84. Green and Lipton, "*The Swan* Controversy," 61.

85. Sanford Gifford, "Cosmetic Surgery and Personality Change: A Review and Some Clinical Observations," in *The Unfavorable Result in Plastic Surgery: Avoidance and Treatment*, ed. Robert Goldwyn (Boston: Little Brown, 1984), 21–43.

86. Virginia L. Blum, *Flesh Wounds: The Culture of Cosmetic Surgery* (Berkeley: University of California Press, 2003), 109.

87. Davis, *Reshaping the Female Body*, 161.

88. Susan Bordo, "Braveheart, Babe, and the Contemporary Body," in *Enhancing Human Traits: Ethical and Social Implications*, ed. Erik Parens (Georgetown: Georgetown University Press, 1998), 193.

89. See Bordo, "Braveheart, Babe, and the Contemporary Body," 193; Cressida J. Heyes, *Self-Transformations: Foucault, Ethics, and Normalized Bodies* (Oxford: Oxford University Press, 2007), 93–97.

90. Heyes and Jones, "Cosmetic Surgery in the Age of Gender," 6.

91. Nely Galán, *The Swan Curriculum* (New York: Harper Collins, 2004), 9.

92. Ibid.

93. Davis, *Reshaping the Female Body*, 74.

94. One of several interviews with Cindy Ingle for Wegenstein and Rhodes, *Made Over in America*.

95. Davis, *Reshaping the Female Body*, 76. Davis also mentions that people who desire a surgical change usually start by listing all the body parts that they would never change and that they love. In one of the focus groups conducted at the University at Buffalo (see note 73), Amy started by saying that she felt beautiful, noted things that she would never change, and ended up with two features that she would change: "I like my hair. My hair is good. Um, my face is a little wide. It should be thinner [laugh]. My eyes: I love my eyes. I always get compliments on my big blue eyes. Nothing about my eyes I would change. Um, my skin: I would like to change my skin a little bit. Um, my chin: it's not the most shapely chin."

96. Interview with Ken Ingle for Wegenstein and Rhodes, *Made Over in America*.

97. As the case of Scottish reality TV star Susan Boyle (*Britain's Got Talent*) show, reality stars, who are unused to media frenzy, may suffer from severe anxiety

or depression. See http://articles.latimes.com/2009/jun/02/entertainment/et-boyle
-clinic2, last accessed July 22, 2011.

98. In addition to nose surgery, Cindy received a "free" endobrow lift, a midface
lift, cheek-fat removal, fat removal below the eye, lip augmentation, liposuction and
shortening of the chin, a photofacial, laser hair removal, collagen and lasic eye
surgery, a breast augmentation, liposuction of the inner thighs, daVinci tooth
veneers, and a tummy tuck. See chapter 4 for further commentary on these "addi-
tional" procedures that Cindy had to have done by her contract with Fox Reality
TV.

99. Interview with Randall Haworth for Wegenstein and Rhodes, *Made Over in
America*.

100. Cindy's bone structure is ideal for surgical interventions.

101. See http://www.drhaworth.com.

102. Interview with Randall Haworth for Wegenstein and Rhodes, *Made Over in
America*.

103. Blum, *Flesh Wounds*, 82.

104. Sander L. Gilman, *Making the Body Beautiful: A Cultural History of Aesthetic
Surgery* (Princeton, NJ: Princeton University Press, 1999), 332.

105. Unused footage from an interview with Cindy and Randall Haworth for
Wegenstein and Rhodes, *Made Over in America*.

106. Data came from the survey cited in note 73, which was conducted at the
University at Buffalo and the University of Southern California together with Mike
Farrell and July Albright.

107. Carl Elliott, *Better Than Well: American Medicine Meets the American Dream* (New
York: Norton, 2003), 3.

108. Ibid., 173.

109. Gilman, *Making the Body Beautiful*, 333, quoting William Butler Yeats's poem
"A Woman Young and Old."

110. Joanna Zylinska, "Of Swans and Ugly Ducklings: Bioethics between Humans
Animals and Machines," *Configurations*, 15.1–2 (special issue "Reality Made Over:
The Culture of Reality Makeover Shows," ed. Bernadette Wegenstein) (2008): 137.

111. Ibid., 137; see also Joanna Zylinska, *Bioethics in the Age of New Media* (Cambridge: MIT Press, 2009), particularly the chapter "Of Swans and Ugly Ducklings:
Imagining Perfection in Makeover Culture," 101–125.

112. Zylinska, "Of Swans and Ugly Ducklings," 133.

113. Giorgio Agamben, *Homo Sacer: Sovereign Power and Bare Life* (Stanford: Stanford University Press, 1998).

114. The images are of "regular" people, not criminals.

115. Email exchange between Chris Solomon, E-FIT software engineer, and the author.

116. Gilbert Simondon, quoted and translated in Ekman, *Throughout*, 22.

117. Adrian Mackenzie, quoted in ibid., 25.

118. Email exchange between Chris Solomon, E-FIT software engineer, and the author.

119. Seth Schiesel, "Finding Escapism in the Minutiae of Daily Life," *New York Times*, June 2, 2009, C1.

120. Charles Paulk, "Signifying Play: *The Sims* and the Sociology of Interior Design," *International Journal of Computer Game Research* 6.1 (December 2006), http://gamestudies.org/0601/articles/paulk.

121. Ibid.

122. Celia Pearce, "Sims, BattleBots, Cellular Automata God and *Go*: A Conversation with Will Wright," *International Journal of Computer Game Research* 2.1 (July 2002), http://gamestudies.org/0102/pearce.

123. Paulk, *Signifying Play*. See Jean Baudrillard's *The System of Objects* (1968), which Paulk uses for this analysis.

124. Cathy, quoted in Wegenstein and Rhodes, *Made Over in America*.

125. For example, choices for the eyes include eye scale, eye height, rotate, eye distance, eye socket height, and eye depth.

126. See Bernadette Wegenstein, *Getting under the Skin: Body and Media Theory* (Cambridge: MIT Press, 2006). This agrees with what I researched for *Getting under the Skin*—that in the digital age, the borders between inside and outside, inborn and made up, have been blurred.

127. Charles Paulk, *Signifying Play:* The Sims *and the Sociology of Interior Design*, http://www.gamestudies.org/0601/articles/paulk.

128. Ibid.

129. *Bioshock 2*, http://www.bioshock2game.com.

130. Ben Bell, http://www.pcworld.com/article/165526/countdown_to_the_sims_3 _a_chat_with_executive_producer_ben_bell.html.

131. Ibid.

132. Ibid.

133. Ibid.

134. Olivia W. in a filmed interview with the author, June 8, 2009.

135. Ibid.

136. See also G. Alan Rhodes, "Future Cinema and Self-ploitation," http://garhodes .com/writing.html.

137. For critical and feminist perspectives on Internet pornography, see *The Porn Report*, ed. Alan McKee, Katherine Albury, and Catharine Lumby (Melbourne: Melbourne University Press, 2008), 128–149; Zabet Patterson, "Going On-line: Consuming Pornography in the Digital Era," in *Porn Studies*, ed. Linda Williams (Durham: Duke University Press, 2004), 105–126; Kath Albury, "The Ethics of Porn on the Net," in *Remote Control: New Media, New Ethics*, ed. Catharine Lumby and Elspeth Probyn (Melbourne: Cambridge University Press, 2003), 196–211. These perspectives emphasize that pornography need not be exclusively objectifying toward women, but my point in drawing attention to such "self-ploitation" sites is that even when women use the camera on themselves, they are still submitting their self-presentation to the dictates and contours imposed by the cosmetic gaze. See, for example, McKee, Albury, and Lumby, *The Porn Report*, 101–127.

138. Rhodes, "Future Cinema and Self-ploitation." See also Ken Hillis, *Online a Lot of the Time: Ritual, Fetish, Sign* (Durham, NC: Duke University Press, 2009), particularly chapter 5, which focuses on the queer/gay vanguard "that used webcam technology to transmit live images of themselves and their immediate personal home environment for some considerable period of time on a regular basis" (203).

139. See http://www.ishotmyself.com/public/general.php?p=about.

140. Rhodes, "Future Cinema and Self-ploitation."

141. Slavoj Žižek, *Looking Awry: An Introduction to Jaques Lacan through Popular Culture* (Cambridge: MIT Press, 1992).

142. Rhodes, "Future Cinema and Self-ploitation," unpublished ms., p. 8.

143. Lev Manovich, "Spatial Computerisation and Film Language," in *New Screen Media: Cinema, Art, Narrative*, ed. Martin Rieser and Andrea Zapp (London: British Film Institute, 2002), 64–65. In this analysis, Manovich refers to one of the first experimental documentaries, *A Man with a Movie Camera* (Dziga Vertov, 1929).

144. Manovich, "Spatial Computerisation and Film Language," 66.

145. Jean Baudrillard, *Plastic Surgery for the Other*, November 22, 1995, http://www .egs.edu/faculty/jean-baudrillard/articles/plastic-surgery-for-the-other, last accessed July 22, 2011.

146. Brenda Weber, "Beauty, Desire, and Anxiety: The Economy of Sameness in ABC's Extreme Makeover," *Gender* 41 (2005), http://www.genders.org/g41/g41 _weber.html.

Chapter 4

1. Elizabeth, C. Mansfield, *Too Beautiful to Picture: Zeuxis, Myth, and Mimesis* (Minneapolis: University of Minnesota Press, 2007), 20.

2. Here I am aligning myself with the "postmodern feminism" identified by Margrit Shildrick. She contends "that the feminist agenda must go further than the appropriation of culture for our own ends; it must deconstruct the implicit link between women and nature by challenging the appeal to biological determinism which shows itself in the notion of maternal instinct." Margrit Shildrick, *Leaky Bodies and Boundaries: Feminism, Postmodernism, and (Bio)ethics* (London: Routledge, 1997), 195.

3. As Vivian Sobchak points out, Barbra Streisand did not follow this route in her own real-life makeover "attitude adjustment." Vivian Sobchak, *Carnal Thoughts* (Berkeley: University of California Press, 2004), 51.

4. *Il volto e l'anima. Interviste a Kim Ki-duk e Lee Il-ho*, ed. Umberto Galimberti and Alberto Pezzotta (Milano: Feltrinelli Le Nuvole, 2007), 66 (my translation).

5. Both of these theses are developed in Jacques Lacan, *The Seminar of Jacques Lacan, On Feminine Sexuality, The Limits of Love and Knowledge*, book 20, *Encore 1972–1973*, trans. Bruce Fink (New York: Norton, 1998). See also Joan Copjec, *Imagine There's No Woman: Ethics and Sublimation* (Cambridge: MIT Press, 2002).

6. Joël Dor, "The Distinction between Symptoms and Structural Traits: Illustration in a Case of Hysteria," *Structure and Perversions* (New York: Other Press, 2001), 23–44.

7. Ibid., 30.

8. Ibid., 34.

9. Ibid., 38.

10. The trope of the fascination with the flesh wounds caused by a car accident has been narrated in J. G. Ballard's novel *Crash* (1973) and visualized in David Cronenberg's 1996 film version. The sexual pleasure stimulated by the idea of disarticulation can be traced on such sites such as http://www.ampulove.com.

11. See E. Ann Kaplan, *Women and Film: Both Sides of the Camera* (New York: Methuen, 1983).

12. See Teresa de Lauretis, *Technologies of Gender* (Bloomington: Indiana University Press, 1987).

13. Anneke Smelik, *And the Mirror Cracked: Feminist Cinema and Film Theory* (New York: St. Martin's Press, 1998), 17.

14. Jacqueline Rose, *Sexuality in the Field of Vision* (London: Verso, 1986), 28.

15. Only the movie version reveals Frannie's real name, Frances Avery.

16. Susanna Moore, *In the Cut* (New York: Penguin Books, 1999), 19.

17. Ibid., 63, 98.

18. Ibid., 51. This conversation does not take place in the film version. The film scene is misogynist in its own way but does not use the violent language of the novel.

19. Ibid., 60.

20. Ibid., 174.

21. Ibid., 78.

22. Ibid., 178–179.

23. Ibid., 71.

24. Jane Campion explains the use of this lens in the director's commentary to the 2004 DVD edition of the film. She adds that this kind of lens is often used in advertising.

25. Andy Klein, "Something about Frannie: Meg Ryan Finesses Her Vague Character in Jane Campion's Unimpressive 'In the Cut,'" previously posted on Web site of LA City Beat, now defunct.

26. The reason for this name change is a clearer class and race attribution. Giovanni Malloy is of at least partial Italian descent. The director comments in the director's commentary: "Frannie is attracted to Malloy because he is himself. It's also a class thing."

27. One of the main causes for this ambiguity is that Malloy shares the same tattoo with the real perpetrator.

28. The novel treats this narrative moment differently. It is expressed earlier that Frannie thinks Malloy is the murderer. She says to him: "I want to know what you did to her" (Moore, *In the Cut*, 152). Malloy, who does not defend himself, starts his speech quite differently, too: "She must have been moving" (152).

29. Moore, *In the Cut*, 169.

30. Although *Dans ma peau* seems to lack such a myth and is trying to be anti-psychological, its narration is not myth-free. Viewers of modern myths can

attribute possible childhood traumas or important events as causes for Esther's self-mutilations.

31. In the novel, Moore alludes to the Geneva episode in conjunction with other disappointments throughout Frannie's life, including the most recent disappointment about Malloy: "I am so ashamed by the things that used to make me unhappy. That I was upset because he lied to me about his wife and then went on vacation with her. That Yale University won't give me permission to use the letters of C. K. Whitney. That my father forgot me in Geneva." Moore, *In the Cut*, 152.

32. Campion in the DVD commentary for *In the Cut*.

33. The original version of the song "Que Sera Sera" was written by Jay Livingston and Ray Evans for Doris Day's character Jo in Hitchcock's *The Man Who Knew Too Much* (1956), who sang the song to let her kidnapped son, Hank, know that she was in the same house. Many versions of the song have been used in films, such as Syd Straw's version of the song in Michael Lehmann's 1989 parody of U.S. high school life, *Heathers*.

34. Moore, *In the Cut*, 127.

35. For further analysis of the history of body art, see my "If You Won't SHOOT Me, at Least DELETE Me! Performance Art from 1960s Wounds to 1990s Extensions," in *Data Made Flesh: Embodying Information*, ed. Robert Mitchell and Phillip Thurtle (London: Routledge, 2004).

36. *Nackt & Mobil: Elke Krystufek*, catalogue published on the occasion of the exhibition February 12 to April 27, 2003 (Klosterneuburg: Sammlung Essl, 2003), 102.

37. Peter Gorsen, "I Am Your Mirror: The Construction of Self-Portrait," in ibid., 63.

38. Ibid., 62.

39. Elke Krystufek, Interview with author, May 3, 2008.

40. For Lacan, the symbolic *je* has the function of suturing together fragments of the imaginary body. Jacques Lacan, *The Four Fundamental Concepts of Psychoanalysis, The Seminar of Jacques Lacan*, book 11, trans. Alan Sheridan (New York: Norton, 1981), 145.

41. William Egginton, *How the World Became a Stage: Presence, Theatricality, and the Question of Modernity* (Albany: SUNY Press, 2003), 25–26.

42. Lisa Dickson, "Hook and Eye: Violence and the Captive Gaze," *Camera Obscura* 56 (2004): 75–103.

43. Ibid., 78.

44. Ibid., 78.

45. Meredith Jones, *Skintight: An Anatomy of Cosmetic Surgery* (Oxford: Berg, 2008), 12.

46. "Self-care" refers to the subtitle of Michel Foucault's *Histoire de la sexualité*, vol. 3, *Le souci de soi* (Paris: Gallimard, 1984).

47. In some recent Hollywood dramas, such as *The Black Swan* (2010), the cosmetic gaze reveals itself as destructive, but it does so in the service of the male gaze and our enjoyment of Natalie Portman's body image disorder.

Index

Note: Page numbers appearing in *italics* indicate illustrations.